Surviving Fame

Surviving Fame

Memoirs of a TV Princess

by

PANDA

Spectrum Publications Melbourne 2001

First published in Australia in 2001
by Spectrum Publications Pty Ltd
PO Box 75, Richmond, Vic, 3121
Telephone: 1300 540 736
Facsimile: 1300 540 737
e-mail: spectrum@spectrumpublications.com.au

Copyright 2001
All rights reserved.
No part of this publication may be reproduced
in any manner without prior
written permission of the publisher.

Cover Photograph: Athol Shmith. Courtesy of his son Michael Shmith and the Performing Arts Museum.
Cover design: Spectrum Publications

Typesetting by SpectrumPublications
Typeface: Goudy

National Library of Australia
Cataloguing in Publication Data
Includes Index
ISBN 0 86786 318 8

1. Panda.
2. Memoirs.
3. Television.
4. Theatre.
5. Entertainers.
6. Modelling.

*Dedicated to
Jimmy and Robin*

ACKNOWLEDGMENTS

I would like to sincerely thank the following publications for their permission to reproduce excerpts from their published articles:

The Age, Pages 183, 241.
The Australian Women's Weekly, Page 103.
The Herald, Page 183.
Listener In-TV, Pages 126, 150, 157, 190, 205.
The Sun News Pictorial, Page 183.
Truth, Pages 163, 187.
TV Times, Pages 196, 230.
TV Week, Pages 100, 104, 112, 115, 128, 164, 173, 176, 193, 204, 217.

I gratefully acknowledge the following picture sources:

Barry Bell, pages 170, 171.
Bruno Benini, pages 71, 87.
*Catherine Perkins, page 65.
The Laurie Richards collection, courtesy of the Performing Arts Museum; pages 114, 188, 203, 258.
Athol Shmith, courtesy of his son Michael Shmith and the Performing Arts Museum, pages 87, 174, 181, 200, 201.
Vernon Spencer, page 106.
TV Times, page 202.
TV Week, pages 136, 138.
Chris Whitehorn, pages 105, 107, 111, 162.

The remaining photographs are from my personal collection.
Disclaimer: Every effort has been made to trace and acknowledge source material contained in this book.. The author and publisher would be pleased to hear from authors in order to rectify any omissions.

TABLE OF CONTENTS

1. Boxing Day	1	
2. Bruce Rock	4	
3. Garden House	7	
4. Spider House	11	
5. Autogyros and Biplanes	14	
6. Grandma's House	19	
7. Return to Bruce Rock	21	
8. The Big City	24	
9. Audition	34	
10. Tivoli Girl	38	
11. Comedy Sketches	41	
12. The Acts	43	
13. Kalgoorlie	46	
14. Melbourne	51	
15. Nullabor	53	
16. Family of Friends	55	
17. J.C.W.	58	
18. Return to Melbourne	64	
19. Carnegie	67	
20. The Modelling Game	70	
21. Flashbulbs and Cameras	76	
22. Catwalks and Runways	81	
23. Darrods and GTV-9	85	
24. Signing with Channel 9	99	
25. New Horizons	103	
26. Busy	113	
27. Outside B'casts	119	
28. Stalkers	123	
29. World Tour	126	
30. London	130	
31. New York	134	
32. Hollywood	140	
33. Home Again	149	
34. 1960 Surprises	151	
35. Twin Lakes	155	
36. Letters	157	
37. End Darrods	159	
38. Magic	161	
39. Wedding Plans	167	
40. Wedding Day	172	
41. IMT Return	178	
42. Signing with Channel 7	185	
43. Princess	199	
44. Tulle and Tiaras	214	
45. All in the Game	225	
46. Biding Time	238	
47. U.S.A. Here We Come	247	
48. Epilogue	257	

1

BOXING DAY

n the afternoon of Boxing Day 1939, there was a foreboding in the air. My brother Norm was keeping a watchful eye on the gate, while the rest of the family waited anxiously in the kitchen. Sister Val, brother Ron and I were quietly playing a game of Ludo as our small brother Ian looked on. Grandma and mother were sitting at the end of the table, nervously sipping tea. Dad had not come home for lunch and his meal was waiting for him in the oven. When we heard the screech of the gate, Norm peeked through the curtains and announced, 'Dad is coming and he is surely full as a boot.' As the door latch opened and dad staggered into the room with his intemperate action the atmosphere suggested a pernicious event.

Taking his warmed meal from the oven, mother placed it on the table, explaining that we had eaten lunch at the usual hour. Infuriated, dad picked up the plate of food, hurled it back into the oven, then lunged at mother, inflicting a crushing blow to her mouth. Sixteen year old Ron ran to mother's rescue and with all his might, drew back his fist landing it on dad's jaw, seemingly with no effect. Dad in turn grabbed Ron's shirt front with one hand, and punched him with such force that Ron went flying through the back door, across the verandah into the yard where he lay unconscious. Dazed, mother's maternal instincts were

My beloved grandmother

now aroused, and in defense of her son she wielded a poker from the wood stove, striking dad across the forehead, leaving an open wound. Blood streaming down his face, dad charged from the room calling for his shotgun and ranting about revenge, while Norm unsuccessfully tried to pacify him.

Grandma hustled five year old Ian and me to a neighbour's garden where we hid, crouched in the shrubbery. Meanwhile, Norm had joined mother and Val and between them, they managed to carry the still unconscious Ron across the back lane to another neighbour's house. Dad, armed with his loaded shotgun, had taken off into the streets looking for us.

Grandma directed Ian and me to the house where the rest of the family were hiding out, everyone fearful of being discovered. Ron was laid out on a bed. Grandma took control, calling for someone to fetch a doctor while she raised his legs allowing the blood to rush to his head. The doctor arrived promptly and found Ron to have a dislocated jaw as well as a badly sprained wrist. Mother's mouth was bruised and bloody but she brushed aside aid for her own pain to comfort her injured son.

In the meantime, the police constable had been notified and had the dangerous task of searching for dad to disarm him. Eventually mother received word that he had been located. The constable had calmed him, confiscated the shotgun and placed him in the 'drunk tank' for the night. This news alleviated our terror, enabling us to return home. Drawing near the house, it was obvious that dad's anger had been vented on the two remaining turkeys from a clutch raised for Christmas sale. With necks wrung, their carcasses lay in full view for all to see. Following the day's events it was an alarming sight. Mother and grandma managed to scrape together a meal and after the dishes were done, we bathed and shuffled off to bed. I was still afraid and sleep was elusive.

Lying in bed, my mind kept flashing back to episodes of dad's past violent behaviour. When under the influence of alcohol, he became another person, not the loving husband and father we knew. It was like a hideous dream when sometimes late on a Saturday night he came home drunk. Val and I would be awakened. Our bedroom adjoined the kitchen, with its door opening directly opposite the ever-smouldering wood stove. Dad usually stormed into the kitchen where he either selected a carving knife, or heated a poker to white hot then disappeared from sight while yelling and threatening mother with these weapons as she lay in bed. We could hear punches as they landed and mother's muffled whimpers and sobs escaping from their bedroom. On those nights we all lived in terror, afraid for mother's safety. But now with dad being held in custody, the house was quiet and my fears were put on hold. As these unhappy thoughts faded I drifted into a deep sleep. The following day a feeling of solemnity permeated the house. About mid morning mother ordered each of us individually into her bedroom where dad was waiting. When my turn came, I entered the room with trepidation to find dad sitting on his side of the bed, arms outstretched, beckoning me to be hugged. Filled with remorse and apologising for his actions, dad was ashamed and crying and I was overwhelmed by his tears. We wept quietly. It was the last tender moment I would share with my father. Memories of that Boxing Day in Merredin, Western Australia are indelibly imprinted on my mind, but most childhood memories are fleeting.

2

BRUCE ROCK

orn on mother's birthday in 1928 to Phillip and May Kelly, my earliest recollection of home was in the country town of Bruce Rock, Western Australia. These were depression days and almost everyone was in need. A former farm hand on his father's property in Rutherglen, Victoria, dad's efforts to find enough work to support a wife and family were challenging to say the least and the obstacles must have seemed insurmountable.

The rented four roomed house in which we lived, was also where dad kept bees in the backyard. He had collected scraps of timber, assembled them into bee hives and searched the countryside for swarms of bees, stocking his hives and providing us with a source of food. Whenever he 'robbed' the hives, we each received a piece of fresh sweet honeycomb, better tasting than any lollies bought at the store. Mother boiled the honey to rid it of impurities and any surplus was shared with neighbours who were struggling to survive, or sold to those who could afford to pay, thus supplementing dad's meagre income. Bees in the backyard were a hazard and the blue bag used to brighten the family washing, also alleviated the pain of bee stings.

In 1934, while living in this house my brother Ian was born, the

Mother, Dad and brother Norm

Dad with his trusty axe

youngest of five children. Our ages ranged from, Norm 14, Ron 11, Val 9 and Joan (me) 6. A new baby in the house meant endless loads of washing. Our laundry facilities consisted of a copper perched over a wood fire, complete with its own copper stick (a broom handle) used to remove the boiling clothing, two kerosene-tin buckets for carrying water to and from the copper, a dipper for scooping out the boiling water and our portable galvanised iron half-bath to rinse off the soap. After filling the copper with water and lighting a wood fire underneath, mother whittled flakes off a large bar of soap into the water. When all was ready she poked, prodded and agitated the clothes utilizing the copper stick, until it all came to the boil. It was then rinsed, wrung out by hand and hung on the line to dry.

In the midst of one of these herculean days, a playmate stepped backwards and fell on her backside into a freshly ladled bucketful of hot water. Screaming, she was rushed home and examined by our mothers. Not seriously burned, she was greased with butter, (not recommended in today's climate) and the only damage was to her pride.

Our home had two bedrooms, one occupied by mother, dad and baby Ian, the other by Val and me, sharing a three-quarter sized bed. One end of the rear verandah was enclosed in canvas, making a third

Panda with brother Ian *Panda with sister Val left and brother Ian*

bedroom where Norm and Ron also shared a same sized bed. To prevent the boys from freezing to death in the winter months, mother made them a large kangaroo skin comforter to throw over their bed. Dad had hunted the animals, skinned and tanned the hides, then mother sewed them together on her hand operated portable sewing machine. The kangaroo meat was shared by those who were most in need. Mother made soup and potted meat from the tail, which we relished.

After my first year of schooling in Bruce Rock, our family moved to Merredin where dad had received an offer of steady work.

3

GARDEN HOUSE

Merredin was a cultural shock. The population of Bruce Rock was about five hundred and now we were in a town of almost three thousand people. It was an important junction for the railway and the commercial hub of the wheat district. The rail expansion and maintenance afforded Dad steady work as a linesman.

Living fairly isolated, about two miles from the outskirts of Merredin, our house had three bedrooms, allowing Norm and Ron to sleep inside. With no electricity connected to the property, our homework was done by the light of a glass based kerosene lamp. An additional kerosene hurricane lantern was used at night to illuminate the path to the toilet situated some distance from the rear of the house. The toilet was a wooden structure with a pan beneath the enclosed bench seat and a pan sized wooden flap-door at the rear for the night-cart man to pick up the used pan, replacing it with a fresh one. Bottles of phenyl stored in the toilet for use, guaranteed it odourless and germ free. Sounds pretty primitive by today's standards, but everyone had the same facility, even the town hall.

Mother and dad wasted no time in establishing a practical vegetable garden and setting up a chicken coop on the acre of land. This was our

'Garden House.' Planted in rows were peas, beans, cauliflowers, carrots, radishes, pumpkins and rock melons. It was green, lush and meticulously cultivated, resulting in copious crops of fresh vegetables.

Our Rhode Island Red chickens travelled with us wherever we lived. Daily, they provided fresh eggs and when the coffers were empty, one of the mature hens would be sacrificed and prepared for the table. Giblets, heart, liver, neck and un-laid egg yolks were made into soup, while the usually very large chicken made a roast-feast. Mother's knack of turning the most mundane cheap cuts of meat into delicious meals was legendary. Although not to my taste today, lambs fry in gravy, creamed tripe, stewed lamb flaps and pot-roasted stuffed ox heart are some of the meat dishes we regularly savoured.

The humble rabbit, brought to the table via dad's skill as a marksman, was served in a myriad of disguises. Rabbits stewed or curried, stuffed-baked or braised, were a staple in our diet. Mother was also a wizard when it came to desserts. Every kind of steamed pudding, rhubarb or apricot pies, dumplings in golden syrup and hot jam tarts were on her dessert menu.

Unlike our Bruce Rock school where more than one grade was taught simultaneously in each classroom, the Merredin school had only one grade per room, enabling teachers to pay more attention to individual students. Every day before school began, a general assembly was held. The Headmaster delivered lectures followed by a few 'on the spot' physical exercises, then in single file, we marched into our classrooms where the learning process began in earnest.

At age seven I had never been to a birthday party, so when an invitation arrived mother decided it would be all right for me to attend. Attired in my Sunday school dress and carrying a small inexpensive gift for the birthday girl, the hostess greeted and seated me at the table with about a dozen other small children. After the food and drinks had been consumed, the hostess told us to take hold of the streamer attached to each of our chairs and follow it to its end in another room, whereupon there was a gift for every guest. Mine was a large packet of multi-coloured plasticine and I couldn't wait to get home and share it with Val.

Not far from our house, where the steam train puffed out of Merredin, we would run across the fields towards the railway line to watch the engine drivers returning our waves and when luck was with us, we collected pieces of coal which vibrated loose from the over filled tender. Coal was a great source of heat for the fireplace and best of all it was free.

Gathering mushrooms was another irresistible recipe for adventure. On a sunny morning after a warm spring rain shower we'd head for an open field where mushrooms grew in abundance. With a billy can in one hand and a knife in the other, we spread out to harvest these delicacies. Having never heard that it was the spores that ensured next years yield, we believed a clean cut to the mushroom stem would guarantee re-growth. With this in mind, we diligently harvested each mushroom with the utmost care, rushing them home to mother. She served them in white sauce (bechamel) over a thick slice of bread, toasted over the red hot coals of the kitchen fire.

Late one afternoon, a ferocious storm passed through and blew in the kitchen window. Dad was badly cut by the broken glass. Mother took care of his wounds and dad wasted no time in going out into the raging storm, nailing hessian bags over the window to prevent the rain from flooding the kitchen. It was very scary watching our brave father protecting us from the elements.

The neighbouring wheat farmers warned us about venomous snakes in the area. On a hot summer's day, mother opened the back door to find a large tiger snake slithering past the step. Slamming the door shut, making sure everyone was inside, she ordered us not to move. While we watched from a window, Norm was dispatched by way of the front door to get a shovel. In hot pursuit, mother grasped the shovel firmly, took aim, threw it at the snake, missing it, but getting its attention. The snake turned swiftly, hissed at Mother who lost her nerve and scurried inside whilst the snake disappeared through the wire fence into a wheat field.

A school Gala. Panda second from right

Dad's work on the railway, road and pipeline gangs, was a strain on the family. Some work sites were many miles from town and the men had to be transported there and housed in 'tent towns' for a week or more at a time. The hours were long and the work tough, but I never heard dad complain. The snake incident, the isolation of living two miles out of town with no electricity and five children to care for and protect was too much for mother, so we moved to a house supplied with electricity in the Merredin township.

With brother Ian

4

SPIDER HOUSE

A borrowed horse and cart made shifting from one house to another relatively easy. Our humble possessions were three beds, a cot, dressing table, two small wardrobes, a kitchen dresser, bench seat, table and chairs, kitchen utensils, laundry equipment, mother's sewing machine, dad's tools and our chickens. A problem arose which we had not encountered before. Something or someone was getting into the coop and killing the baby chicks. At first dad thought it was a fox, but investigating a disturbance early one evening he caught the culprit, a cat, inside the chicken coop. In hopes of being reimbursed for the slaughtered chicks, he lugged the cat around the neighbourhood in search of the owner. No one admitted to ownership, so he solved the problem in the manner some folks did when their livestock was attacked or destroyed. He simply took the cat out into the scrub and wrung its neck. The depression had deepened and in those wretched times dad refused to allow food to be stolen from our table by a cat or by any other means. We never lost another chicken.

Apart from the usual childhood ailments such as measles and the like, the whole family seemed to be a healthy lot. Mother and dad became alarmed when I started suffering regular bouts of croup and so began a lengthy period of ill health. One night while mother was administering my usual inhalation treatment, she was bitten on the arm by a red-back spider. The swelling around the bite was intensely painful. She was nauseous, perspiring profusely and became seriously ill. We were afraid she would die. The doctor's treatment was effective and mother recovered slowly, much to our joy.

Ian was just a toddler, but Ron, Val and I attended school, while Norm had taken a job as trainee sales boy at the Co-op, the busiest store in town.

Co-op stores were the forerunners of today's supermarkets. Excepting meat and vegetables, everything else could be bought there. It was stocked with general groceries including fresh farm butter.

Nothing was self service and cooking ingredients like sugar, flour, rice and so forth, were not packaged, but hand measured, weighed and scooped into brown paper bags at the counter. One could purchase large sacks of wheat, bran and pollard for chicken feed, chaff and oats for horses, fuel for fires and kerosene for lamps. Clothing, shoes, toiletries, haberdashery and almost anything else was somewhere on the shelves. In fact, if you couldn't get it at the Co-op, you couldn't get it.

Dad was injured at work and had to travel to Perth for treatment. Mother was well by now and with grandma's help the entire family excepting Norm who had to work, accompanied dad by train to Perth where we stayed in a small boarding house. It was so exciting none of us slept a wink on the overnight train trip. Neon signs outside the city stores were absolutely fascinating. They were all turned on in broad daylight and I wondered about the electric bill, as we were never allowed to leave an unattended light switched on. Grandma treated us to a night at the theatre where we were enthralled by a dazzling vaudeville show. I didn't think any of us would ever stop laughing at the comedians and the music, costumes and talent astounded us all. We were only in Perth a few days, but grandma wouldn't let us leave without a trip to the ocean. The cold day didn't stop us from collecting seashells for souvenirs. A brief respite from the depression, they were memorable days.

Returning home, mother and dad decided our current house was too small for a family of seven and a coop full of chickens. The yard was cramped, with no room for a vegetable garden, so we were on the move again. They found a four-room home on an acre of land right in the middle of town. Once again a portion of the back verandah was enclosed to accommodate Norm and Ron. Dad and mother soon had the chickens ensconced and our new vegetable garden bearing the fruits of their labour.

A large apricot tree next to the house supplied loads of fresh fruit for eating and preserving.

5

Autogyros & Biplanes

orm had saved enough money from his wages to buy a flashy new racing bicycle, his pride and joy. Dad owned a second hand bicycle for the purpose of riding to many of his jobs. It was a heavy duty model and with no gears must have been hard to pedal. It had a tool kit suspended from the back of the sprung saddle-seat, a pump clipped on the vee bar, an old fashioned canvas water bag on the cross bar and his lunch bag on the handle bars. The bicycle was used strictly for work or hunting rabbits, never for recreation and no one was permitted to touch it.

Dad took great pride in his two axes, keeping them finely honed. The wood pile was the beneficiary of one, but the other was special, it was used only in wood chopping competitions for which the winner received a handsome sum of money. The wood chop was a social event, usually a picnic with other competitive sports and free ice cream for the children. We puffed up with pride whenever dad won, for he was the hero of the day. His skill with an axe won him enough prize money to purchase a dining room suite (buffet, table and chairs) as a gift for mother. Having no lounge suite, this setting became our living room furniture.

Although we did have a gramophone of sorts at one time, the operating spring broke and left us with a dozen unplayable records, so having no radio we created our own entertainment. Some evenings, gathered around the table, dad and Norm played the button accordion and harmonica respectively. We sang songs and laughed at Norm's antics (he was the family clown). Ron also played harmonica and we all played the Jews Harp. Our maternal grandmother Mary came to town a couple of times a year and each time was a merry making occasion. She had her own button accordion and brought us the latest melodies which were adapted by dad and Norm for future get-togethers. She was our only living grandparent, each of the others had passed away before I was born. We all loved grandma, but probably nobody more than me. She was affectionate, kind, loving and as generous as she could afford to be. When Val was taking dancing lessons, grandma decided I should learn as well. She produced the money and paid my way. Val and I attended the matinee performance of a touring vaudeville show playing in town. Like the show we witnessed in Perth, we were agog with amazement. Our enthusiasm gained impetus and stimulated our zest for dancing lessons.

Community Concerts were an additional form of entertainment. Words of standard popular songs were projected on to a large screen and to a piano accompaniment, the master of ceremonies led the exuberant singing audience into raising the rafters with songs like, *Beautiful Dreamer, Silver Threads Among The Gold, Red, Red, Robin, K-K-K-Katy, Shine On Harvest Moon,* and *Home On The Range.* The special attraction of the evening was a talent quest. It was open to anyone who had either the talent or nerve to perform in front of an audience. First prize was one pound, second ten shillings and third five shillings, a fortune to most and there were plenty of people willing to participate. Both dad and Norm won first prize individually and once as a duo.

I first appeared on stage at a local theatre in a school production in which Val portrayed the Principal Boy, Bonnie Bobby Shafto. Although just a small child, I played a Spinning Lady dressed in costume with a tall cone shaped hat from which flowed a long cascade of tulle. My primary role was to keep the spinning wheel in motion. Was this an omen of things to come?

Grandma owned a small Ford runabout in which she volunteered to drive us to a lake many miles from town. In those days, to be a passenger in any automobile was exciting. Mother and Ian travelled in the cabin with Grandma and the rest of us sat in the rear tray with dad, who caringly watched over us. The temperature was hot and the bush flies thick, but no one could have been more in awe of the lake or had so much fun splashing and cavorting in the water than our family.

Back in town again, one of Ron's friends invited us to visit his parents' property to pick mulberries. Armed with billy cans we descended on the mulberry tree climbing high into its branches collecting the juicy dark purple fruit while eating equal amounts. By the time we arrived home, we were covered in fruit stains, but mother forgave us in exchange for the large haul of mulberries, which she made into pies and jam. Another luxury for the table. Measured doses of Hearn's Bronchitis Cure for ongoing bouts of croup became unpleasantly routine. Shortly after we arrived at the 'Apricot House' I had recurring tonsillitis with an intolerable sore throat and swollen glands. Mother had her own remedies. For this complaint she took a hen's wing feather, stripped the shaft leaving a small tuft on the tip as a paint brush, scalded the feather with boiling water, dried it by the fire and dipping it into the iodine bottle, she painted the swollen glands with the brown antiseptic liquid, which usually gave me a rash.

A more serious situation arose when on another occasion while mother was applying an iodine treatment, my heart began an irregular rhythm. Becoming extremely weak, slowly everything within my visual range began fading to black and I lost consciousness. On awaking, a dreadful feeling of malaise overcame me and my head was sore where it hit the table as I collapsed. These episodes occurred every once in a while and as I always bounced back, mother never sought medical attention. However, fainting was to become part of my life.

In rural Western Australia in the mid 1930's, any sighting of an aircraft was a rarity. One could not imagine how we were roused into action when an autogyro landed in a field on the outskirts of town. An airplane with a supplementary propeller on a vertical shaft, its blades and shaft were rotated by the aeroplane's motor lifting the machine vertically. Every child within a radius of ten miles showed up to stare at this peculiar contraption with its leather clad pilot. We stared in amazement, bombarding the pilot with endless questions, learning that it had not long been invented by J. De La Cierva in 1923 (the helicopter didn't arrive until 1939).

Another aerial highlight came about when the manufacturer of a custard powder sent a small biplane on a promotional stint through the country areas. To see a plane actually land and the occupant distribute free samples of custard powder was beyond anyone's expectations and the talk of the town for weeks. A couple of months later, mother and dad were burning off yard debris when we heard another plane. Walking slowly backwards and looking skyward at this wonder I stepped right in the middle of the fire's hot embers. This put me out of action until the blisters healed.

Mother was the driving force in the family in terms of our religious instruction. Dad had been raised Catholic, but had no problem with mother's decision for all of us to be christened at the Church of England. Each Sunday morning we siblings attended Sunday school and on our return home, mother had the main meal of the day ready to eat. Sunday evening church services were attended by the entire family and it was this unqualified support from our parents that imprinted on each of us a moral integrity for life.

The church social club held a picnic in the bush and every member paid a nominal fee to cover the expense of hiring a train to transport the horde of takers to the picnic location. Many sporting events were held for the children. One was the obstacle race in which I entered. The competitors had to run through old car tyres, climb over several obstacles and finally crawl under a huge heavy railway truck tarpaulin, exit the other side and dash for the finish line. I was about even with two other competitors until we came to the tarpaulin, when, on hands and knees we started crawling in pitch black darkness. Almost choking to death on coal dust which coated the entire tarpaulin, I thought I would smother, so I took off with every bit of energy I could muster until I saw the light, then scrambled to my feet and sprinted for the finish line to receive my first place reward of two shillings. We were a sight to behold, covered from head to toe in the black coal dust. Everyone laughed at us.

Entertainment came in many guises. A large gathering of Aborigines came to town and invited the townsfolk to attend a celebration. They turned on a spectacular corroboree under the stars, on the outskirts of town. The intricate artistry of the dancing was not completely understood, but there was obvious pleasure experienced by the participants and the audience. The dancer's body paint was applied in great detail creating an artistically mysterious atmosphere. The accompaniment was provided by the rhythmical beating of sticks and the haunting, pulsing drone of the didgeridoo. The dancers represented birds and animals with uncanny accuracy and identifying each action was a wonderful way to experience the corroboree.

In contrast to the corroboree, another occasion found us in the audience of a travelling circus. Work was scarce when dad was engaged as a casual circus hand and given a family pass to the show. There are no words to describe the joy this event brought our family. The animal acts, acrobatic flyers on horse back, tight-rope walkers, clowns and the stars of the circus ring, the trapeze artists, overwhelmed us all. What a night!

When no work could be found, dad took advantage of a Government bounty plan. Eagles and foxes were considered pests and by submitting a fox pelt, or the claws and head of an eagle, a cash bounty was paid for each specimen. Although our family was self sufficient at growing vegetables and hunting meat, some cash flow was necessary to meet rent, clothing and utilities. The bounty plan, along with selling rabbits, helped keep a roof over our heads during unavoidable bleak periods.

It would be hard to find a Christian family who did not remember Christmas as being the most wonderful time of the year. For each of us, mother and dad always managed to afford a small red mesh Christmas stocking. The toe was stuffed with lollies while the rest of the stocking contained small play-things like a putt putt boat, a very small tin toy, driven by the heat of a tiny lighted candle. It putted around a dish of water until the candle burned out. Other goodies were a miniature celluloid pan flute, whistles, a hooter with thin coloured streamers flowing from it, a cardboard game and comics. Grandma came to visit and on Christmas eve the family attended church to sing and enjoy the carols. Christmas day was celebrated with a roast feast, including Christmas pudding containing threepenny bits. The luckiest person was the one who found the only sixpence in the pudding. Crepe paper streamers strung from the single central light fitting in the kitchen festooned across to the walls. As the Christmas bon-bons popped around the table we retrieved the party hats from within. There was much joy in the house and I love to remember those days.

6

GRANDMA'S HOUSE

hese recollections of a happy family life were stored in my memory, for following the Boxing Day calamity, mother felt that threatening his family with a gun had established a new level of violence in dad's behaviour and this she was not prepared to endure. Taking action, she obtained a legal separation. Dad was obliged to leave and we became a single parent family. Grandma transported us back to Bruce Rock. We all clambered aboard her run-about and somewhere between towns, the vehicle broke down. Night had just fallen and the road was deserted of any kind of traffic. Grandma announced we would sleep in a wheat field not far from the road. Norm and Ron held down the barbed wire fence as we climbed over it into the field. We flattened a small area of wheat, spread blankets over the top of it and settled down to try and sleep. It was a horrid night, we were uncomfortable and assorted bugs continually crawled all over us. At the first sight of dawn, we were on our feet. During the night, Norm and Ron had taken off on foot for Bruce Rock and notified the church minister who drove out in his car to rescue us. Dad had also learned of our predicament and riding his bicycle, appeared on the scene. We were afraid when we saw him approaching, but he was his normal warm self and had simply come to offer help to his estranged family.

Our situation altered rapidly. Mother organised our furniture removal from Merredin back to Bruce Rock and while this was going on, Grandma took temporary custody of me and I spent a few days at her farmlet. Grandma's small cottage, situated on a few acres of land, had tank water but no electricity. Her cow Bess had just calved and milking the cow provided gallons of rich creamy milk. Grandma poured the milk into a huge enamel saucepan and placed it on the wood stove bringing it to just boiling point, then before it had a chance to boil over she quickly lifted it on to the table to cool. When it was cold the rich yellow scalded cream, about an inch thick, was scooped off the top and served on hot scones and jam or whole baked apples. On farms, there seemed to be an endless supply of this epicurian delight.

Accompanying Grandma into the bush, carrying the always handy billy can, we gathered quandong fruit (native peach) from a tree. She made this red, thin fleshed fruit with its edible kernels into jam, saving some of the fruit's stones for a Chinese checker game. The stones were perfectly round, about the size of a marble and covered with tiny indentations. She stained them different colours with vegetable dye then set about to make the checker board.

Taking a square piece of thin plywood, she smoothed it down with sandpaper, sketched the pattern of a Chinese checker board on one side then heated a round poker in the wood stove to the appropriate temperature and applied its tip to the small circles sketched on the board. After some time and a lot of heating and re-heating the poker, she achieved her goal. All of the circles had been burned through to the other side of the board and after another sanding, she coloured different sections of the board with dye matching the quandong stones, then set about teaching me how to play Chinese checkers. Grandma also taught me how to play cribbage, poker, euchre, bridge and two kinds of solitaire. She loved card games but never gambled on them.

7

RETURN TO BRUCE ROCK

inally, mother, my siblings and I were re-united in Bruce Rock where there was a dramatic change in our lives. The declaration of war in Europe impacted on all Australians, calling for men and women to enlist. Dad and Norm were accepted into the armed forces and were in training. Living in town in another two bedroom house, mother was forced to secure employment in a local shop. Val had turned fourteen and was working as a dental assistant, while Ron worked and lived on a farm in nearby Doodlakine. Ian and I attended the same small school where each teacher taught multiple grades in their individual classrooms. It was my responsibility to escort my little brother safely to and from school each day. I was his minder during lunch hour and at home until mother or Val returned from work. At age eleven I was the responsible authority figure during half of Ian's waking hours. On Saturday nights mother rewarded us by allowing Ian and me to attend the latest movie showing at the local theatre. I was given enough money to purchase two front stall tickets at threepence a seat and a penny each for a selection from the penny lolly tray which offered various sweets like sherbet filled envelopes with a licorice straw to suck the fizzy powder into one's mouth, an ice-cream cone filled

with sherbet sealed with marshmallow and dipped in hundreds and thousands, crunchy candy bananas, large marble shaped gum balls, pink musk sticks, hard candy bulls eyes which lasted almost through the whole movie, and dozens of other choices.

We were worried when dad embarked for the Middle East conflict. World War II brought petrol rationing and many changes to the way of life in Australia, but perhaps none so drastic as the lives of rural women. Until this time, the manual chores and hunting were the sole domain of dad and later, Ron. Before leaving to live on the farm, Ron brought Val and me up to date in the art of wood chopping and how to set traps at a rabbit warren.

Finally the day came when trapping a rabbit became Val's and my responsibility. Leaving early in the morning, we headed for a rabbit warren. The trap had two jaws of steel at one end and a spike attached to a short chain at the other. We followed Ron's instructions, hammering the spike into the ground at the entrance of a rabbit burrow, springing the jaws open, catching the plate on its latch then concealing it with scattered grass. Eyeing it off, we left, confident we would have rabbit for dinner. Returning late that afternoon, as we cautiously approached the warren, we heard a high pitched screaming and discovered a rabbit caught by its leg in the cruel and unforgiving teeth of the trap. Getting a firm hold on the injured animal, we quickly released its leg. Ron's instructions on how to kill it (grip the hind legs in one hand, the head in the other and give a sharp pull severing the spinal cord assuring a painless and instant death) a neat and tidy theory, but when the moment of truth arrived, we almost lost our courage. Val's action was sure and swift and we scurried home with the wretched animal for mother to gut and skin. Alas, when she opened it up, we were horrified to see that it was a very pregnant doe. Mother took the rabbit and its contents and buried them at the rear of the yard. It was the first and last time we set a rabbit trap.

Various chores fell on my shoulders, including feeding the chickens, collecting the eggs, cleaning the coop, and retrieving washing from the clothes line if the weather was threatening. When a red dust storm was imminent, if precautions weren't taken, everything would have to be rewashed. On a scorching hot day, water from the tap equalled the outside temperature so filling the hessian water bag and hanging it under the verandah kept us supplied with cool drinking water. Before mother left for work each morning, she checked the water level in the top of the Coolgardie safe. This was a galvanised metal framed safe, with a water tray on top and a drip tray underneath. Its walls were comprised of hessian and squares of wet wool flannel emanating from the filled water tray draped over the side onto the hessian, dripping water down all four sides keeping the entire safe wet and cool, and the butter, milk and other perishables safe from spoilage. The drip tray at the bottom spilled out into a container which had to be emptied regularly.

While running an errand to pick up some medication for my croup, I heard music coming from a house. It was loud and clear and I asked a small child standing by her gate what it was. She told me it was the radio playing *The Road To Gundagai* and that the *Dad and Dave* radio show was about to start. It was the first time I had heard a radio. Rushing home with my medicine, excitedly I declared,

'Oh mother, I wish we could have a radio!' Her standard reply to impossible requests was, 'Just wish in one hand and spit in the other and see which gets full first.' However, she did add that nothing is impossible, but it was many moons before a radio graced our mantel. I enjoyed school and received good grades. To boost self motivation and confidence, students were encouraged to enter the school concert talent quests held in the Town Hall. For my first entry, I gave a rendition of Brahm's *Lullaby* and was runner-up to a girl who interpreted a very sad song. Thinking this was a good idea, next time around I searched and found the saddest country song I'd heard, *Please Mr Conductor, Don't Put Me Off The Train*. It told the story of a sorrowful boy, travelling on a train, without a ticket. The conductor was about to eject him, when the boy pleaded not to be put off the train because he had to reach the best friend he had in the whole world, who was about to die at any moment from an excruciatingly painful illness and was hanging on by a thread awaiting his arrival. If that tale of woe is not sad enough to touch your heart, the final gut wrenching development of the story revealing that the friend was his own mother removed any doubt that the audience would be reduced to tears.

This soul searching tale is followed by a second verse in which a young girl, overhearing the story, takes up a collection from the passengers and pays his fare.

At the next concert I offered this song to the audience. There wasn't a dry eye in the house and I carried off first prize of five shillings. Lucky me!

8

THE BIG CITY

randma's health became fragile. She sold the Ford run-about and moved to Perth where she was closer to specialist treatment for her ailing heart. Dad, Norm and Ron were all members of the armed forces and we felt defenceless and vulnerable. Mother responded to Grandma's pleas of moving to Perth and living with her. We were on the move again. At age thirteen, I was sent to Perth to stay with and help Grandma, while mother and Val prepared our chattels and chickens for removal from Bruce Rock. Soon we were all reunited and living in Grandma's East Perth three bedroom weatherboard house, with its galvanised iron roof. It was quite remarkable to us, for it had features we had never enjoyed before. A bathroom with plumbing, a wash-house with a built in copper, two wash troughs (one for washing, the other for rinsing) and even though the toilet was at the rear of the yard, it had a cistern and we were amazed at how well it worked. The biggest and most wonderful surprise was that Grandma had a radio. We were in awe of this brilliant little wooden box with its speaker and two little knobs for volume and station control.

Mother received regular dependency payments from dad's military allotment and was able to stay at home and take care of Grandma, Ian and me. Val derived great pleasure from working again, while Ian attended the East Perth State School and I was enrolled at the Perth Girl's School. In addition to the usual High School subjects, there were to be swimming lessons and domestic science classes, both of which I was anticipating with pleasure.

Circumstances kept changing my life. No sooner had I started at the Perth Girl's school, when each student received notification that due to the danger of a Japanese invasion, the school would close until further notice and we should all seek enrollment at the school nearest our home. This happened to be Our Lady's College, a Catholic girl's school adjoining St Mary's Cathedral in Victoria Square. Settling in was easy going, but the nuns had not had a Protestant under their tutelage before and they eyed me suspiciously. Once, during a religious instruction period for the Catholic students, I was alone in the classroom studying algebra when two nuns approached me and suggested changing my Protestant standing to Catholicism. On hearing this mother advised me that it was not compulsory and to carry on as usual. I liked the college. Although discipline was strict, there were good educational opportunities, including book-keeping, touch typing, short hand and French language tuition all of which I enjoyed, but alas, there were no swimming lessons.

For my fourteenth birthday Grandma's gift to me was a permanent wave. An after school appointment was made and I felt apprehensive sitting in the hair-dresser's chair with huge hot iron curlers all over my head. When the procedure was complete my face was framed with curls and I felt special, except for a scalp burn resulting from an over heated curler. Next day at school, one of the nuns told me I would have done better to have put the time into study instead of vanity. This diminished the pleasure derived from Grandma's generosity.

There was hardly a family in Australia untouched by World War II. In the early period, many of our service personnel were sent to the Middle East. They were a long way from home and with unsophisticated communications, plus censorship clouding our knowledge of exact locations, every piece of adverse news was received with dread, for fear of possible loss or wounding. Towards the end of 1942, the war office notified mother that dad was missing in action. We were beside ourselves with worry. However, he managed to make it back to his unit and we were informed of his safe return.

Our personal risk at home seemed very remote until Japan entered the war and their relentless drive south to the very shores of Australia made our vulnerability apparent. In 1942 the rationing of petrol allowed each motorist to travel approximately sixteen miles per week. Each person was allowed half a pound of tea every four weeks and one pound of sugar per week. Ration books were issued to every civilian and only 112 clothing coupons were allotted to each person per year. Coupons required for a woman to buy just one complete outfit were: Overcoat 27, suit (jacket and skirt) 23, blouse 7, hat 3, shoes 8, stockings 4, gloves 2, slip 8, panties 4, brassiere 4, a total of 90 coupons. To add to the list a dressing gown 14 and pyjamas 12, would have exceeded the annual allowance of clothing coupons. The restriction on men's clothing was even more severe, as each equivalent article of apparel required more coupons. A man's overcoat used up 40. However, maternity corsets and jock straps were exempt.

Air raid shelters were constructed by the government and many of them were dug out in suburban backyards. Val and I attempted to dig one but the earth was so sandy that as quickly as we dug it out, the sides caved in and we gave up.

Then there were the blackouts. All blinds were closed at night. Street, shop and all outdoor lighting was banned. Strips of brown paper were stuck in lattice work design across our windows to prevent glass from fragmenting in the event of a bombing. The lights of automated vehicles wore covers with cut-out slits illuminating precious little. It was proposed that white lines be painted in the centre of roads to aid night motorists. All signs and mile markers on major highways were removed in case the enemy too easily found their way around.

Every child was supplied with a percussion aid, consisting of a length of string with a small foam rubber ball attached to each end and threaded through a three inch long rubber tube. In the event of an air raid, we were to place the rubber tube between our teeth and stuff the foam rubber balls into each ear, protecting teeth and ear-drums. Women knitting khaki or navy blue scarves, socks, mittens and sweaters for our troops, were a regular sight on public transport.

My fainting bouts were still bothersome. Standing on a chair on the front verandah, hammering a loose nail back into place, the familiar signs of irregular heart beats, total weakness and diminishing vision overcame me. Usually these symptoms gave me time to sit or lie down to avoid injury, but this time the episode happened more rapidly. Collapsing again, I fell off the chair onto the concrete floor of the verandah, hitting my head hard causing bleeding from an ear. As a precaution, mother kept me home from school for a couple of days and I bounced back one more time.

Brothers Norm (left) and Ron

Our house was quite close to the Swan River. On a pleasant sunny day, a group of neighbourhood children built a raft to paddle across to a small patch of land in the river known locally as Rabbit Island. The raft could accommodate only two at a time so it took a few trips to land us on the shore. Once there, a couple of the more adventurous boys embarked on a sight-seeing trip around the island. Unfortunately the skills employed in building the raft fell far short of perfect and it sank leaving one proficient swimmer to drag his non swimming friend back to land. By this time, we were very worried. Fully clothed and two of us unable to swim, we were stranded. A young sculler training on the river answered our cries for assistance and came to our aid. His long narrow racing boat could accommodate only one person at a time, so loading, swimming and pushing his fragile boat, he went back and forth until he'd rescued all of us. This incident undoubtedly ruined his day's rowing but his patience and kindness saved us from getting into deep trouble at home.

Grandma became very ill and needed twenty-four hour a day nursing care. Her doctor recommended a Catholic nursing home on the other side of town. Mother, Val, Ian and I delivered her to the facility where she appeared to be comfortable. Thursday and Sunday afternoons were the only visiting days, so mother arranged with the nuns at the college for me to take Thursday afternoons off to visit Grandma and deliver anything she needed. I loved visiting her and she was always pleased to see me. One request was for some home-made junket which I carried in a jar across town in two buses and managed not to shake it up or turn it into mush. The only time I heard her complain was when the staff neglected to cut her finger and toenails and she requested a small pair of scissors for me to take care of them. She was confined in a tiny room, alone with no radio. Mother and the rest of us visited her on Sundays, cheering her every way we could, but mother always left in tears, especially the day Grandma told us a priest had visited and

Sister Val

given her some rosary beads. Mother considered the priest's gesture to be a token of farewell. The following week Grandma died. I was deprived of grieving. Mother would not allow me to attend the funeral, instead I was to be minder to Ian and a horde of unknown cousins.

Heartbroken, a few days later, I found my way to Karrakatta cemetery and said goodbye to my beloved Grandma.

After Grandma died I felt a great loss and to add to my pain, dad was wounded in action. After weeks of medical treatment for his injured leg, he was assessed as no longer fit for active service and returned to Australia to serve in a non-combatant capacity. He came to see us once in a while and we hoped mother and dad would reconcile, but it was not to be.

It seemed our family was slowly being depleted, with the men of the house absent and Val at work, I wanted to grow up. In December 1942 I applied to work during the school holidays, at W.L.G. (Westralian Leather Goods) a luggage manufacturer situated in Wittenoom Street, a stone's throw from where we lived. The manager, Harry Reed, interviewed and hired me for the pre-Christmas season. Starting at 8:00 a.m. and working until 4:30 p.m., my first assignment was making suitcase handles, then long leather luggage straps. For five days work, my first pay packet contained nineteen shillings and sixpence.

My taste for pocket money was whetted and sparked me to ask mother to let me leave school and become a member of the work force. This sent mother into a spin. Her response was an unequivocal 'No!' My schooling was too important. After much pleading, she reluctantly agreed only if I continued my education at night school. Following the holiday season I was working by day, studying by night and paying mother ten shillings a week for board and lodging.

Although it was initially interesting, the work became boring.

Mentioning this to Mr Reed, he advanced me to making attaché school cases. Cutting, milling, bending, rivetting, attaching frames, latches, corners and handles, I was a regular little 'bee' and in spite of my physically immature stature, it wasn't long before I was making full size suitcases. Much to mother's chagrin, later in 1943 I abandoned night school, but continued at W.L.G.

Butter rationing was introduced, allowing only a half pound of butter per person, per week. If at any time we ran out of butter coupons, we breakfasted on eggs and wholemeal toast spread with leftover drippings from roast meat.

Val, my beautiful sister, was being courted by a young American Naval Officer, 'Barney' Harry Eugene. He was likeable, confident and pleasant to be around. His work in the United States Navy was on shore, so the house was frequently filled with his presence. When Ian and I contracted the mumps, he thoughtfully brought us large icecreams every day until we recovered. The distribution of American candy bars and chewing gum was commonplace and he introduced us to the taste of Coca Cola. One evening he brought home some dried corn kernels and demonstrated how to make pop-corn, by pouring the kernels into a pan, covering it and placing it on the hot wood stove. We watched and waited until the sound and aroma of popping corn perked our taste buds.

Barney purchased a bicycle and attached a small motor to the rear driving wheel, which, after pedalling to start, propelled the bicycle along at about twenty miles per hour. On this bicycle he double dinked me on the cross bar to the Perth baths, promising to teach me how to swim. Arriving at the baths we walked around the wooden decking and without notice he pushed me into the deep water. It was a very bad idea. Like a lead weight, I plunged straight to the bottom and almost drowned. Realising his swimming lesson was a failure, he jumped in and hauled me out of the water just in time. The baths were part of the Swan River where American flying boats were moored. On our way home we stopped and watched one of them take off, return and land amongst the jelly fish.

In 1943 Val and Barney married and moved into a house just five hundred yards from where we lived and we were happy to have them nearby. Mother, Ian and I were now the sole occupants of our house. My life was quite routine. I was working five days a week, lunching at home daily with mother, attending as many movies as my spare change would allow, reading and enjoying weekend visits to Scarborough beach.

Norm and Ron came home on leave at different times and got to meet their new brother-in-law, Barney. We begged Ron to show us his marching routine and how to 'present' and 'shoulder' arms as we had seen in the movies. This he did with gusto and put on a grand military show. Norm, on the other hand, clowned around and told absurd stories of his adventures. He beguiled us with tales of grateful Sultans welcoming his battalion to their palaces, where they sank up to their knees in deep carpet. They feasted on outrageous gourmet delicacies of hummingbird tongues, accompanied by peeled grapes and washed down with pomegranate nectar, served in exquisite golden goblets by elegant hand maidens. Servants dressed in silken robes and shoes with rolled up pointed toes wafted fans of colourful ostrich feathers to cool and soothe the men after a long day on the battle field, while beautiful belly dancers in exotic costumes entertained them. My youth and naivety afforded me the luxury of believing these fanciful adventures and coloured my imagination.

1944 saw the birth of Val and Barney's first child Valda. It also ushered in my sixteenth birthday and the blossoming of my womanhood. Val and Barney invited me to accompany them to dances at various venues while mother lovingly cared for her first grandchild.

Rationing was becoming more severe. At two and a quarter pounds per person per week, meat was added to the list and butter was reduced from eight to six ounces for the same period of time.

Manufacturers required to aid the war effort were assigned military contracts. At W.L.G. I installed protective anti-percussive linings in helmets and as each one passed through my hands, I hoped my efforts would save someone's life. Service personnel from Australia, England and the United States were everywhere, snatching moments of rest and recreation from the horrors of war.

Work at W.L.G. had become both tedious and dangerous. At one time I cut a small piece off the end of a finger, which luckily grew back. Another time, the milling machine pedal whacked me on the shin breaking the skin, whereupon an infection set in causing an enormous swelling. Mr Reed sent me to a worker's compensation doctor, my first consultation with any member of the medical profession. Limping into his gloomy little surgery, he told me to take a seat, then bathed the wound in antiseptic, produced a scalpel and without anaesthetic proceeded to lance my excruciatingly painful shin. Barely able to walk, I returned to work and was given simple chores until the wound healed.

Every day at 11:00 a.m. Mr Reed turned on the speakers throughout the building and treated us to an hour of light classical music which I loved, because it helped blank out the racket coming from the operating machinery. Working on some luggage at a rivetting machine during one of these treats, I heard someone call my name. Looking up, I saw a young apprentice, who had been cutting metal frames on the electrically operated guillotine, pleading for help. I ran to him to find the machine's safety bar missing and part of the boy's fingers on both hands had been severed. He was bleeding profusely, was ashen and in shock. Holding him, I screamed to the foreman who rushed to his aid. Grasping the boy's wrists and pressing on the arteries, he instructed me to tell Mr Reed to call an ambulance. I felt so bad for the boy. It was a dreadful experience to have witnessed and was made even worse when the foreman returned to the machine to retrieve the severed finger parts and I never got over the shock. It is beyond my comprehension to imagine what police, firemen and other rescuers mentally endure when attending horrific accidents.

This terrible episode spurred me to consider alternative employment. The Land Army was always calling for young women to replace those young men who were recruited into the armed forces. Having come from the country I knew I could handle anything they dished out, but being under age, mother would not give her consent. Remembering grandma's words, 'Good things come to those who wait,' I decided to persevere at W.L.G. until good things came my way.

1945 introduced Val and Barney's second child Kim into our lives. Valda was only thirteen months old when her baby brother was born. They were adorable babes and received much attention from the family. On my way home from work each day, I called in to see them and to lend Val a helping hand.

Authorities in Western Australia took special precautions against a possible invasion. Japanese bombing raids were carried out, not only in Darwin, but as far south as Exmouth Gulf almost midway between Darwin and Perth. Newspapers carried large block advertisements advising about air raid shelters, protecting children, crowd dispersal and anything which could be of assistance to minimise casualties during an attack. This continual barrage of information had the citizens on alert and continued relentlessly until the tide turned. May 7, 1945 the Germans surrendered unconditionally, followed three months later by the Japanese, on August 15. VP day 1945 was the party to end all parties. The entire city and suburban population was out on the streets. On this day there were no strangers. Everyone was an instant friend and the jubilation was simply that.

The euphoria continued for some time as the veterans returned. Dad was out of the Army, Norm returned home and Ron, who had last been in action in Balikpapan, Borneo, was on leave, but soon after was transferred to the occupation forces in Japan.

Until I turned seventeen, other than my brothers, my only association with boys came about when accompanying Val and Barney to ballroom dances. My introduction to this pastime was the formal Old Time Dance which included the Veleta Waltz, Pride of Erin, Gipsy Tap, Parma Waltz, Boston Two-step and the much loved Progressive Barn Dance. The latter gave one the opportunity to change partners, giving everyone on the dance floor the chance of an informal introduction, which was the reason for its popularity.

Fifty-fifty dances mixed the old time with the new, including the Modern Waltz, Fox Trot, Slow Fox Trot, Quick Step, Tango and the Jitterbug (taught to us by Barney) and danced to a rendition of *Golden Wedding*. The bands played popular music of the time like *Cow Cow Boogie, Elmer's Tune, In the Mood, Serenade in Blue,* and *Sentimental Journey*. The really big dances had a band with Saxophones, Trumpets, Trombones, Piano, Bass and Drums playing the music of Glenn Miller, Benny Goodman and Artie Shaw. A 'lucky spot' dance highlighted the evening. The lights dimmed, the band played a romantic slow song and at a prearranged point, a spotlight hit the floor and the lucky couple standing in the circle of light received a prize.

Most people relied on public transport to travel to and from dances, so all dance halls closed in time for patrons to make a connection with the last bus or train home.

The younger set owned dozens of song books costing about sixpence each. They contained the lyrics of the most popular melodies played on radio and we knew them all. Favourites like *Don't Get Around Much Any More, You'll Never Know, Begin the Beguine, Boogie Woogie Bugle Boy, Don't Fence Me In,* and *Saturday Night Is The Loneliest Night Of The Week.*

Barney was recalled and stationed in the United States. Letters and gifts for his family arrived frequently. A big decision about where he, Val and the children would live, had to be made. Barney wanted them to settle in the United States, but Val wanted to live in Australia, so the situation was at a stalemate.

By 1946, Val decided she could not leave Australia. Barney's naval career firmly anchored him in the United States, so a divorce was inevitable. Val was granted custody of the children, but vowed to keep in touch with Barney and his family enabling them to have a close relationship with Valda and Kim. Keeping her promise, she corresponded regularly, sending photographs and information on the progress of their offspring.

Norm's steady girlfriend Ursula was a weekly visitor to our home. Tall like Norm and with striking good looks, she was well mannered and pleasant company. They were both interested in antiques and travelled from place to place on and in Norm's motorcycle and sidecar.

Almost twelve years old, Ian was an agreeable child with typical boyish behaviour. One of his pranks was to enter any room in which I might be alone and start yelling loudly and calling for mother. When she appeared on the scene, he declared I was hitting him. Mother soon got tired of his mischievousness and one day hid behind the bedroom door while I brushed my hair. Alas for Ian, when he started his hoax, mother stepped out from behind the door, admonished him and reminded him of 'The Boy Who Cried Wolf,' putting an end to his prank. Ian was an excellent student and played football for the East Perth State School team. Due to his influence mother became an enthusiastic football follower. In spite of his unmerciful teasing of them, Valda and Kim adored him like a big brother.

Christmas 1946, mother asked for a volunteer to behead a chicken for Christmas dinner. The family had witnessed this ritual dozens of times, so Val said she would be the executioner.

First we caught the chicken. Val tied its legs together and held them with one hand, laying the chicken's neck on a chopping block at the wood heap. She gripped the axe handle as dad would have done, but just as she was about to strike, the chicken retracted its head. This happened several times, so Val ordered Ian to tie a length of string around its neck and hold it in a stretched position. Ian did as she asked and with one sharp blow, the chicken was ready for plucking. Hanging the bird from the clothesline post, she boiled a kettle of water, poured the contents over the chicken, doused the feathers and proceeded to pluck it. Rolling up a piece of newspaper and lighting it with a match, she singed off the remaining hairs. Now it was ready for mother to gut and dress for the oven, in readiness for our annual roast-feast.

Back at work following the January 1947 holidays, the pommelling and crushing blows my hands received from the tools and machinery were taking their toll on my joints. Suffering incessant swellings, aches and pains, I was not prepared to put up with it any longer.

9

AUDITION

etermined to get away from the dangers at work, I started searching the newspapers every day for alternative employment. Weeks went by with nothing appealing to me, until one day an advertisement appeared for a 'Tivoli Girl' at the Tivoli Theatre. Giving the idea some serious consideration and discussing the situation with Val, I asked what she thought about me attending the auditions. Well, much to my delight, she was very enthusiastic and said, 'You have nothing to lose'.

When mother heard about it, she was understandably negative about any scheme that would take me away from what she perceived to be permanent employment. Borrowing one of Val's playsuits, consisting of crisp white cotton shorts with matching midriff top and hastily rehearsing a simple routine learned at dancing classes years before, I took time out from work and set off for the audition.

Arriving at the Tivoli with tap shoes in hand, I was surprised to find some budding Ginger Rogers devotees had already auditioned and were leaving the theatre. With absolutely no point of reference as to how difficult it would be to secure a position with the famous Tivoli circuit, I had no choice but to play it by ear. On entering the dimly lit theatre, I noticed a handful of people sitting in the front stalls. An attractive tall girl with platinum blonde hair approached me. Asking my name, she beckoned me to follow her up some steps onto the stage. Introducing herself as Lorys Blencowe, she advised me to put on the tap shoes. When this was done, there I stood in a pool of light, centre stage, the focus of everyone's attention. Lorys announced my name and from the darkness of the theatre, a male voice asked, 'Have you had any theatrical experience?' 'Nothing except school concerts, dancing classes and singing competitions,' I replied.

There was a moment's silence, which seemed like an eternity. I felt that my opportunity had passed by without being given a chance, but then I was told to confer with the Musical Director Geoff Robertson who had handled many auditions with inexperienced performers. We talked through the music and with a four bar introduction, I sang and danced my way through Cole Porter's *Anything Goes*. It had been used regularly at the dancing classes and was a simple, straight forward thirty-two bar song and dance routine.

When it was over the voice indicated that I should join the group in the front stalls. Lorys introduced me to Producer-Director Bruce Carroll, Assistant Producer-Stage Manager Hal Lennon and Choreographer Madge Wilson. Bruce asked if I could tell a joke. As it happened, mother had related her favourite joke only days before, so with a confident 'Yes,' I told the following story:

> *The Lady of the Manor was expecting dinner guests. She was experiencing post nasal drip and was concerned that the guests would notice her problem before she could rectify it, so she told her butler to discreetly inform her should he notice anything. The code he was to use was, 'James is at the door!'*
>
> *Soup had been served, when the Butler noticed the tiny drip on Madam's nose.*
>
> *'Madam! James is at the door' he announced. Unfortunately, 'Madam' was so engrossed in conversation with her guests that she ignored the signal.*
>
> *The Butler persisted valiantly, 'Madam! James is at the door!'*
>
> *Finally, Madam turned to the Butler and snapped, 'What is it?'*
>
> *The Butler replied, 'Madam, James WAS at the door, but he is NOW IN YOUR SOUP!'*

To my surprise and relief, everyone laughed. They made their decision and I took my first step into the entertainment industry.

Choreographer Madge Wilson initiated me into the language and ways of the theatre, explaining things like when facing the audience, the left hand side of the stage is referred to as the *Prompt Side*, and alternatively the right side is *Opposite Prompt* or *O.P.* The rear *Up-Stage* and the front, *Down*

Stage, behind the scenes *Back Stage*. The *Wings* of the theatre are large canvas covered pieces of scenery used to extend the set off stage. They are very unobtrusive but are critical as they conceal the off-stage activities from the audience. The expression *Waiting in the Wings* means that the performer waiting to go on stage is hidden behind this scenery awaiting his or her entrance. *Footlights* are a series of lights along the front of the stage near the floor with reflectors to throw the light back on to the performers. *Spotlights* are also used with reflectors, throwing a strong light on any given thing or person. The musicians sit in a *Pit* in front of the stage. It took no time at all to become acquainted with these and many other theatrical terms.

Everything was a new experience and to be backstage was thrilling. Lorys escorted me into the wardrobe department to take measurements and have costume fittings. The mystique and ambience of the theatre was exemplified in this large room. There were endless racks of sparkling costumes, shoes and exotic head-dresses. The costumes for the Tivoli Girls were designed to look spectacular under the bright lights. The wardrobe mistress Florence Devine instructed me to purchase two flesh coloured 'Hollywood Maxwell' net brassieres (bras) as part of my personal Tivoli Girl effects. The bras would be the basis for many decorative flowers, sequins, feathers, diamentes and other suitable adornments as required for each costume.

The dressing rooms were downstairs and I followed Lorys as she entered one of them. It was just like something out of a Hollywood movie musical. Facing us and extending along one wall was a bench style dressing table. Over this were four individual large make-up mirrors, each mirror surrounded by bright light bulbs for perfect make-up application. Under the dressing table was a small drawer in which to store one's personal items. On the opposite wall was a long rack which held in sequence all of the costumes needed for the show. On another wall was a large full length mirror used for a last minute all over check before going on stage.

Lorys sat me down in a chair in front of one of the mirrors, produced a pair of tweezers and proceeded to pluck and shape my eyebrows, reminding me to take note, for it would be my responsibility in the future. As it was the first time and was done by someone other than myself, the procedure was quite painful, but through experience I learned how to master this without pain. On a piece of paper, Lorys wrote out a list of theatrical cosmetics otherwise known as grease paint. This theatrical make-up was invented by Wagnerian opera-singer Ludwig Leichner in the latter part of the nineteenth century. It came in thick sticks with each shade numbered. There were also thin sticks to outline eyes and lips and for many other dramatic effects. These days one has the choice of a wide range of theatrical cosmetics, which includes the well known Max Factor line. Adding to her list were false eyelashes, a jar of cold cream for removing make-up and a large tube of leg tan. She explained that the application of make-up is personal and to make changes later would be my prerogative. In the meantime, her basic list would see me through.

The natural colour of my hair washed out under the bright stage lighting, so a demonstration of how to apply a henna rinse was made available to me and the change in appearance was dramatic. The auburn colour adapted well to my green eyes and overall I was happy with the result. All of the courtesies offered me have never been, nor will be forgotten.

Tivoli theatres were started in Australia by the late Harry Rickards in approximately 1910. His Perth theatre was originally built by Mr T. Shafto who also owned the adjacent hotel which was called the Shaftsbury. The theatre's name was later changed to the Luxor and later still the Hollywood, before reverting to the Luxor once more. On Friday November 2nd, 1945 it became the Tivoli and by that time there were Tivoli theatres in all mainland capitals, each a vaudeville house except the Brisbane Tivoli which was a movie theatre.

10

TIVOLI GIRL

y position with the Tivoli was that of showgirl-dancer and the required skills had to be mastered. I was about to learn a great deal about the theatre. Being a Tivoli Girl was a glamorous assignment. Good deportment and elegance was a prerequisite. Prior to this time I had only once worn spike heeled shoes when my sister loaned me a pair of her fashionable *Baby Dolls* to wear to a dance. They were dainty in appearance but difficult to walk in and almost impossible to dance in. However, the Tivoli soon changed that.

Wearing spike heeled shoes, a fabulous costume and a weighty headdress, it was expected that without looking down, I climb and descend precarious staircases, glide effortlessly across the stage, carefully manoeuvre around gowns without catching a heel in the trains and maintain eye contact with the audience. It was almost like an intricate balancing act and certainly new to me. Every movement was choreographed so there would not be any collisions between those entering or exiting the stage and I can't recall one mishap in this area.

Preparing myself for the times when the showgirls would be asked to augment the dancers, it was my obligation to both stay in shape and keep on top of my dancing. Madge gave me a set of exercises for this purpose and I

Wearing a 'G' String and bra. The centre of attention in a Tivoli scena

indulged in them daily. Working on my limited tapping repertoire of time steps, toe-heel taps, shuffles, pickups and so forth, I built up my confidence to be included in the ballet line at any time. Thus another step forward was made and prepared me for the future. The dance routines were challenging and Madge Wilson was exceptionally patient as she led us through each movement. Whenever we were included in the ballet line, she never choreographed anything we showgirls couldn't handle. It was thrilling to be part of the dance troupe and one couldn't help but feel the camaraderie that existed at the Tivoli.

On one occasion, arriving at rehearsal for a French flavoured theme show, I was summoned by Bruce Carroll, whereupon he disclosed his plans for me to be featured in one of the scenes. High on a slowly revolving rostrum, in subtle lighting, standing absolutely stationary, with arms outstretched in a statuesque pose, I was to be the central figure in a dramatic finale. At a given point, a brilliant spotlight would focus on me, dressed in nothing more than a flesh coloured G-string. As these words were tumbling out of his mouth, my mind was racing to come up with an excuse for not agreeing to this preposterous suggestion and at the same time, not losing my job. Explaining that mother would never agree to nudity in any form, Bruce quietly withdrew the suggestion, almost as though he had expected this response. The end result was that I played the scene wearing a sequin covered G-string and bra, (much less revealing than today's string-bikini,) and the words nude or semi-nude were never mentioned again.

Tivoli scena. Panda – eighth from left next to Ike Delavale and Maggie Buckley (centre)

Panda – front row left with full Tivoli cast and visiting dignitaries

11

Comedy Sketches

long with headline comedian Ike Delavale, darling of the patrons and Maggie Buckley, leading lady of comedy at the Perth Tivoli, soubrette Doris Whimp was a major player in the sketches. At times Lorys and I would be called upon to be a foil for any one of the comedians who required additional talent. These sketches were played in front of the tableau curtains, more commonly referred to as the 'front tabs,' which were divided centrally and drawn sideways for opening, or in reverse for closing. While the sketch was being performed in front of the tabs, behind them, the stagehands were striking the set and setting up the next scene with the speed of a Grand Prix pit crew. A stage black-out signified the tag to a sketch and during the black-out, one would scurry off stage to change costume in preparation for the next scene.

Major sketches were like self-contained mini-plays within a show and would encompass almost the entire stage and incorporate most of the cast. The 'COURTROOM SKETCH' was a perennial favourite and required a jury, witnesses, clerk of court, prosecutor, defense lawyer, the judge and the accused. There were many variations of this theme, so the audience could never anticipate which direction the action would take. This sketch was one of my favourites. Many times the cast was caught breaking up with laughter at the hilarious physical and verbal ad-libs delivered by Ike Delavale and Maggie Buckley. In fact many of the sketches, more often than not, contained ad-libs and this kept the material fresh, interesting and each show a new adventure.

These experienced practitioners of comedy had their own individual style of attaining optimum results from their material. Each had a different delivery and their timing was always spot on. It was a great feeling to work with these exceptionally talented entertainers who had the power to make an audience shake with laughter. I loved it.

To compete with the picture theatres, where they were able to change the movies frequently, it was necessary for the Tivoli to maintain a similar policy.

The shows changed approximately every two weeks, so as one started, we were already preparing for the next. This meant that at all times there were two shows going on in your head at the same time and if concentration lapsed, it could be the end of your career. New acts would be engaged every two to three weeks. People from vaudeville had the ability to absorb and perform material accurately and with a minimum of rehearsal, so the changing shows were never a problem.

12

THE ACTS

he shows started precisely at 8:00 p.m., and the entire cast had to be in the theatre by 7:30 p.m., so punctuality was strongly emphasised. Arriving at the theatre as early as 7:00 o'clock allowed me a leisurely hour to apply make-up and time to relax before curtain-up. This gave me the opportunity to get to know the various acts in each show. Observing them was like attending a school of Vaudeville. Some of the great acts with their fanciful show business titles were, 'The King of Fun,' Ike Delavale, a veritable mine of talent. At that point in time, Ike held an Australian record of appearing continuously at the one theatre for two years, varying his seemingly bottomless well of material. His popularity was such that, after a short break, he returned to the Tivoli and continued his amazing nonstop career.

Ike's partner, Maggie Buckley, was also a highly prized performer. Billed as the 'Queen of Syncopation,' she was more than a singer and comedienne. She was recognised as one of the foremost character actresses of her time. As a team, she and Ike rightfully held court at the Tivoli as King and Queen, their titles were well earned and their talents held in the highest esteem by all other performers.

'The Atomic Comic,' Morrie 'Slim' Barling was another of the Tivoli's regular comedians. A South African, he headlined several shows and being part of the team kept him in demand to work alongside other international artists.

Heather James, Great Britain's leading Piano Accordionist, was known as 'The Mighty Scotch Atom.' She had that intangible something extra that can transform a fine musician into an entertaining act of International stature.

Desiree, another import, came to the Tivoli direct from the Follies Bergeres in Paris. She was a fan dancer with a unique way of presenting her act. Wearing only a G-string and working with two exotic ostrich feather fans, she manipulated them with the grace of a swan and not at any time did she reveal her hidden treasures. One could see the audience craning their necks to perhaps get a glimpse of her nakedness, but alas for the audience, she was able to outsmart them. The women admired her courage and the men felt the illusion was worth even more than the price of admission.

For many years Wee Georgie Wood was a major international vaudeville sketch comedian and B.B.C. variety artist. He first toured Australia in 1926 and was exceedingly popular. Twenty-one years later he had returned to fulfil engagements at the Melbourne, Sydney and Perth Tivoli Theatres. Born in England, his natural growth had stopped as a boy, leaving him wanting in height and his tiny stature was accompanied by a pre-adolescent boy soprano voice, effectively used in the sentimental songs with which he usually closed his act. It was a sign of the times that he was able to take these seemingly insurmountable obstacles and turn them to his own advantage.

No greater star appeared at the Tivoli than Will Mahoney, 'The Man who made the King laugh'. He was a comedy genius and at the same time he could not have been a more generous, helpful, patient and encouraging human being. Questions asked about show business were answered forthrightly and with encouragement. Will was the first person I heard describe the difference between a comedian and a comic. A comedian is someone who does funny things, while a comic is someone who *says* funny things. Sight acts, he explained, were so called because they did not rely on dialogue to entertain. Acts like Amazing Gymnasts, Sensational Whirlwind Skaters, Acrobatic Wonders, jugglers, illusionists and an endless variety of unique entertainers, could appear anywhere in the world without language difficulties. Anyone who was fortunate enough to see a live performance of will Mahoney would never forget the experience. The sheer depth of talent was remarkable. His various routines included, 'The Ballerina,' in which Will appeared dressed in a Tu Tu and toe shoes. The shoes resembled a pair of football boots with extremely elongated toes designed to support his every comical move without having to worry about toppling off his mobile perches. His witty dialogue, his mischievous attitude and his prancing around on point was something to behold and made this a classic piece.

Many comedians presented a bathroom sketch, but Will's version had to be one of the funniest. With Lorys Blencowe playing the lady in the bathtub, he extracted howls of laughter from the audience with his slapstick antics. Skidding and falling about in the bubble-bath suds which had splashed all over the set, was intentionally chaotic.

His now famous Xylophone act was a unique Vaudeville masterpiece. With xylophone mallets attached and protruding from his shoes, he danced on top of the key bars of the instrument and cleverly tapped out melodies, delivering comical anecdotes with abandon. In all of the intervening years, I have not seen nor heard of this act being duplicated.

Another show stopper during his Perth engagement, was a duet performed with teen-age violinist Peggy Mortimer to the tune of George and Ira Gershwin's *Let's Call The Whole Thing Off*. (Peggy later married musician Enzo Toppano and presented show business with the gifted actress Peta Toppano.)

Good comedy is timeless and these routines performed today would still be accepted with the same enthusiastic response. Will's advice and encouragement played a major part in my decision to ultimately leave the Tivoli in Perth and venture to the east coast to further my career.

Dozens of outstanding entertainers passed through the stage door of the Perth Tivoli whilst I was there, each one leaving an indelible imprint on my mind.

13

KALGOORLIE

he Gold mining town of Kalgoorlie was about to embark on its racing carnival. Bruce Carroll had announced that the Tivoli Company would present shows there during this spring event so we were all excited about travelling to Kalgoorlie for a three week season. Just before the last show *Clowns in Clover* closed at the Tivoli in Perth on Thursday August 21 1947, it had been decided that as a farewell gesture, Tosti's *Goodbye* would be included in the show. This created a certain amount of trepidation because in theatrical superstition this particular song is considered very bad luck. However, we soon overcame our apprehension and after the crew struck the sets, the wardrobe department packed the costumes, and our luggage and props were stacked on top of the chartered bus, dubbed 'Miss Tivoli.' We climbed aboard and were on our way. Everyone was dressed comfortably for the long journey ahead and spirits were high. Chatting amiably and tossing jokes around the bus, it wasn't too long before exhaustion replaced enthusiasm and most of those on board were sleeping as best they could.

Travelling at an average speed on the open road and approaching Bodallin, all on board were relaxed and everything seemed normal. Suddenly, for some unexplained reason the driver lost control. The bus started to rock from side to side and with the heavy props and baggage on top, the bus was already listing. First we were riding on the left wheels then the right wheels, back and forth from side to side. The bus was making a hair-raising racket and all of the cabin hand luggage was being flung around like missiles, creating a very frightening situation. By this time everyone was wide awake and watched horrified as the driver frantically tried to gain control. There was a final terrifying lurch and with a thundering crash the bus rolled over onto its right side. The sound of grinding metal and shattering glass was like an explosion. Those on the left side were hurled across the bus with some landing on those who were seated opposite. I was catapulted through the air head first onto the opposite wall of the bus and was rendered unconscious. On awaking, the pain in my jaw was so excruciating I mercifully fainted again.

Regaining consciousness and realising that my jaw was locked and immovable, the refrain of Tosti's *Goodbye* rang in my ears. Someone told everyone to get out of the bus as quickly as possible in the event there might be a fire. I don't remember exiting the bus, but found myself sitting on the side of the road with head between my legs to stave off fainting. Looking towards the bus, those who were uninjured were milling around trying to sort out their luggage from the props which were strewn all over the side of the road.

We were on an isolated stretch of the highway so had to wait until help arrived. Eventually some workmen in a utility truck stopped to offer assistance. Those of us who were injured were placed on the tray of the truck to be taken to the Southern Cross Hospital about thirty miles away. When the driver set off, we couldn't believe how painful and nerve shattering it was bouncing around in the back of the truck.

A short while later, in his haste to get medical attention for us, the driver accidentally steered on to a shoulder of the road into gravel, causing the truck to slide down an embankment into a culvert and by some miracle, stopped almost at the point of overturning. For the second time in one day we'd been involved in an accident. In total disbelief and suffering shock, we then had a further delay waiting to be towed out of the culvert.

Finally arriving at the hospital, with my face very swollen, jaw locked tight and speech almost inaudible, I thought things would be just fine. However, as this was a small hospital, very limited medical facilities were available and those of us who were not suffering from lacerations were in for quite a long wait to see a doctor. Jimmy Haines, a specialty tap dancer had his arm severely lacerated and it took some time to complete his treatment.

When I was finally attended to, the doctor said he suspected my jaw was broken and as there was no X-ray equipment in Southern Cross, I would have to go on to Kalgoorlie for treatment.

The train trip from Southern Cross to Kalgoorlie was a mental nightmare for me. The shock of the events that had preceded this journey was starting to have an effect. As the old steam train trundled toward Kalgoorlie with its 'clickety clack' sound, its jerking and swaying motion, it seemed like there might be a third accident for the day.

Bruce Carroll had been alerted and was at the station to take care of me. He rushed me to the radiologist for X-rays and there we received the first positive news of the day. The results were negative, no broken bones. The problem was a burst blood vessel which had caused trauma to the jaw. The swelling was the size of a clenched fist with severe bruising which would take days to dissipate.

The injuries Jimmy Haines had sustained resulted in his hospitalisation back in Southern Cross. This situation left a large gap in the show, as Jimmy had been featured in some of the comedy sketches and scenes, so it wasn't easy to replace him at a moment's notice. Ike Delavale, Maggie Buckley, Hal Lennon and Bruce Carroll had a meeting and quickly cast Tom Carroll, Phil Moran and Alan Barry to cover Jimmy's roles. Bruce also asked me to

Our bus, 'Miss Tivoli' after the crash

perform that night. Trying to speak through a locked jaw was impossible, so my position in the sketches was temporarily cancelled. Necessary changes were made to my grooming. The swelling and bruises had to be disguised and this was accomplished by draping my hair over the swelling, while the bruises disappeared under some skillfully applied make-up. Although feeling a little unsteady, when the curtain went up, it was on with the show.

As the racing carnival was in full swing, hotel accommodation was unavailable. Bruce Carroll had been able to place the cast in private homes and as only breakfast was provided we ate our other meals in restaurants near the theatre. Due to my jaw injury, solid foods were impossible to chew, so for the next few days, my only nourishment would be soup, fruit juices and malted milk.

Another of our casualties was specialty act Louise Gay. A violinist, she incorporated a flock of love birds into her act. The birds balanced on the violin bow while she executed her musical repertoire. Prior to her arrival in Australia from Singapore, all of her wardrobe and birds were destroyed in riots. Her first job on arrival had been to obtain a new flock of love birds and train them for the act. It was hard for her to imagine that she might have lost another set of feathered friends, but the birds were unscathed. Bruce's son Roger, who was just a child at the time, insisted that when the bus rolled over, he finished up with his head in Louise's bird cage and thought he had gone to bird heaven. The schedule was hectic. For fifteen days we trekked back and forth from the town halls of Kalgoorlie and Boulder performing five different shows. They were: *Artists and Models*, *Naughty Nineties*, *Hits and Highlights*, *Follies Bergeres*, and *Clowns In Clover*. Also included was a special farewell children's matinee.

Bruce offered a thank you to the people of Kalgoorlie for the many courtesies shown us after the bus accident and for their more than generous hospitality that ensued. Because of the racing carnival, a great number of tourists had taken up the available accommodation and most of the company were in a crisis situation with the possibility of having to live in the bus during our entire stay. More than enough residents volunteered to have members of the cast stay in their homes and yet one more seemingly insurmountable hurdle simply melted away. It was as though the whole project had a fairy godmother looking after us and there could not have been any situation that the entire community couldn't take in their stride.

Whilst performing each night, most of the daylight hours were spent rehearsing for the next production. Whenever free time was available, we were invited to participate in the events of the racing carnival. We also had the opportunity to take an escorted tour of the famous gold mine. Most of us were still too shaken by the bus accident to even consider going down a mine shaft. We were readily identified as being members of the Tivoli and were lauded wherever we went. To our great relief, the cast was told there would be no return bus trip to Perth and that arrangements had been secured for the company to travel by train.

I have treasured the display of generosity shown by the people of Kalgoorlie and this tour has always had a special place in my heart. Upon our return to Perth, we soon settled back into the routine of new shows. Apart from Jimmy Haines, the remainder of the performers had all made full recoveries by this time, making an acceptable ending out of what could have been a disastrous tour.

14

MELBOURNE

 young raven haired beauty and former J.C. Williamson's soprano, June Phillips, came to Perth for a three month season at the Tivoli, including the Kalgoorlie engagement. We became good friends and her many stories about the theatre in Melbourne had me spellbound. Like Will Mahoney, she talked about the Melbourne Tivoli and J.C. Williamson's Musical Comedies, including the new smash hit, *Annie Get your Gun*, starring Will's wife Evie Hayes, which opened in Melbourne on my birthday, July 19, 1947. I was fascinated and wanted to see these shows for myself. Towards the end of June's contract in Perth, her mother Vera came over to spend some time. During a conversation about my future, Vera pointed out that Melbourne was a good central location for theatrical opportunities and suggested I would be most welcome to stay with her family if I relocated there. Of course I was overjoyed at this generous offer.

After Vera returned home, June and I often spoke of the potential opportunities. June's father Norm, was in staging at J.C. Williamson's, His Majesty's Theatre, and Gerry, the elder of her two brothers had theatre interests. My only concern about leaving on this adventure was that mother wouldn't hear of it. June assured her my well-being would be in good hands with the Phillips' family. Armed with mother's approval, a charming family to stay with, letters of introduction from Will Mahoney to Ginger James at the Melbourne Tivoli theatre and producer Carl Randall at J.C. Williamson theatre, I boarded a train and set off for Melbourne on the east coast with nothing more than a couple of suitcases, twenty pounds cash borrowed from my sister Val, and a heart filled with dreams of what might be in the future.

15

NULLABOR

ravelling second class on the old steam train meant sharing a cabin with another woman who had already claimed the lower of the two berths before I arrived for the overnight trip to Kalgoorlie. Changing trains, it was each passenger's responsibility to collect their luggage from the Perth train in Kalgoorlie and transfer it to the baggage car of the 'Trans-Australian' which we boarded to travel across the Nullabor Plain.

The Steward advised passengers there would be three sittings for each meal and calls would be announced at the appropriate times. Meals were served in a dining car, with good rib-sticking food, typical of that served in country hotel dining rooms at the time. Cereal, bacon and eggs, toast, marmalade and hot beverage for breakfast. Soup, hot bread rolls, Shepherd's pie, vegetables, and dessert trifle for lunch. On the dinner table were hot soup, roast pork with crackling, baked vegetables with peas and gravy, followed by steam pudding and boiled custard. The meals varied slightly each day and in addition a morning a cup of tea was brought to the cabin as a wake up call and another at bed-time. The psychology of this was to get you out of and into bed at the staff's convenience.

A memorable moment during the journey happened when sharing a table in the dining car with a married couple. They were discussing the desolation of the Nullabor Plain when the wife said, 'All the Nullabor needs to become the garden oasis of the world, is good people and water.'

'Yeah!' replied the husband, 'that's all Hell needs!'

The Nullabor Plain scenery left a lot to be desired. The terrain is quite flat and mostly uninteresting with its vegetation of mainly salt-bush, mulga and spinifex. The train made many stops along the way to take on water for the steam engine. Most of these stops were small stations with a house or two, practically all of which were occupied by railway personnel such as maintenance crews. Passengers would alight from the train at some of the stops just to stretch their legs and break the monotony. I participated in this activity occasionally, but was more interested in my book *Gone With the Wind* authored by Margaret Mitchell.

The high point of the journey occurred when at one of the stops, the train was met by a tribe of Aborigines selling hand made souvenirs of boomerangs, bull-roars, bark paintings and an assortment of other collectables. Trading was brisk and both buyers and sellers enjoyed the encounter. Before the train steamed off, passengers raided their personal hampers and handed the traders gifts of fruit, biscuits and chocolates.

At Port Augusta was another change of train, then on to Adelaide where a third and final transfer took place before making the overnight trip to Melbourne.

16

FAMILY OF FRIENDS

eering through the carriage window, I saw June Phillips standing on the platform waving frantically as the train pulled into Melbourne's Spencer Street Station. Greeting me warmly with a big hug, we collected my baggage, hailed a taxi and set off for her home in Moonee Ponds. Her parents Vera and Norm and her siblings Gerry, Donald and Maisie welcomed me. Their warmth and friendliness made me feel at ease immediately and I was about to experience what hospitality was. June's father Norm was an amiable man with considerable knowledge of theatre production and gave generously of this knowledge. His wife Vera, was genuinely loving of her children and brooded over them night and day. Her caring extended to my welfare also and at night she would come to my bedside and tuck in the blankets, making sure I was comfortable.

June was aware that I needed coaching to enable me to compete for theatre work in Melbourne and began by sending me to her singing teacher for voice lessons, giving me a goal to strive for.

Having never seen a live performance of a Musical Comedy, I was beside myself with anticipation when we obtained tickets to see *Annie Get Your Gun* at His Majesty's Theatre. Will's wife, Evie Hayes starred as Annie,

American Webb Tilton as Frank and Claude Flemming as Buffalo Bill. The principal roles were of world class and ably supported by a superb cast. Not only was I going to see my first musical comedy, but it happened to be one of the greatest shows of the twentieth century. The story is about a simple outback girl Annie Oakley whose prowess with a gun is miraculous. She is employed as one of the stars of a Wild West show run by Buffalo Bill Cody. This severely bruises the ego of crack shot Frank Butler, who leaves the show and joins an opposition troupe, which in turn ruins the business of both companies. Eventually the two shows merge, but the friction between Annie and Frank continues. Annie is romantically interested in Frank and is persuaded by Chief Sitting Bull (Sydney Wheeler) that if she can bring herself to lose a shooting contest with Frank her fortune in the game of love will be greatly improved. Hence the song, *You Can't Get a Man With a Gun*. The entire show was filled with the wonderful music of Irving Berlin: *Doin' What Comes Natur'lly, Sun In the Morning, They Say That Falling in Love Is Wonderful*, and the show stopper to end all show stoppers, *There's No Business Like Show Business*. On leaving the theatre we were bursting with exhilaration. In fact, the whole experience was overwhelming.

Swinging quickly into action, appointments had to be made with Ginger James at the Tivoli Theatre and Carl Randall at His Majesty's Theatre. Heading first for the Melbourne Tivoli Theatre in Bourke Street, with Will Mahoney's letter of introduction, an audition with Ginger James was secured. He was very complimentary and offered me an upcoming position as showgirl with the proviso that I would be prepared to appear topless. Although declining this offer, the possibility of a non-topless position was still an option should a vacancy occur.

Next, an appointment was made with New York Producer, Carl Randall, who produced *Annie Get Your Gun* for J.C. Williamson's His Majesty's Theatre. Will's letter of introduction was very helpful in breaking the ice and the audition went off without a hitch. Although there was no immediate vacancy, he asked me to stand by, as there was a possibility of touring with two shows yet to be named.

Returning to Moonee Ponds and announcing the good news to June and family was cause for celebration. Norm, who worked for "The Firm" (as J.C. Williamson Theatres Limited was known) assured me that Carl would never have proposed the offer if it was not genuine. What a wonderful boost for my morale. However, the reality was that a pay check was needed to pay my board and lodging and to sustain me until the tour began.

A successful interview for sales personnel at Coles, led to a training course at the Bourke Street store. It was enjoyable and dealing with the public sent me on another upward learning curve.

During this period of time, Melbourne offered a varied choice in entertainment fare. 'The Kiwis,' a New Zealand troupe of all male thespians were at the Comedy Theatre with the third of their famous revues *Bengrazi*. This was on the 'must see' list for all theatre-goers. Then there were the Opera *Carmen* playing at the Princess Theatre, world famous pianist Eileen Joyce packing them in at the Town Hall and following close on her heels was Gladys Moncrieff. Top radio 'Shell Show' personality Willie Fennell, was touring with his "Ow are yer Mate' show. A memorable night out at the Tivoli was to see American stage and screen star Chico Marx, member of the famous Marx Brothers comedy team. A wide selection of movies was also to be had. Amongst them *The Best Years of Our Lives* starring Fredric March and Myrna Loy. *The Root of all Evil*, starring Phyllis Calvert and John McCallum, *Son of Frankenstein*, with Boris Karloff and Bela Lugosi, also Abbott and Costello in *The Exile*.

One Sunday, Norm and Vera invited me to attend a match at the Melbourne Cricket Ground between the *Annie Get Your Gun* cricket club and members of Parliament. Norm played for the 'Annie' team, so I had the opportunity to mingle with the cast and crew. It was good fun and they even included me in a picture for the *Age* newspaper.

After a very short time at Coles, the call came from J.C. Williamsons that the tour with *Follow The Girls*, and *White Horse Inn* was confirmed. Realising that the tour may not offer employment forever, it was important not to sever the connection with Coles. The supervisor placed value on my job performance and approached management for a temporary leave of absence. The manager did not agree to this arrangement, so my resignation was tendered and with the Phillips' family blessing, I boarded the train for Perth.

17

J.C.W.

hose of us who were fortunate enough to be chosen, would join 'The Firm's' Musical Comedy company in Perth, following the success of their two previous presentations, *No, No, Nanette*, and *The Girl Friend*. The latter would play until we opened with the third production of the season, *Follow the Girls*. Luckily for me, as a member of the chorus, I was able to lay my hands on the lyrics, so the four day journey from Melbourne to Perth was put to good use learning the show. Some of the choristers travelling with me were: Jean Campbell, Joan Cowan, Roma Kent and Valerie Meehan. Time spent on the train going over and over the songs from *Follow the Girls*, helped pass the time and gave me a fundamental knowledge of the show, which in turn added to my confidence when we went into rehearsals in Perth.

Although homesickness had not been a major problem for me in Melbourne (thanks to the atmosphere in the Phillips' household), it was good to be back home with my family.

During rehearsal for *Follow The Girls*, two of the featured dancers were practicing a classical *Pas De Deux* for the show. When they had completed their routine, I noticed the young man staring in my direction. I smiled and he came over and introduced himself as Francois Lisner. We talked for a short time and he invited me to join him for coffee following rehearsal. Adjourning to a neighbouring coffee shop, I found him to be a very personable, articulate young man. He was a former member of the famous Borovanski Ballet Company, which had temporarily disbanded earlier that year (1948,) thereby creating the opportunity for him to transfer to J.C. Williamson's Musical Comedy Company. His family had migrated to Australia in 1937, from Paris, France. He had two siblings, Paulette and Charles (a dancer with the Royal Ballet in London.) His mother Malka and father Joseph took up residence in North Carlton, Melbourne, where they ran a

Francois

successful tailoring business. His family was of the Jewish faith, so it was most fortunate that they left France when they did, although the terrible holocaust which wreaked havoc upon Europe touched his family in many ways. While living in North Carlton, Francois (who had changed his first name from Tauvia for professional reasons) had learned piano and with his brother Charles, studied ballet at the Borovanski Ballet Academy, eventually joining Borovanski's Ballet Company. Eleven years after his arrival from Paris, he still spoke fluent French, Yiddish and perfect English.

The long hours of rehearsals continued and we took every chance to exchange greetings, arrange dates and generally behave like two young people forming a relationship. By the time the season was under way, we were inseparable and referred to as 'an item' by the cast. Each day after exercises, we would either take trips to the beach, go on sight-seeing tours, visit the many beautiful parks, or catch up on some matinee movies. On Sundays, we visited my home, making the most of mother's good home cooking and enjoying the company of sister Val and brothers Norm and Ian. Brother Ron, was still in the army.

Follow the Girls was not a very complex plot, which was ideal for my debut into Musical Comedy. The musical score was written by Philip

Charig, the lyrics by Dan Shapiro and Milton Pascal and the book by Guy Bolton, Fred Thompson and Eddie Davis. Pat Keating, Fred Murray and Colin Croft headed the cast. Other talented players were, Robert Burns, Albert Chappelle, Wilma Harrison, Phil Jay, Miriam Lester, Bobby Mack, Betty Meddings, Lily Moore and Betty Sparks. The plot centred around the 'Spotlight Canteen,' a recreational club for servicemen on Long Island. A sailor named 'Goofy Gale' (Fred Murray) and Burlesque beauty 'Bubbles La Marr' (Pat Keating), romped through this World War II piece of fantasy, with 'Bubbles' wowing them every night with her saucy rendition of *I Wanna Get Married*. There were other delightful moments provided by songs like *Today Will Be Yesterday Tomorrow, I'm Gonna Hang My Hat, Twelve O'clock and All is Well* and many others. Encouragement received from Producer Carl Randall, benefited all of us. The glamorous costumes were designed by Norman Hartnell, Berkeley Sutcliffe, William Chappell and Edgar Richard. My favourite was a beautiful, slinky, full length white crepe sheath.

When rehearsals began for *White Horse Inn*, it was pleasing to renew my acquaintance with Phil Moran, with whom I had worked at the Tivoli and was now also a member of the chorus. During the run of the show we happily reminisced about our Tivoli days. The schedule became hectic. We were performing in *Follow The Girls* every night and by day, rehearsing *White Horse Inn* which was a complete three act Operetta. When Francois and I weren't dancing, we were singing, learning dialogue, or being fitted for the twenty or more costume changes required. Our social life dwindled to coffee breaks, but our affection blossomed.

A three day break between the two shows, allowed time for the elaborate sets of *White Horse Inn* to be assembled in the theatre. With the complications of setting the revolving stage, everything had to be checked and double-checked to ensure that the mechanism worked flawlessly. In addition to the cast, there were farm animals tethered on the revolve, including goats who left their calling cards every show, causing us to tread gingerly. Also scattered around the set were twelve children under the watchful eye of dance director, Hazel Meldrum.

The music for *White Horse Inn* was written by the Austrian composer Ralph Benatzky, with additional numbers by Robert Stolz, Bruno Granichstaedten and Robert Gilbert. The libretto was adapted by Hans Müller from the Blumenthal and Kadelburg comedy *Im weissen Rössl*. One of the most elaborate musicals of the 1930's, it continued successfully right through until the 1950's. Even as late as 1954 it was completely revamped in London, to become *White Horse Inn on Ice* and proved to be a box office triumph. With exquisitely reproduced costumes of colourful velvets, brocades and other rich fabrics, we were dressed as villagers, waitresses, dairy maids and tourists. In one scene, Francois and his fellow dancers performed an exciting Tyrolean 'Slap Dance', wearing authentic leather costumes. The company provided us with dressers, who would help us in and out of our costumes, doing and undoing the many hooks and eyes, buttons and bows. Zippers were discouraged in stage productions because of the possibility of them bursting open during a performance. The plot centres around an Austrian Inn where the head waiter Leopold (Colin Croft), endlessly courts the Inn's proprietress Josepha Voglhuber (Miriam Lester). The lives of the Inn's guests are interwoven to create tensions and misunderstandings. The Emperor Francis Joseph (Percy Martin) arrives at the Inn and through his benevolence for his people, soon has everyone united, including Josepha and Leopold, which brings the show to a satisfactory and happy conclusion. The best known songs from the show were *It Would be Wonderful*, *The White Horse Inn*, and *Goodbye by Robert Stoltz*, (Remembering the 'Miss Tivoli' bus crash, I thanked God the latter was not written by Francesco Tosti.) It was a big and happy cast numbering approximately sixty and this company helped nurture the talents of several members. One of the principals, Betty Meddings, became a successful television choreographer at both Channels Seven and Nine in Melbourne. Judd Laine was a choreographer for channel Seven in Melbourne and became one of the most innovative personalities in dancing for both theatre and television. Talented actor singer, Colin Croft expanded his career to include all avenues of theatre and television, while chorister Richard Hennessy created a fashionable custom jewelry boutique in Collins Street, Melbourne. Dancer Tikki Taylor, was featured in other J.C. Williamson productions and was one

In costume for 'White Horse Inn'

of the stars of *The Pajama Game*. Later with her husband John Newman, they provided entertainment for thousands at their theatre restaurant and showcased a succession of talent at this venue.

By the time *White Horse Inn* closed in Perth, Francois and I were already planning to be married and looked forward to the next season in Adelaide, where both shows would be re-staged.

Following the final show, a night club was reserved by the management exclusively for a cast farewell party. Not having been to a night club before, this social affair was something special and caused great excitement for both Francois and me. A wonderful supper was provided and even though I didn't partake of the available alcoholic beverages, the night itself was a natural high. Traditionally, theatricals always have special material on hand just for these occasions and this night was no exception. Our principals Miriam Lester and Fred Murray sang their favourite duets and one by one the other performers including Betty Meddings and Colin Croft displayed their own special talents. An unexpected highlight was provided by one of the chorus girls Valerie Meehan as she rose to the occasion, entertaining us with a piano recital of DeBussy's *Clair De Lune*. The evening was a fitting finale to our sellout season.

A trans-Australian railway veteran by now, it was double the fun traversing the Nullabor with my future husband by my side. In Adelaide, the cast settled into an old, but comfortable hotel near the theatre and unlike hotels today, the bathrooms were shared by everyone. Following exhausting rehearsals, the dining room would fill to capacity, keeping the hotel chef busy satisfying our ravenous appetites.

At one time Mr Edgar Forwood, a theatrical devotee from Adelaide, invited a group of us for a Sunday outing into the Adelaide Hills. The spectacular scenery was a contrast to hotel living and after a wonderful time, this kind man escorted all of us into a country chemist shop, where he told us to select anything we wanted, at his expense. Some of the girls took the opportunity to obtain cosmetics or perfume. At the conclusion of the excursion, he handed each of us a book as a memento of our visit to the country and to this day, I have it still, (*Fauré*, by Norman Suckling).

Edgar had been in the Army in World War 1 and his humanitarian achievements began soon after, taking hospitalized servicemen on weekend excursions around Adelaide and the surrounding areas. He became a well known philanthropist who, throughout his life, gave unstintingly to people in need. His love of theatre allowed us to be included in his unselfish, giving ways. Approximately two years later, on June 26, 1950 the worst commercial air disaster in Australia's history, (at that time) occurred in rugged, isolated country near York, Western Australia. An ANA Skymaster aircraft, bound for Adelaide from Perth, carrying 49 passengers and crew, crashed. The sole survivor was Mr Edgar Forwood, aged 67. He suffered severe shock and third degree burns. Unfortunately, he succumbed to his injuries and died on July 1, just six days later. The photographs recorded and presented to us of that Sunday in the country with Edgar are forever treasured.

All was smooth sailing at the theatre until my old problem of sporadic fainting spells caught up with me. Awaking one morning, not feeling particularly well, but not expecting anything unusual to occur, my irregular heartbeats and accompanying symptoms started once again and barely able to stand, I struggled to Francois' room and weakly knocked on his door, just in time for him to catch me as I entered the twilight zone of syncope. A doctor was summoned to the hotel. During his examination, he detected the irregular heart beat and knowing that the company was moving on to Melbourne, referred me to a cardiologist. As an after-thought, before he left, he advised me not to mention the heart condition to anyone, or there could be discrimination whenever seeking employment whether it be in theatre or elsewhere. With this information at hand, my decision was to stay tight-lipped about it and was a secret maintained throughout my working life.

Towards the end of the season, before our departure from Adelaide, a picnic and sporting event for the entire cast and crew was held at a country sports oval to celebrate the successful run of the show. On a bright sunny Sunday morning, the only non-working day for theatricals, we all boarded a bus for the big event. Fun is the primary objective and even though competition is the mainstay of the day, congenial rivalry makes for happy memories. Such events as the three legged race, egg and spoon race, sack race, assorted trivial ball games and relay race, made for much joyous behaviour. There were also many jokes exchanged that day, especially the theatrical variety. My contributing story was:

> *The Producer of a Road Show Company, telegraphed the manager of a theatre in a tiny town where the company was due to appear.*
>
> *The telegram read: 'Will hold rehearsals Friday at ten. Have your carpenter, electrician, stage hands and manager ready.' A few hours later the theatre manager replied: 'O.K! He'll be there!'*

Everyone had a great time and through exhaustion, probably the best night's sleep of the tour.

18

RETURN TO MELBOURNE

rancois and I were married on arrival in Melbourne following the closing of *White Horse Inn*. We found and leased a delightful, but small apartment in Spring Street, right in the heart of Melbourne's theatre district. Resuming my relationship with the Phillips family was top of the list and they warmed to my new husband. Francois was back into the ballet dancer's life of rigorous gymnastic workouts, as well as resuming acting lessons. I reported back to J.C. Williamson and was engaged to work in the Opera *La Bohème*. The Opera season was almost at an end and we now needed alternative work.

Mr Leo Curtis, who was later to become Lord Mayor of Melbourne, had a chain of fashion stores which operated under the name of 'Bradmans'. Some stores specialised in handbags and others in lingerie. Engaged as a sales girl in his Collins Street 'Lingerie Boutique,' I became Assistant Manageress.

Ecstatic about expecting a baby, our first Christmas together was spent with a group of Francois' friends, former Borovanski ballet dancers, including Kathleen Gorham, one of Borovanski's Prima Ballerinas. A petite young teenager, with a cute pixie face, she had a charming and witty

With Robin on Mother's Day *Robin aged 3*

personality to match her extraordinary talent. She was affectionately known as Kathy and reminiscing about their ballet years with Borovanski was fascinating and enlightening. They talked about *Giselle*, *Swan Lake*, *Sleeping Beauty*, and other ballets, none of which I had seen at this point in time. Later, Francois introduced me to another of Borovanski's shining stars and one of Kathy's ballet partners, Martin Rubinstein, also a brilliant dancer. His bright future was threatened when he became ill and had to abandon his distinguished career. After a long convalescence, he returned to the scene as an exceptional ballet tutor and director. Those who studied under him were indeed fortunate.

After auditioning, Francois secured a small role in the play *Born Yesterday*, which opened at the Comedy theatre on January 8 1949. During the run of the show it seemed the right time for me to resign from Bradmans. Mr Curtis personally asked me to reconsider, as he had plans for me to manage one of his stores. However, he was understanding when I explained my impending motherhood. Being at home preparing for our baby was a busy time. Actors, dancers and singers popping in and out of our Spring Street apartment was a regular occurrence. To catch up with those with whom I had worked previously and making new friends was stimulating.

When *Born Yesterday* closed in May, Francois joined the cast of *Oklahoma!* Winter was now upon us and after a particularly long and difficult labour, our son Robin, was born by Caesarean section. This marked another turning point in my life.

Although hospitalised for ten days following Robin's birth, ill-health circumvented my homecoming, so I was transferred to a convalescent hospital for another three weeks. At the same time, a problem arose when Francois received the unwelcome news that babies were not permitted in the Spring street apartment. This placed a lot of unwanted stress upon us both. Francois was in *Oklahoma!* six nights a week plus Wednesday and Saturday matinees. Now he had to search for alternative accommodation and during those few daylight hours available, somehow find time to visit baby Robin and me. It was a long and isolated five weeks until I was released from the convalescent hospital and moved into our new temporary living quarters, just a stone's throw from our doctor in Camberwell.

In the short time we were there, a fire broke out in another tenant's quarters. When Francois returned from the theatre, he found the fire brigade in attendance, the building evacuated and all the tenants huddled together in the freezing cold. The firemen quickly extinguished the flames, which caused no injuries, little damage, but scared the daylights out of everyone.

19

CARNEGIE

alka and Joseph (Francois' parents) had retired from their tailoring business and purchased an attractive brick duplex in Carnegie. They lived in one unit and leased the other. Shortly after the fire, at the most opportune time, the lease for the second unit became available and it was offered to us. We moved in immediately. The house was clean, airy and well appointed. My health was improving and the future was looking rosy.

An unwritten rule for theatricals is, 'Never purchase anything you can't fit in a suitcase.' Bearing this in mind, it is understandable how ill-equipped we were to move into unfurnished quarters. With limited funds, we purchased a few items of furniture and Francois' family rallied to help. His uncle gave us a radio, his sister an ice-chest and his parents, utensils and other essentials, enabling us to settle in and establish a home.

The environment was new and I was now part of a European family, whose day to day language was either French, Yiddish or English. Francois would scold his family if they broke into a foreign tongue and insisted they speak English in my presence. Malka eliminated this problem by introducing some basic Yiddish into my vocabulary and as time went on, we all got the hang of how to express ourselves. My cooking skills were basic and in this area, Malka was a veritable mine of information, not only in the preparation of dishes I had never heard of, but in the traditional ways of selecting what to cook and the stringent rules of *Kosher* cleanliness. Some of these rules sound rather quaint today, because modern facilities make them almost redundant, but their application has provided successful hygienic conditions over many centuries. Her recipes for Potato Kugel, Gefilte Fish, Apple cake and home made Cottage Cheese were some of my most successful culinary achievements.

At the same time the Lisners migrated from Paris, the Benini family arrived from Italy and also settled in Carlton, where they all became friends. The Beninis had three children, Mario, Bruno and Hilda, each approximating the ages of the Lisner siblings. I met them at their house, when we attended a welcome home dinner for Bruno, who had just returned from a tour of Italy. A fashion photographer, he was on the threshold of opening his own photographic studio in Melbourne. His brother Mario was studying medicine at St Vincents Hospital and their sister Hilda held a position with the Italian Consulate. They were a charming family and a grand time was had at the reunion. We were to visit each other regularly, sharing many happy hours together.

Francois' brother Charles returned from London after a successful season with the Royal Ballet Company. He had contracted a severe bout of pneumonia whilst in England and returned to Australia, where the moderate climate would be more beneficial. Francois, Charles and I spent many hours talking about the London ballet scene, listening to classical music and following the English librettos to Operatic recordings. Charles longed for a warmer climate and decided Queensland would be perfect, so he moved to Brisbane and opened a School of Ballet. For his contribution to the arts, in 1976, he was awarded an OBE.

Oklahoma! had closed in Melbourne and instead of touring to Adelaide, Francois left the show and accepted a temporary position as a technical assistant at the Princess Theatre in Spring Street. It was during this period that he decided to move away from the theatre. He tried his hand at several different avenues of employment and finally found his niche in advertising. He liked the medium and was happy and successful in this environment.

To supplement our family income, when Robin was old enough, I secured a position as Usherette at J.C. Williamson's His Majesty's Theatre.

Even though it was the other side of the footlights, this was a heartening experience and for many months to come, I absorbed the kaleidoscopic talents displayed in shows like the revival of: *Annie Get Your Gun, Song Of*

Norway, Ice Follie, and across the street, at the Comedy Theatre, a very funny New Zealand revue, *The Kiwis*. I knew the dialogue of every show and the lyrics to every song. Immersing myself in the show made it possible to absorb the quintessence of each actor's performance. In *Annie Get Your Gun* Evie Hayes was the consummate Annie and thoroughly deserved the thunderous applause that followed every show. The adulation for her didn't end when the curtain fell. Each night when she left the theatre there was a host of admirers at the stage door waiting for autographs, or presenting her with flowers. She greeted each of them warmly and disappeared in a large black limousine. At that time, Evie was J.C. Williamson's number one asset.

I contracted a severe bout of the flu and instead of resting in bed, continued to work through. Like most viruses, one thinks it's just a matter of time and it will all go away. Unfortunately, the virus hung on for weeks. When finally seeking medical attention, breathing had become very difficult and the doctor diagnosed me as suffering from asthma. This dreaded disease plagued me on and off until it worsened to the point of having to resign from J.C. Williamson. Eventually injections of adrenaline were administered and this proved to be incompatible with the irregular heart beats, so a medical merry-go-round of medications were tried until a suitable one was found.

At age four, our sweet little son Robin who constantly brought us untold joy, was enrolled in kindergarten. He was extremely bright and each day couldn't wait to attend his preschool classes with his new found pals. Purchasing the appropriate equipment for developing and printing at home, Francois was able to pursue his photographic hobby and became quite engrossed in it, often utilising Robin and me as his subject matter. He considered me to be photogenic and the potential of becoming a photographic fashion model was discussed in detail. With his support, the decision was made. A professional name change was thought to be appropriate and various monikers were bandied around. 'Pandora,' mother's second choice name for me, was the final decision. Considering the title to be a little grandiose, I abbreviated it to 'Panda,' and enrollment at the Mannequin's Academy of Melbourne became a reality. Years in the theatre had established the confidence necessary in this arena and I successfully graduated in April 1953.

20

THE MODELLING GAME

fter graduation I put together a portfolio of professional photographic images and personal details. I then hand-delivered them to the various fashion houses, advertising agencies, department store fashion co-ordinators, commercial photographers and magazine fashion editors.

Before April was over, Peter Fox Photographic Studios published a full page cover lay-out of Robin and me for a special Mother's Day edition of *Our Studio News and Views*. *Woman's Day and Home* Fashion Editor, Isobel Kennedy, had visited the Mannequins' Academy during my training and booked me to do a fashion spread in the magazine, with more to come in the near future. Modelling engagements began to escalate.

To help many worthy causes and at the same time gain exposure, I accepted invitations to model at charity fashion parades. The patrons of these events were usually the most charming of Melbourne's society and models were so valuable to their fund raising, each of us was treated like gold.

This was a productive time and was my first experience of self-employment. Well-known photographers such as Bruno Benini, Gordon De Lisle, Peter Fox, Harry Jay, Latrobe Studios, Helmut Newton, Ritter

Modelling

Jepperson, Carden Rofe, Kenneth Ross, Athol Shmith and Sutcliffe Studios were among those who secured my modelling services.

Although some of the photographers had dressing rooms stocked with a selection of their own preferred make-up and accessories, in the 1950's it would have been a very naive model who turned up for an engagement without her ever present beauty case containing a good supply of make-up, costume jewelry and a large sheer scarf for covering one's head when changing, to protect garments from make-up. It was essential to have a wardrobe with a broad selection of shoes, scarves, gloves, hats, hosiery, handbags and anything else required for a photo-shoot.

No hairdressers or make-up artists were provided and although in retrospect, we would have taken full advantage of these luxuries, being responsible for all facets of our appearance gave each of us the chance to develop our own individual style.

Designer, Robert Millesi, sent me to Buckley and Nunn's Department Store to purchase a length of black wool boucle, whereupon he cut, draped and fitted exclusively, a beautiful formal dress which turned out to be the envy of many. This basic black dress was to be the foundation for modelling coats, millinery, jewelry and any number of other accessories.

By this time I was an established member of the Mannequins' Association, a voluntary Association of Mannequins whose policy was to improve working conditions, promote employment by advertisers, stores, manufacturers, and speak with a single voice for its members. It was founded by Margaret Edwards, Betty Jackson, Judy Lancet, Gretta Miers, Karen Scammel, Bambi Shmith and Gweneth Webber. Having approximately one hundred members, the association agreed that only graduates from approved schools would be accepted. It also operated an agency for their employment and this service was free to both members and employers.

The office of the Mannequins' Association was situated upstairs at 243 Collins Street, adjoining the Peter Fox Studios. Peter Fox was a strong force behind both the photographers and models. He was understanding of their needs and volunteered his expertise whenever it was required.

Helen Violaris was engaged to manage the association. A lovely blue-eyed girl of Greek descent, she was extremely efficient in her role and kept everything and everyone on an even keel. She was a well known jazz singer and appeared with some of the dixieland jazz bands playing in and around the Melbourne club scene.

'The Gown of the Year' was to become an annual event presenting the finest achievements by designers and manufacturers in a dazzling Fashion Parade organised by the Mannequins' Association. Each designer, manufacturer or retail store was represented by an Association mannequin and the details of each gown to be shown were zealously guarded prior to the big event. The opportunity to present the finest gowns at such an illustrious parade, had designers putting forth their most exquisite creations, for to win 'The Gown of the Year' meant good publicity, prestige in the trade and even more importantly, sales at the cash register. Being selected to model any one of the entries meant devoting a lot of time to fittings and design consultations which had to be kept in the strictest of confidence. This glittering evening was a must for the fashion fraternity and all proceeds raised were donated to charity.

Just as everything was falling into place and my foot was in the door of

Myer's fashion parades, more frequent asthmatic attacks struck with a vengeance and all of my accomplishments were at risk of crashing down around me. Cancelling engagements was a recipe for disaster, so I had to diplomatically curtail acceptance of many offers due to this indisposition. During this period of ill~health, many days were spent in bed, with little Robin playing next to me on the carpet. He would run his small match-box cars up on to the pillow, over my face, forehead and down my neck whispering, 'I'll take care of you mummy.' One morning he insisted I stay at the breakfast table until he called. When he was ready he took my hand and we entered the bedroom to find he had made the large bed by pulling the coverlet up over the top of a heap of crumpled blankets, saying, 'This will save your breath and make you better.' Leaving the bed exactly as it was until Francois arrived home, gave us a much needed laugh.

Val had decided to visit Melbourne, so we invited her and her two children Valda and Kim to stay with us. They had hardly set foot on Melbourne soil when a telegram arrived with the news that our brother Ron had died. This came as a terrible shock. He was only twenty-nine years old and his young widow Betty, caring for their nine month old baby daughter, was also expecting their second child.

Val, her two children, Robin and I set off for Perth to be with our family. Shortly after we arrived, Betty also lost her brother in a road accident. Perhaps the only positive note in this entire sad episode was that mother, who had just lost a son, met her grandson Robin for the first time. The visit home also improved my health and being free of asthma attacks seemed like a miracle. With Robin, I returned to Melbourne, picked up the threads and began the entire process of re-establishing my position as a model.

By early 1954, all modelling activities had once again re-generated and my services were sought for the most prestigious events on the Fashion calendar. Other top models of the time were, Pauline Kiernan, Leah McCartney, Ronnie Goodlet, Jeanette Elphic, Marie Auckett, Elly Lucas, Judy Lancet, Gretta Miers, Karen Hill, Bambi Shmith, Janice Wakely and Helen Homewood. The Institute of Photographers engaged a group of us for their one week convention at the Melbourne Town Hall. As a result of the expertise of both members of the Institute and the *crème de la crème* of the models involved, the photographic achievements attained helped keep the bookings coming in for each of us and the studios buzzing with activity.

The Royal Melbourne Show was another excellent showcase. German model Christine Kollis and I were booked for the run of the show by 'Jeldi' to model dressing gowns. The engagement was not only well paid, but provided the opportunity to be seen on a personal level by hundreds of thousands of people, something that is not always attainable in the fashion industry.

There were offers of commercial movies for a lip-stick and another for Remy Martin Brandy. With television looming on the horizon, more doors were soon to open. Quality commercials shown in movie theatres during intermission had always proved to be a creative and successful selling point and with a burgeoning public profile, a lot of this work was to come my way. On any given day, I could have a commercial movie call in the morning, two or three photo-shoots at different studios in the afternoon and a fashion parade in the evening. To do the job successfully was all consuming and personal sacrifices were sometimes made.

Publicity photograph

By the end of December 1954, with advertising approaching its annual slow period, Francois returned to the Princess Theatre in his capacity of stage technician to work in the Pantomime production of *Aladdin* and by early 1955, with Robin now in school, my appointment book began to fill rapidly.

Up to this time, my hair had been waist length and worn in a French *Chignon*. Figuring it was time for a change, I took the plunge and ventured into a hair styling salon where a whole new look transformed me. As the hair stylist was about to make a major cut of the long tresses, he bunched it all into one hand and said, 'This is your last chance! Are you really sure?' With my approving nod, click went the shears and off it came. Called an *Urchin* look, the new hair style was short, meticulously tailored and very fetching. An excellent style for modelling and easy to manage.

Leah McCartney, (a former Miss Australia) was unable to fulfil a one week engagement at the Australia Hotel for a Sydney manufacturer to present his range of suits and coats, so she recommended me. The garments were of excellent quality, the manufacturer a delight to work for and the success of the showing was reflected by the sales. At the end of the engagement, we were usually given the opportunity to purchase any of the merchandise at wholesale prices, so I acquired a chic silky grey suit to add to my expanding wardrobe.

Interstate manufacturers usually leased a suite at a city hotel to accommodate the buyers. However, the prominent local manufacturers featured their own show rooms to enable buyers from retail outlets to view garments in the best possible light. Putting together a range of clothing, they engaged a model, or if it was an extensive range, sometimes two or more, and invited prospective buyers for individual private showings, which continued until the last buyer had viewed the range. These were regular seasonal events and if a manufacturer felt that you had shown his range to the best advantage, return engagements were assured. These were especially tiring days. Climbing in and out of garments over and over again for each client, without appearing dishevelled in any way was an achievement in itself, but totally exhausting. One couldn't wait to plunge into a hot bath at the end of the day.

Luckily for us models, the professional photographers and fashion houses were all above reproach and the term *sexual harassment* was unheard of in the fifties. However, an occasional fly in the ointment would sometimes be uncovered alive and well.

Once, while I was modelling in a show-room, my colleague was changing for her next appearance. Suddenly, there was an electrifying scream. The manufacturer looking distinctly pale, emerged from the dressing room, limping and mumbling that the clothes rack had fallen on him. However, the truth was that as my colleague (dressed in her underwear,) was pulling a gown over her head with arms in the 'I surrender' position, this opportunist had entered the room, seized the chance to become a bosom buddy, and clamped his hands over her breasts. Instantly she went into self defense mode. With a swift action knee jolt to his 'crown jewels', she forced him to make a royal retreat and gave new meaning to the term a *Royal Flush*.

Some of the fun photo shoots were those posing for *Woman's Day and Home* magazine's short stories. Photographs representing a principal character in various poses, were taken. These photographs were then delivered to the magazine illustrator, who in turn used the images to create a character from the story line. This was then reproduced in the magazine to catch the reader's eye. As opposed to the camera, I found it interesting to see how these talented illustrators perceived me.

21

FLASHBULBS & CAMERAS

he *Industries Fair*, located in the Exhibition Building was Australia's largest Fashion Parade, featuring the latest fabrics and designs including sleep-wear, day-wear and sophisticated evening-wear. Some of the girls working with me on this plum engagement were, Jeanette Elphic (who later moved to the United States of America and achieved international acclaim as movie actress Victoria Shaw), Marie Auckett and Pauline Kiernan (who later became one of Europe's top fashion models). An attraction at the fair was the inclusion of male models, which unlike today, was not commonplace. With a story line set to music, this unique display of fashion was devised by John and Esta Handfield and organised by the Victorian Chamber of Manufacturers.

Following the huge success of this engagement, there was a same day return plane trip to Sydney by special invitation to audition for Myer's Italian Fashion Parades. It was most prestigious to be included, for it opened more doors and as a result I was booked by Sydney's June Dally Watkins agency for the upcoming Bob Hope Show. Work with *Home Beautiful* was added to my calendar after a successful photo-shoot with Mr Yates.

Next on the agenda were several consecutive photo-shoots for *Woman's*

Day and Home, by photographer Helmut Newton, prized for his beautiful *Vogue International* spreads. Helmut has since achieved the status of being one of the world's most distinguished photographers.

When Bob Hope came to the Palais Theatre to do his season of live shows, a handful of models and I were to perform with him in 'Bob Hope's Australian Fashion Parade.' Amongst the other girls were Shirley Lester and Joan Bilceaux who became a popular identity on HSV 7's *Hit Parade*. Each of us was to model a garment (mine was a rich bronze taffeta strapless evening gown,) and exchange comedy dialogue with Bob. Another one of the models must have thought she could make an impact by ad-libbing around the script and make an impact she did, although not in the manner she anticipated. At the conclusion of the first show there was a knock on our dressing room door, Bob Hope entered, singled out the hapless girl who had presumed to improve on one of America's top scriptwriters and gave her a dressing down which I'm sure she never forgot. However, he forgave her and was gracious enough to allow her to complete the season. Dorothy Gitsham, who had provided the gown for Bob Hope's Show, called me to participate in a special Australia Hotel Parade, with Helmut Newton to do the photo-shoot.

By this time, Francois was deeply involved in advertising and my schedule had become increasingly busy. Although neither of us saw it coming, by the end of June 1955, our marriage had disintegrated.

Robin was our first priority. In his best interests, we decided he would not be moved from his home environment. His extended family Malka and Joseph next door and his friends and school nearby would all stay intact. This was the first time I had ever lived alone and being *lonely* was an understatement. In order to minimise this solitary existence, as many bookings as possible were accepted and having daily contact with Robin was my only consolation.

'Treasure Island's' jewelry parade showcased my theatrical experience. Covered from neck to toe in a black wool leotard, featuring necklaces, brooches, bracelets and ear-rings, a male dancer paraded me down the runway in a series of ballet *lifts* which revealed each piece of jewelry to the audience. The creative choreography was fun to perform and my knowledge of elevation was greatly appreciated by the dancer. This novel concept was the brainchild of Shirley Stevenson from 'Treasure Island' boutique and was lauded by both the press and all who attended, as nothing like it had been seen before. Pictures of the event and a cartoonist's impression were featured in the press.

The Gas and Fuel Corporation presented staff seminars in a large conference facility on the premises. Speakers were regularly invited to lecture on wide ranging topics of interest such as theatre, home economics, travel, sports etc. I was invited to lecture on fashion. The audience was most receptive and the questions asked, gave me invaluable experience in audience participation.

Because of the war time restrictions, new cars had been as scarce as hen's teeth so advertising had been minimal, but by 1955, the market was again opening up and lavish advertising was becoming necessary. Model, Joy Fountain and I were booked for an eleven day filmed commercial shoot for Standard Cars (one of Britain's top car makers). With the producer and camera crew, we left Melbourne on a cool winter's day, stopping off at Sale and on to Lakes Entrance where filming began. Because of the multiple locations in which we would be shooting, varying from seaside to snow fields in the Bogong High Plains, an extensive wardrobe had been packed. A picture in sunshine does not necessarily mean it was shot on a hot summer's day, so we were prepared for any contingency. Passing through flood waters and snow covered mountainous roads was a little alarming, so we were glad to arrive safely at our base Omeo, in the snow fields, where comfortable country accommodation awaited us. Every morning we were up at the break of dawn and by nine o'clock at night we were ready for the sandman. Shoots took place at the most picturesque locations, which included Joy's and my valiant attempts at skiing and horse back riding. At the completion of the tour, we returned to Melbourne to fulfil a long list of engagements.

Shortly afterwards, Francois and I talked about a reconciliation, but it did not eventuate. He became more and more distant and without my knowledge, later moved away from Carnegie to another address. This sent me into a panic. Robin was no longer within my reach. I searched for weeks trying to locate him. One day, Helen Violaris said that she had spoken to Francois and although he would not divulge his address, the suburb was mentioned. Armed with this information, I headed for the State School and waited for each child to exit the school gate until Robin appeared. This was jubilation for us both. We promised never to lose touch again and we didn't.

Daily appointments at the studios were ever increasing and as life had always been disciplined for me, arranging schedules and fulfiling them was relatively easy no matter how complex. Public transport was the only means of getting from one place to another and with mobility essential to the modelling profession, I had to be on top of all the bus, tram and train schedules and if this network didn't work out, taxis filled the gap. Keeping fit to cope with this hectic schedule was important so Helen (who had become a good friend) and I decided that we would do something about it. Enrolling at the Borovanski Ballet Academy and under the direction of Francois' old colleague, Martin Rubinstein, we undertook the strenuous exercises set out for us. Although knowing classical ballet training was extremely difficult, we didn't realise what physical pain we would have to endure. Dame Ninette De Valois suggested classical ballet training commence at age ten and being long past our use-by date, we were heroic just to enroll. To this day, I can still envisage the look of astonishment on Martin's face as he observed our feeble efforts. Naturally the pain didn't last long, as we abandoned the classics for less physically challenging classes in modern ballet with David Hamilton McIllwraith. Enjoying regular evening classes with David and improving my physical condition was a great diversion from the every day modelling schedule.

When collecting my mail one morning, a surprise letter arrived from Terry Vaughen of J.C. Williamson Theatres, inviting me to audition for their up-coming Broadway show *Can Can*. My head was swimming at the thought of returning to the theatre, however, my contractual modelling commitments were signed and sealed. Although doing the shows every night would have been manageable, the rehearsals and matinees were out of the question. Very reluctantly, the offer was declined, which I regret still.

As we often did, Helen and I were lunching at a small Collins Street restaurant when from a nearby table a young man approached us. Helen knew him and introduced me to Brian Goldsmith. He was very friendly and we exchanged pleasantries. During the conversation, Helen mentioned she would be attending the 'Fashion Ball' and Brian asked me if I would accompany him to the event. I looked at Helen, she nodded approvingly so I agreed. This invitation led to many others and we became good friends.

Between modelling engagements and dance classes there really wasn't a great deal of time for socialising and to squeeze in a ten-day, manufacturer's showing in Sydney was tightening the strings a little. Brian told me his father was expanding his business to New Zealand and that he (Brian) would have to move there temporarily to run the operation.

Taking off for the Sydney showing was routine until about an hour out of Melbourne, when the car in which we were travelling was involved in an accident. By a stroke of good fortune, no one was hurt, but due to the delay we had to stop in Albury overnight. Such a delay meant time lost for preparation of the Sydney showings and when there was a further delay by flood waters in Goulburn, we were beginning to doubt the wisdom of car travel. The Sydney excursion was financially successful for the manufacturers and they were obviously pleased. Before leaving we met up with Mel Torme who was on an Australian tour, Terry King one of Australia's great jazz singers and band leader Lee Gallagher who invited us to his home for brunch. On his departure to New Zealand, Brian called to say goodbye and although we exchanged greetings for a while, we eventually lost touch.

Back in Melbourne, settling into a normal routine and with Christmas approaching, I was looking forward with anticipation to sharing the festive season with Robin. As Francois was not agreeable to any Christmas get together, returning to Sydney and spending this otherwise lonely time with friends seemed like a reasonable alternative.

Immediately after Christmas, a chance meeting with photographer Henry Talbot from the Helmut Newton studio was fortunate indeed for he was leaving by car on New Years Day to return to Melbourne and offered me a ride back, which I promptly accepted. It was a very pleasant journey except for a severe thunder-storm we encountered. We were both a little shaken when a lightning bolt demolished a tree a few hundred meters from us. Undaunted, we drove on through the driving rain, thunder and lightning and arrived safely, just in time to keep my promise to substitute for Helen at the Mannequin's Association, while she took her vacation.

22

CATWALKS & RUNWAYS

eter Fox asked if I would be interested in an interview with his friend Mr Epstein who was looking for a well groomed, experienced receptionist-cashier at the newly refurbished Claridges restaurant and night club in South Yarra. Peter explained the rather exclusive clientele was made up mostly of Melbourne's elite social set. The position paid very well and left every day free to continue modelling. Agreeing with him that it would fill my evening void, an interview was arranged. Mr Epstein was impressed with my resumé and the job was mine. Because of the late closing hour, he suggested that nearby accommodation would be desirable and recommended the Gower family's St Ives boarding house just a block away. This became my new address.

The ambience of the beautifully appointed Claridges made it the *in* place to be. Accomplished English pianist Arthur Young with his band and stylish singer Paula Langlands provided the musical entertainment and in between sets, piano-accordionist Hans Blau strolled from table to table playing requests. When Paula left to fulfil other engagements, singer Shirley Simmonds joined the ensemble. Both girls also resided at St Ives and we could often be seen on weekends lunching at Brummells Coffee Shop in

South Yarra. Courtesy of Mr Epstein, the chef would have Maitre d' Robert Blau deliver a delicious meal to my desk each evening. As my rent included breakfast, and dinner was complimentary, lunch was the only meal I had to provide. Apart from the normal activities of a receptionist, my duties included taking care of the waiters' accounts, then balancing the books before the night was over. When first starting out, Maitre d' Robert Blau was extraordinarily helpful to me and I am forever grateful to him. 3DB radio announcer Geoff Corke had been Master of Ceremonies at a charity fashion show we shared. He was a young man of disarming charm and wit. When he learned I was at Claridges nightly, he confided that he too worked late at 3DB. Once in a while, by invitation, he attended a late night show business supper party and declared that when the next invitation came around he would call Claridges and escort me to the party for a bite to eat. As models and radio personalities were sometimes victims of unwanted attention, being unaccompanied at some functions was not desirable, so our mutual working hours afforded us both the luxury of protecting one another from unwanted advances. Because of the lateness of our appearance, most parties were almost over by the time we arrived, but a good meal was always reserved for us and we enjoyed many late suppers together.

When Arthur Young left Claridges to do a series of radio shows for the Australian Broadcasting Commission, Charles and Beryl White were contracted to fill the entertainment needs. They had been working the top cabarets in the United States and recently returned to Australia. An exciting cabaret act, Beryl was a power-house performer, Charles a consummate musician and the rapport developed with the audience was remarkable. Beryl was always on top of the current show tunes and while *Can Can* was playing at Her Majesty's Theatre, *I Love Paris*, and *C'est Magnifique* became a part of her nightly repertoire. A few pangs of disappointment flashed within me when listening to these haunting refrains, which made me wonder how differently life might have unfolded if I'd not declined the offer to do *Can Can*.

Working six nights a week at Claridges and modelling every day made me stop and think about the latest offer to teach Saturday morning children's classes at the Athol Shmith Model College. Although adding more hours to my already arduous schedule, accepting the offer caused no regrets. It was the beginning of my communicating with groups of children.

Although as a married couple, Francois and I never reconciled, Robin was a bond that made our association more amicable. Francois had moved to South Yarra and with me still residing at St Ives, my personal contact with Robin was more accessible. He was a well adjusted boy, who was already showing signs of academic skills and his regular presence enhanced my personal happiness immensely.

Here I was, ricocheting backwards and forwards from the studios of Peter Fox, Kenneth Ross, Helmut Newton, Athol Shmith, La Trobe Studios and so forth. Now, adding a new dimension to my already diverse portfolio, were store demonstrations which provided a well paid comfortable climate in which to speak to people extemporaneously. This facet of the industry was appealing and Foy and Gibson department stores created these opportunities. Success in this area led to demonstrations at other stores for products such as, Ansell rubber gloves, Taffle and Shone Paints, Besters Sweets and Family Games, just to name a few.

During an all day shoot for a 'Pimm's' Movie Commercial, a series of abdominal pains wracked my body. Up until this time my health had been consistently good, in fact no asthma attacks had occurred for a long time. However, misgivings about my general health made me seek medical attention. Following an examination, the doctor advised me that surgery would be required for an ovarian cyst. Another tour was in the pipeline, so the surgery had to be delayed.

As my relationship with Claridges had been most cordial, my resignation was given with mixed feelings, but the impending Australian tour for G.J. Coles stores showing their latest range of clothing was too important financially to pass up.

At the conclusion of the Coles' parades in Melbourne, a handful of us including Judy Lancet and radio personality Moira Farrow set out to tour Adelaide, Perth and Launceston. This tour helped minimise my anxiety over the forthcoming surgery. On returning to Melbourne, engagements had to be reduced until finally the overdue surgery took place. The operation took it's toll and once again I was admitted to a convalescent home.

It was during this period, when recovering from surgery that television came into our lives. ABV-2 and HSV-7 were on the air in November in time to cover the Olympic Games from Melbourne. Although GTV-9 did not officially open until January 1957, they provided a continuous live telecast using the talents of Geoff Corke, Eric Welsh, Tony Charlton, Ian Johnson, Bert Bryant, Jack Russell, Ted Harris and Jack Kramer as commentators. There were noticeably no women, but this strong team gave an indication of how formidable the Nine Network would be.

Peter Fox's brother Ernest invited me to attend the Olympic Games and on this single memorable visit I exchanged greetings with the Prime

Minister Sir Robert Menzies, who was later dubbed 'Lord of the Cinque Ports' by Her Majesty, Queen Elizabeth 11.

Most people in television circles think that my television debut was made on GTV-9, but the truth is, my initiation was in a live Saturday night show on HSV-7 called *Wedding Day*. It started at the beginning of television's transmission, long before there was a *Late Show* on HSV-7 or *In Melbourne Tonight* (*IMT*) on GTV-9. The show was hosted by John Stuart and a bride and groom who had been married that day were invited into the HSV-7 studios in Dorcas Street, South Melbourne where the fun began. A great fuss was made of them and my role on the show was to give advice to the bride on how to stay well groomed and attractive to her husband. The show lasted well into 1957.

23

DARRODS & GTV-9

A mountain of appointments began to stack up. Still teaching at the Athol Shmith Model College, somewhere along the trail it had a name change to the Bambi Shmith Model College (Bambi was Athol's wife). My communicative skills were utilised by both Coles and Foy and Gibson in a steady stream of store demonstrations. The giant J. Walter Thompson Advertising Agency, Nixon Advertising, Pan Public Relations, Fashion Promotions and others vied for my time. The diversity of photo shoots for Aspro, Kelvinator appliances, Holden automobiles, Caravans, Esther Lights gas heaters, tiles, Allen's Butter Menthol and any number of other varied merchandise; the store demonstrations; teaching; and the numerous fashion showings in establishments such as Comtesse d'Espinayls millinery at Myers, swimsuits at Cole of California, Richard Hennessy Jewelry, Hicks Atkinson, Darrods, Foy and Gibson, Douglas Cox, Holeproof, Sutex, Lincoln and Paton's knitting wools were regular fare. As a full time professional model, top newspapers, the *Sun*, *Herald*, *Age* and the *Argus*, commissioned my services for their fashion pages. So too did the leading magazines of the day, *The Australian Women's Weekly*, *Woman's Day*, *Pix*, *Australasian Post* and *Home Beautiful* feature me in their various fashion pages and covers. The weeks were flying by in an endless whirl.

On May 2nd, 1957 having just completed an early photo-shoot followed by a demonstration for Besters Sweets at Coles, by sheer chance, I bumped into Peter Fox on Collins Street. He said that as we spoke, Phillip Goldstone owner of Darrods 'the style store in the heart of Bourke Street,' was holding interviews for a model to appear on television and they (Darrods) were trying to reach me. Explaining that my portfolio was at home, he advised me to forget the portfolio and get there swiftly. Doing exactly as he suggested, I arrived to find that some girls had been interviewed and departed, while others were waiting. When my turn came around, Phillip Goldstone welcomed me and introduced his staff manager Ian Rainsford and his two executive nephews the Lefler brothers. Asking innumerable questions about modelling, they appeared to be especially interested when my theatrical background was mentioned. The interview went well, with an invitation to appear in an on-camera audition the next day at GTV-9 studios in Bendigo Street Richmond.

It was rather exciting sitting in the studio of this brand new medium, cheerfully discussing the possibilities and opportunities. Suddenly the lights came up and my good pal Geoff Corke appeared in the centre staging area. Greeting me warmly, he whispered that seated in the control room were several people including, general manager Colin Bednall, program director Norm Spencer, producer Tom Miller and from Darrods, Phillip Goldstone and Ian Rainsford. Responding to Norm Spencer's instructions from the control room, Geoff proceeded with the auditions. At the conclusion, Geoff confided in me that the girls they were interested in for the two major roles were Gretta Miers and me. Summoned to Phillip Goldstone's office, I was engaged as one of the two Darrod's Girls.

In the meantime my contractual obligations continued with Besters Sweets and G.J. Coles, plus a full calendar of fashion parades at Myers and Woolworths, photo shoots and teaching at the College, so time was at a premium. To be squeezed into this schedule were Darrods' conferences, meetings and fittings. Gretta did the shows Tuesdays through Saturdays and I did Monday nights, but shortly afterwards, Gretta resigned and I was engaged to do all six shows as 'Panda, the Darrods Girl.'

Phillip Goldstone's plan was to establish a fashion model as Darrods' representative on GTV-9's new night time television variety show *In Melbourne Tonight*, affectionately known as *IMT*. Darrods, GTV-9 and Clemenger's Advertising worked a successful format into the show, where a purchase was made at Darrods and the shopper was given a coupon on which they filled in their name and address. The coupons were collected,

Publicity photographs

taken to GTV-9 and deposited in a barrel for the Darrods' segment of *IMT*. I was modelling fashions from each of the store's departments and working with the show's host, Graham Kennedy, in a game of chance with a Darrods' contestant which turned out to be a smash hit with viewers.

Discovered at the top of a staircase when introduced on the show then descending the stairs to a musical theme and a Clemenger script read by a booth announcer, I modelled the chosen fashion for the night. Graham joined me on the set where we exchanged extemporaneous dialogue. The lucky contestant was introduced and in turn, spun a large wheel featuring numbers corresponding with prizes. When the wheel came to a halt, from a little black book of prizes the contestant was informed of their winnings. Next, a barrel was wheeled onto the set, spun around and another shopper's name was drawn for a future show.

Phillip Goldstone also featured me as hostess of the 'Darrods' Television Theatre' on Saturday nights, introducing two half hour American dramas *Mr District Attorney* and *Crosscurrent*, and in between the two dramas, I hosted a ten minute fashion show live to air, in which several lovely girls, amongst them Joy Fountain, Arlene Andrewatha, Dorothy Moore, Shirley Lester, Wendy Marshall and others, modelled the latest fashion offerings from the store (Darrods rotated a stable of models in their television fashion parades).

There was a feeling that something special was happening. Television brought a new enlightenment into my life and to everyone else it touched. Achievements in the fields of theatre, modelling, public speaking, demonstrations, teaching and my collaboration with journalists and photographers, put me in very good shape to cope with the unexpected avalanche of attention and publicity. Television collectively incorporated all media and swallowed up talent with its insatiable appetite.

Operating from my own office on the top floor of Darrods, 9:00 a.m. to 5:00 p.m. Monday through Friday, the days were filled with television discussions, decisions and photo shoots for their newspaper advertisements. Phillip Goldstone, a shrewd business man, was an extremely nice person and his son-in-law Ian Rainsford, in charge of handling all of the merchandise for *IMT* was too, a very likeable man which made my association with the two of them pleasurable.

It was hectic racing home to St Ives after every day in the office, to shower and without a hair dryer, wash, dry and set my hair in curlers, apply make-up, then by taxi, hightail it to the GTV-9 studios. Once there, there would be a meeting with John Clemenger to familiarise myself with the Darrods fashion script and in the meantime try to grab a bite to eat, dress and ready myself for the show.

Saturday nights, after hosting *Mr District Attorney, Crosscurrent* and the *Fashion Parade* on GTV~9, I sometimes joined Joy and Geoff in the audience of a live amateur boxing program taking place in another studio. Geoff offered us his expertise on the sport by explaining the technicalities like: a short punch is a jab, bringing the fist up under the chin is an upper-cut, the fist coming from the side is a hook, hitting below the belt is a penalty and so forth. It was the first time I had been present at any boxing event and the youngsters vying for the titles were serious about their sport. One young boy who was hit hard received a bloody nose and burst into tears. Because they used soft padded boxing gloves, it was never apparent to me that the punches hurt. Armed with this knowledge I have always felt uncomfortable about the safety of the sport.

IMT was a variety show hosted by former Melbourne 3UZ radio announcer Graham Kennedy, who was young, energetic and strikingly novel with his sharp repartee. Youthful in appearance, of average height, fair haired and with large brilliant blue eyes, he won his viewing admirers the first time he stepped in front of the *IMT* audience. The show had a simple format of music, comedy, dance, song and sight acts, more or less a vaudeville show with a Master of Ceremonies, interrupted by commercials.

In charge of the whole presentation was Program Manager and 'star-maker' Norm Spencer, a director everyone respected. He had the uncanny ability to know if and when a performer would be successful and without hesitation gave those he deemed worthy every opportunity and encouragement. In spite of his young age, he was like a father to everyone and was surrounded by his talented troupe of directorial proteges and camera crew, including Rod Kinnear, Ian Holmes, Billy Beames, Ian Crawford, Brian Phillis, Dennis Rawady and Ron Davis (who, like Norm had trained overseas). His right hand man was producer Tom Miller. Tom booked acts for the show and was tirelessly proficient. Sight acts were eaten up like bird seed in an aviary. Five new shows every week put enormous pressure on Tom to provide the show with fresh talent.

At a social event, dancing with Graham Kennedy

When *IMT* first went to air, the band was small in number and was under the direction of Sydney pianist Lee Gallagher. The earliest regular singers featured were Val Ruff, Max Bleach, baritone Martin Clark and Irish balladeer, Bill McCormack. Later Elaine McKenna, Diana Trask, Annette Klooger, Dorothy Baker and Johnny Marco joined the line-up of singers. Groups like the Tune Twisters, Horrie Dargie Quintet and the Four Debs provided harmonic excellence and Arthur Young took over musical direction. The *IMT* dancers were young and talented enough to learn new routines every day, as well as partnering singers as back-up dancers. In the beginning of live variety television, minimum thought had been given to the number of dressing rooms required for those of us working in the shows. At GTV-9, all of the men shared one dressing room. The acts, singers, musicians and even Graham, all prepared for *IMT* at the same time, in the same room. The only concession to privacy for Graham was a simple partition which provided only a dividing line from everybody else. As he mentally geared himself to concentrate on hosting ninety minutes of live television, it is hard to imagine how he functioned with the cacophony of singers and musicians warming up their voices and instruments, plus the inevitable high level of general conversation in the room.

It was the same dressing room situation for the women, one for all and all in one except for the dancers. Somehow it worked out. There were no quarrels or contrariety in either dressing room.

Becoming a personality on GTV-9 six nights a week, I was literally entering the viewer's homes, appearing in their living rooms, becoming part of their everyday life. Keeping this in mind, public recognition was unavoidable. It was a very flattering situation to be in, however, my personal life was being restricted by lack of privacy. Most television personalities suffered the same consequence and we were constantly under public scrutiny.

After having my telephone connected, strangers began calling at all hours, so Norm's good advice to acquire a *silent line* eliminated many nights of disturbed sleep. Nevertheless, there was one uninvited incoming call from a phone company operator who had access to unlisted numbers. Simply wanting to say hello, she begged me not to report the incident fearing dismissal for this breach of company security. After promising not to call again, I let her off the hook. Celebrity invites the curious and breaches the bounds of privacy. Inevitably my social life centred around working colleagues, who became an extended family, permitting a degree of relaxation otherwise unattainable.

Working with Graham was great fun and there was an indefinable rapport between us. He was alert and nothing passed him by. I never appeared on *IMT* without being conversationally prepared to feed him material he could bounce off, using his remarkable comedic talent. Every night we experienced many chapters of laughable incidents and as viewers would remember, the whole segment became a regular comedy piece.

Loving good humour and through the years a happy recipient of many jokes, I started relating them to Graham each night on the show. He and the audience were very receptive to these humorous efforts and the joke telling became an anticipated part of my appearances. Limericks were not out of the question and the night I started to relate 'The boy stood on the burning deck,' Graham stopped me and queried the Limerick's morality. Assuring him it was perfectly aboveboard, I continued …

> *The boy stood on the burning deck, With crackers in his pocket, The flames licked all around his feet, And he shot up like a rocket!*

Graham mopped his brow and gave a sigh of relief, stating it was not the version he knew, which brought a roar from his knowing audience who understood only too well what he meant. Like theatre, there was a need for winding down after the show and some of us gathered at 'Gini's' Toorak restaurant. Along with me, Graham, Norm, Geoff, Val Ruff, Jack Little, Joy and others were often seen seated at a table in the rear of the restaurant where we enjoyed a Nasi Goring or Goulash, washed down with spiked hot coffee. When Graham mentioned 'Gini's' on the show, the establishment became jam packed with after theatre patrons, but American proprietor Pierre Versluys had our table reserved at all times. Personalities from HSV~7 frequently joined us for a powwow, where inevitably television and show business in general were the topics of conversation.

After 'Gini's,' often times Graham, Geoff and maybe one or two other colleagues, visited my apartment for a nightcap, a little music and laughter before their tired bodies took them home to sleep. There were other times when we would forego Gini's and go directly to my place where I made toasted ham, cheese and tomato sandwiches which were wolfed down by my hungry guests.

Once in a while Graham mentioned these evenings on the show. He described the beautiful garden setting on the approach to my apartment, explaining how we had to walk with bent posture to reach the staircase leading to the front door, because the gardener, who was small of stature, could not reach above five feet to trim the overhanging shrubs and trees. In particular, he described one rainy night when the trees and shrubs were heavily laden with water, clearance was down to about four feet and we all had to wade through the jungle of sodden garden overhangings to reach the front door of my apartment. Graham burlesqued the scene by bending backwards from the knees, exaggerating our movements so as to be lower to the ground (I think someone watching that night was inspired by his antics and created the 'Limbo'). His physical depiction had the audience falling about with laughter and me dodging the gardener for weeks afterwards.

One evening Joy said she would be attending a barbecue and added that the hosts, Joan and Sam Wilson, a prominent Sorrento family had also cordially invited me. She advised me to bring a toothbrush and pyjamas as we were expected to stay overnight. It was quite a big shindig, with a band and a semitrailer tray set up as a dance floor. Other than Joy, Norm Spencer, his wife Amy and children Diane and Dennis, I knew only a few of the other revellers. Nothing untoward happened, except that the barbecue was great fun.

The following Monday whilst in my office at Darrods, Phillip Goldstone summoned me to a meeting. I was surprised to find GTV-9's general manager Colin Bednall present, who began questioning me about the weekend social event at the Wilson's Sorrento home. He related that an un-named person had reported to him that I was in attendance as an uninvited guest. Challenging me in the presence of my mentor Phillip Goldstone, without checking the authenticity of such an accusation, offended me terribly. Infuriated at the inference, I gave him the telephone number of my hostess, suggesting that he get his facts from the source and if there was anymore to say about the matter, he should phone me direct. In utter disbelief, I swept out of the office in tears.

Phillip Goldstone defended me, giving his full support and encouragement and I added another notch in the learning game. 'There are those who dare to utter odious truths and for every thousand well wishers, there is always someone with horns waiting on the fringe.'

The incident was never mentioned again, but it hurt deeply and left me with a feeling of having been violated. A cordial relationship was maintained with all around me, but from that time on, I was always aware of the possibility of those with invidious preferences being painfully present. Although the un-named perpetrator of this perfidious act meant harm, quite the contrary occurred. Colin regularly invited me into his office to inquire about my well being, making sure I was happy both at Darrods and GTV-9 and I was to make many return visits to Sorrento and the Wilson family.

Phillip Goldstone was a whizz at promotion and decided he would have me represent Darrods at the racing carnival in November. He sent me along to the store's exclusive fashion boutique, where their well known bridal wear was designed and made, to collaborate with his chief designer for an outstanding fashion statement to be worn on Oaks Day at the Flemington racecourse. The designer had already sketched her ideas before my arrival and as the gown was exceptionally eye-catching, we agreed it would be a stunning outfit to grab the attention of the press photographers, thereby promoting Darrods. A navy blue taffeta gown trimmed with white spotted muslin, it was accessorized with white picture hat, hand bag, gloves, parasol and navy blue shoes, all from Darrods. As it turned out, *The Sun* published a half page picture and likewise *The Age* featured the ensemble on their pages. I wore it on *IMT* the same night and the next day it was displayed in the store window where people flocked to see it. The entire effort resulted in another success for Phillip Goldstone and his 'style store in the heart of Bourke Street.'

In the 1950's, Drive-in movie theatres were the latest entertainment innovation to be ushered into Australia. Preceding television, they were enormously popular and became *the* family outing of the week. Accepting extra work at GTV-9 and outside engagements which fitted into my schedule, in November I made a short film for Skyline Drive-in theatres. Dressed in their Drive-in uniform, my role was to explain to the movie audience how to replace the speaker on it's stand before exiting, to drive forward, turn right and follow the well placed signs out to the public carriage-way. The film was always screened at the conclusion of the main feature. Apparently, when Drive-in theatres were first introduced to the world, some patrons were driving forward as others were backing up, turning left instead of right, resulting in minor accidents. Without this filmed information, the potential for chaos was inevitable.

I was travelling daily to Darrods, GTV-9 and home on a newly acquired Motor scooter, my first personal mode of transport. A little scary at times in peak traffic, but it got me to and from without having to rely on the Taxi formula. Darrods and GTV-9 managements provided me with parking space on their respective lots.

On December 7th, following a romantic courtship, Geoff Corke and singer Val Ruff were married at The Little John Chapel, at Scotch College. Many of us from GTV-9 celebrated their union by attending a lavish reception at Chevron Hotel on the corner of St Kilda and Commercial Roads, Melbourne. Val looked beautiful in her pink lace gown, while Geoff exuded pride. *TV-Radio Week* magazine featured the happy couple on the cover of their very first edition.

IMT was extended an extra hour for 1957's New Year's Eve celebration. Norm and Tom had all of us performing additional specially material. The cast and crew were in a festive mood in spite of bordering on exhaustion by the time we rang in the New Year at midnight.

After the show, we were taken to Ciro's Night Club where a table had been reserved for us to partake of a chicken and champagne supper. Seated only about five minutes, irregular heartbeats began to wrack my chest, a deep sinking feeling set in, the blood drained from my face and body weakness started to overcome me. Taking deep breaths, I turned to the nearest faceless person, quickly told them of an imminent fainting predicament and asked if they would help me out into the fresh air. Making it only as far as the foyer, with a diminution of hearing and vision, I collapsed. Coming out of the darkness of unconsciousness in an upstairs office, I heard a doctor's voice saying, 'Her pulse has stabilised and she's recovering nicely.' As Norm had arrived on the scene, it was a great relief to me that the doctor had not made reference to the irregular heartbeats in his presence. Despite being accustomed to these occasional attacks, it never entered my thoughts that one could take place in public and now my greatest fear was that if an episode happened on camera, I might never work in television again. A cab was called and in a very weak state I made it back to my apartment where I was greeted with a 'Happy New Year!' from my neighbour Barry, as he disappeared through his front door.

A bachelor, Barry lived downstairs in accommodation detached from the main building. He was a friendly and charming person who became my saviour two or three times. When arriving home late at night following *IMT*, discovering my keys missing and locked out of my apartment, unfortunately for Barry, I would pound on his door and awaken him. Acknowledging my need for assistance and clad in pyjamas and dressing gown, he defied danger by courageously climbing the heights of the two story building. Venturing in the dark of night to enter my upstairs apartment window, he found his way to the front door, unlocked it and let me in. Thinking nothing of these valiant acts and still groggy with sleep, he would return to his apartment and dreams. Barry was the epitome of gallantry.

Reflecting on the past months made for interesting recall. In 1956, the year television transmission began, the small number of sets in use, made finance for live programming limited, so large scale productions at that time were not viable. At HSV-7, one of the first shows to be established was *Hit Parade*, where Joan Bilceaux, Bernadette Russell, Don Bennetts, John D'Arcy and Don Carter mimed popular songs. Other HSV-7 presentations were *Wedding Day* in which I had appeared, Ernie Sigley's *Teenage Mailbag* with Gaynor Bunning and *Stairway to the Stars* a talent quest where Helen Violaris made her TV singing debut. It was hosted by Eric Pearce and later John McComas. By May 1957 they had introduced Noel Ferrier in *The Late Show*, while at GTV-9, Graham Kennedy's *IMT* hit the air waves. There was instantaneous competition between the rival shows, with both the participating performers and the viewing public holding strong opinions as to their preferences.

GTV-9 studios were also in full flight with Geoff Corke's Saturday *Breakfast Show*; Happy Hammond and Ron Blaskett's Children's Show with Susan-Gaye Anderson and 'Uncle' Ernie Carroll (Ernie also did some very funny *bits* with Denzil Howson on *IMT*). There was also live boxing; and 'Thursday at One' featuring Bernice (Binnie) Lum, Eric Pearce and later, Judy Anne Ford and Evie Hayes joined the team. Other shows included Harry Dearth's 'Charades,' in which *Pyjama Game's* Toni Lamond, Tikki Taylor, Bill Newman, Jill Perryman and Keith Petersen were typical guests

Television was far from settling down and the positioning of personnel engaged the attention of all for analysis. Geoff Raymond resigned from HSV-7 only to return. Eric Pearce resigned from HSV-7, moved to advertising and from there he joined GTV-9's news department eventually becoming their anchor. Judy Jack resigned from HSV-7, transferring to ABV-2 for an alternative childrens' program. Noel Ferrier resigned from HSV-7's *Late Show* and was replaced by Bert Newton. There was a pattern shaping up that showed a propensity for GTV-9 to be strengthening the available talent.

Right from the start, *IMT* personnel were a loyal hard working family. The sense of belonging extended to all departments of the station. Most of this radiated from Norm Spencer's office. Because of his far-sighted vision, Norm was able to make *IMT* the most celebrated show on television and due to its success, the flow on to other GTV-9 shows made the station number one, with advertising revenue exceeding all expectations.

By the beginning of October 1957 there were 70,000 licensed TV sets in the Melbourne area and this number almost doubled by the end of the month. The continuing increase in sales meant more revenue and expanded the budget for shows.

ABV-2 engaged Peggy McCloud, television's first woman producer for a live variety program *Seeing Stars*, while Christopher Muir produced the station's dramas and Corrine Kirby was their leading lady presenter. Corrine was married to another successful ABV-2 producer, Oscar Whitbread.

Crawford Productions had a TV workshop of talent development. Holding auditions for the company brought forth potential talent and provided a data base for their future shows.

Lucky viewers were able to see exceptional variety programs from the U.S.A. like the Steve Allen, Perry Como and Rosemary Clooney shows.

1957 was behind us. By now, radio had been ransacked for established personalities and programs, including the two biggest radio quizmasters Bob Dyer and Jack Davey who had already made the switch. Shows such as *Swallows Parade*, *Leave it to the Girls* and *Raising a Husband*, made the transition with varied success, firmly establishing television in Australian homes.

By early 1958 the situation of celebrity had escalated so rapidly, it was difficult to keep track of everything. Graham was very helpful in many ways. He advised me to engage his accountant to take care of my taxation and business pursuits; to subscribe to *Press Cuttings of Australia* which kept me entirely informed as to how I was being presented by the print media and to purchase a specific kind of scrapbook, properly bound and of substantial size and strength to cope with the volume of press reports arriving daily.

TV Radio Week (later to be known as *TV Week*) decided to present a hypothetical story about Graham's marriage plans. They sent Graham and me dressed as bride and groom to the steps of a Punt Road church in South Yarra, where we were photographed for the magazine's cover. Lo and behold, the phones started running hot and the story was gossiped around Melbourne that Graham and I had secretly married. Denying the rumours didn't stop the tongues from wagging. We shrugged them off, but it was a while before the rumours subsided. Members of the press were harmlessly fond of publicly matchmaking one personality with another, however, readers were a little sceptical of the alleged romances and usually read the stories with tongue in cheek.

A viewer, with the very best of intentions, presented me with a beautiful Great Dane puppy. Living in an apartment didn't deter me from taking this precious puppy home and dubbing him 'Ranji.' Within no time at all he became the size of a small pony and it was impossible to keep him in the apartment. What to do? Fortunately, a good friend Barry Trainor, who co-owned the Peacock Hotel in Northcote, had ample back yard space and needed a deterrent against intruders. He adopted 'Ranji,' bringing an awkward situation to a resolve.

The cast of *IMT* and visiting artists gradually increased in number resulting in our communal ladies dressing room bursting at the seams. One evening I opened the door and there on the threshold, standing next to producer Tom Miller was Evie Hayes. Evie was to make her debut appearance on *IMT* and Tom asked me to see that she was as comfortable as possible in our less than perfect size dressing room.

Enjoying an immediate rapport with her, I introduced her to the girls and we each cramped our space a little to make room for the additional body. When she realised that I was the 'Tivoli Girl' Will had mentioned in his letters from Perth, she confided that Will was delighted he had offered encouragement in my early show business days. Knowing how well J.C. Williamson Theatres had treated Evie during her reign with them, I somehow felt that our communal dressing room may not have been what she expected, but there was no need for concern. To put it in her words, 'It sure beats the heck out of a nail in back of a door.' This down to earth attitude had every one warming to her and once she had appeared on the show, there was no doubt that an international star had joined the *IMT* Company. This was the beginning of a long friendship

Shortly afterwards, the dressing rooms were expanded. Darrods needed a locked area for the week's supply of fashions, so a room was allotted to take care of the situation, at the same time providing me with a dressing room. To kill three birds with the one stone, I used the room at night, Susan-Gaye in the afternoon and Joy whenever she made appearances. As host of *IMT*, Graham was also given his own 'star' dressing room. The new rooms were not large but of reasonable size, a refuge where one could enjoy a little privacy, go over scripts and gather one's thoughts before the show.

GTV-9 publicity department and editors of television and radio publications were already jumping on the bandwagon of those with popular profiles, resulting in never ending articles and cover pictures promoting us and in turn, selling their journals. *Listener-In TV* created a cover for their weekly publication of Graham, me, Elaine and GTV-9's new musical director Arthur Young, with HSV-7's Noel Ferrier, Bert Newton and *Bells are Ringing* star Shani Wallis. An excellent and successful promotion for the first birthday celebrations of both GTV-9's *IMT* and HSV-7's *Late Show*.

Some time in May, there was a slight change in my appearance and I couldn't fathom what it was, until a swelling just below the jawbone on the right hand side of the throat caught my attention. Consulting a general practitioner for diagnosis, he suggested it was a tumour and referred me to a throat specialist who in turn recommended immediate surgery (specialists usually do). Into hospital went I, where the non-malignant tumour was excised, leaving a three inch scar. Not too excited about this very visible, medically induced blemish and challenging the surgeon, he reassured me it would disappear in time, but would not happen overnight. Falling back on stage make-up technique, the scar was successfully disguised and it did eventually fade into insignificance.

A new longer version of the Darrods segment was programmed which provided bigger and better prizes (if that was at all possible) and extended Graham's and my entertainment time. Norm insisted my nightly joke telling was a must, as it had become a much talked about highlight and Graham's reaction was always significant. Every Friday night the two of us sang *The Chum's Song*, a little ditty Graham brought with him from radio.

On the 300th, anniversary of *IMT*, Norm decided to put my theatrical experience to the test and feature me singing to Graham a Rose Murphy song entitled, *Billy*, but programmed it outside the Darrods segment. Not having sung solo publicly since my theatrical years, inspired me to practice my old vocal scales and breathing exercises as often as possible before the night of the presentation. Everything went exceedingly well. The audience liked what they heard and saw and Norm said he would provide me with other winning musical offerings to perform. (He was a walking encyclopedia of popular music, due to his years as producer at 3DB radio.)

This particular show marked Graham's final night before he embarked on an extended vacation in the United States. During his absence, Happy Hammond replaced him on *IMT*. Happy was totally opposite to Graham, but entertaining and easy to work with.

In June, editor Rod Lever, asked me to write a column for *TV Week*, basing the contents on light hearted gossip and topical events from the television studios. Accepting the challenge, there began another adventure in my colourful career. Television journalist Robert Fent was assigned to be my overseer, teaching the do's and don'ts of writing a column. He was a very sweet person and unselfishly helped me enormously through the initial stages. Whilst writing this column, I became pals with Robert, Rod and *TV Week* journalist Jack 'The Ace' Ayling. Television and the newspaper industry were all interconnected and I became as much involved with the press as with entertainment. Acquainted with many journalists, for the most part they were decent, well informed men and women and almost all of them were good humoured. When interviews were requested, many times the reporter preferred an *at home* atmosphere and by allowing them into the inner sanctum of my cozy retreat, friendships were born.

Invitations abounded at the frequent inter-studio *late-night-bites* (suppers) and most of us were willing participants. At a small HSV-7 gathering, amongst the guests were Don Bennetts and Bert Newton, both warm, friendly young men. Bert invited me to accompany him on a Saturday afternoon drive, where he could talk at length about television. Intrigued, I accepted. During the drive we talked about the talents of Graham and Norm, working conditions at GTV-9 and HSV-7 and future aspirations. Bert showed such interest in GTV-9 that the day was sealed with an invitation for him to visit the Bendigo street studios. It was a pleasant, but curious afternoon, as in the not too distant future, Bert switched stations and joined Channel 9.

24

Signing with Channel Nine

n August 1958, Phillip Goldstone decided that his long term business interests had to be protected and to ensure our continuing relationship with 'the style store in the heart of Bourke Street,' he had a two year contract drawn up which would bind me exclusively to Darrods. He was leaving on vacation and left me to ponder the offer in his absence.

The suggestion of a contract took me somewhat by surprise. Always loyal, with a moral obligation to be considerate of Darrods before accepting any free-lance engagements, the proposition of being exclusively tied to one company gave cause to contemplate what my options might be. Primarily, there were only two alternatives. Sign the contract and perhaps have future regrets, or refuse to sign and possibly lose the position as Darrods television representative. Norm sprung to mind as the one person who would understand, analyse the situation and advise me of the best way to handle it. A meeting was arranged with him and all my cards were laid on the table. Like the true father figure that he was, Norm's advice was to sit tight and do nothing for the time being.

Shortly afterwards we had a second meeting. This time in the presence of Colin Bednall, who presented me with a similar, but more attractive, lucrative GTV-9 contract with an option of renewal. Signing this contract ensured the best of everything. As well as continuing in my role with Graham five nights a week, Norm's vision promised a more versatile application of my talent. The contract was signed in August. Graham was in New York and when contacted offered congratulations and was quoted as saying, 'I'm thrilled to pieces.'

There were some misgivings about declining Darrods offer which had been generously made, with consideration of our mutual interests. However, taking chances was part of my life and this was no exception. Phillip Goldstone cancelled his Surfer's Paradise vacation and returned to Melbourne. As a consequence of my signing with Channel Nine, Darrods threatened to withdraw their sponsorship from *IMT* and this caused a storm between them and GTV-9. Darrods demanded complete control over the content of their segment, replacing me with a girl of their choice. GTV-9 maintained that the entire content of the show had always been and would continue to be, under their jurisdiction. The press had a field day, extracting tidbits of information from all concerned. 1958 *TV Week* reported:

> ...'The news SHATTERED THE STORE'S PLANS to tie her up with a similar contract. Mr Goldstone said that the store's future plans for the Darrods quiz on 'In Melbourne Tonight' could not be made public yet. GTV-9 also SCOOPED a Sydney TV Station, which had made a lucrative offer to Panda. The GTV-9 contract makes Panda the highest paid female in Australian TV...'

There was so much ado about the contract and salary, reporters flocked to Norm's office in quest of further details. In response to questions about my representing Darrods in *IMT*, Norm said:

> ...she will stay in the same role in 'In Melbourne Tonight.'...It has snowballed into the high spot of the program. We don't want to put her in any other shows at the moment ... Panda is on Camera each night for twenty to twenty-five minutes and, believe me, that is no small part ...

Those nightly appearances are the equivalent of being on television for a full two hours a week, so finding fresh, funny and interesting material every night was challenging.

When *TV Week* announced a record number of sales following the publication of a cover and feature story of me in the September 4 issue of their magazine, I was amazed when in the editorial they announced that much of the credit was mine. For the first time in Victoria, more than 100,000 copies were sold within a 48 hour period. A very substantial number for a magazine in it's infancy.

There was a furore of continual speculative stories regarding my position at GTV-9 and on September 18, Ian Rainsford of Darrods issued the following press release:

> Panda is leaving the Darrods spot to pursue a full time TV career with Channel 9. Darrods wish her luck and thank her for her services in the past. We regret the parting of our ways, but the Darrods girl must be a Darrods employee or else she is not a true Darrods girl. Panda's contract with Channel 9 is a step up the ladder for her and we don't wish to stand in her way.

When comedian Joff Ellen joined *IMT*, he brought with him a huge library of comedy material. His repertoire of vaudeville sketches and run-on gags expanded *IMT*'s horizons, allowing set designers, lighting directors, costume designers and camera crews to add a new dimension to their ever widening skills. His voluminous material transferred perfectly from theatre to television. There were the wonderful courtroom and hospital scenes, classic school room romps and just about any plot one could imagine. The soda syphon, cream pies and breakaway suits were ideal foils to be used over and over again. Joff's talent was a huge boost for *IMT* and together Graham and Joff were a riot.

The 'TARAX' soft drink company was about to introduce a new tropical fruit flavoured drink for the summer and negotiated with GTV-9 and me to name the drink 'PANDA.' The drink would be launched on a GTV-9 television spectacular called the 'PANDA SHOW.' This was my own Saturday night prime time *special* and was the first time Channel Nine had presented a variety show starring a female personality and I was determined to fulfil the expectations of GTV-9, Tarax and the hundreds of well wishers who wrote letters of encouragement.

The station provided top talent, Joff Ellen, Ron Blaskett, Bob Horsfall and his wonderful vocal group 'The Tunetwisters' (Joan Clark, Jack Bowkett, Brian Rangott and Bob) Bill McCormack, an imported act Katy Delacruz from Manila, Elaine McKenna, the GTV-9 ballet and orchestra conducted by Arthur Young.

What a schedule! Representing Darrods on *IMT* every night, plus daily rehearsals for my own show. There were comedy sessions with Joff, routines to learn with Ron Blaskett and his ventriloquist dolls, Gerry Gee and Adolphus, singing and a high energy tap dancing routine with the talented Bob Horsfall, former Australian tap dancing champion.

The big night was a great success. Receptionist Wendy Hansen at the switch board was swamped with congratulatory calls, the ratings for the time slot were through the roof and Ken Pethard, the owner of 'TARAX' was overwhelmed with the response. Flowers, telegrams and letters poured into the mail room at GTV-9, which more than justified Channel Nine's decision to place me under contract.

Press rumours were always prevalent. One such rumour put to Graham and me was that Graham had been trying to *kill* my jokes in an effort to steal the limelight for himself. In essence, Graham was defensive about the rumour and was quick to point out it didn't matter who got the laughs and that he was fully supportive of me. There are various views about action and reaction in comedy and in his capacity as host, Graham's responsibility of keeping the show moving was uppermost and it was his style of action and reaction to everything that kept the audience mesmerised. It was no secret that those working with Graham were subject to his routine practice of *distraction* or *up-staging*.' It might have bothered some critics, but it didn't bother me. It was all part of the fun.

Anyone who has worked in theatre is familiar with the exercise of *up-staging*. Years ago, when explaining this to me, Tivoli comedienne Maggie Buckley said it occurs when one actor takes a step backwards (up-stage) so that his or her fellow actor is forced to turn away from the audience thus projecting the audience attention onto the *up-stager* who, at the same time might be *mugging* (making faces) at the audience. Although frowned upon, it happened frequently in vaudeville.

25

NEW HORIZONS

n early September, to celebrate Graham's return from the United States, GTV-9 presented what was termed in those days, a 'Spectacular,' namely the Astor 'BIG' Show, starring Graham and along with me there were comedian Joff Ellen, Philip Stainten, Jimmy Parkinson, Toni Lamond, Betty and Eddie Cole (Nat King Cole's brother), the GTV-9 ballet, Arthur Young and the new twenty-one piece orchestra. Aired on a Saturday night, directed by Norm and produced by Tom, it was an exhilarating television event.

As well as working with Graham, I also sang *You'd be Surprised*, whilst Graham performed Sammy Cahn's *It's Nice To Go Travelling*. *Volare*, an Italian hit song sweeping the world at the time was also introduced. It was by their individual talent that everyone in the show excelled. The critics were fairly generous with their kudos, one claiming the best part of the show were Graham's interludes with me. *The Australian Women's Weekly's* Nan Musgrove said of its Sydney airing:

> Melbourne's TV pin up-boy, Graham Kennedy, of GTV9, made his Sydney debut recently when Channel 7, Sydney, showed a film of his big Saturday show, the first one he did after his return from a trip abroad.

> *It was a good hour's entertainment, remarkable for it's smooth production and the fact that it was a real variety show, not just a variety of singers.*
>
> *Young Mr Kennedy, who looked younger, smaller, and not nearly as brash as I expected, was not in top form according to Melbourne reviewers, but his form was better than any of his opposite numbers in Sydney at their best.*
>
> *I've heard Kennedy described as a 'Melbourne phenomenon who simply wouldn't go down in Sydney.' Having seen him, I strongly doubt that remark. Sydney televiewers like good entertainers.*
>
> *I was interested to see Panda Lisner, who seems to be the only female personality yet to make any impact on Australian TV. Panda is a pretty blonde who sings adequately, talks engagingly, and is pleasant to watch.*

Amongst others, these were encouraging tributes for the spontaneous humour and entertainment we generated that night.

Meanwhile we were receiving National attention from Parliament House in Canberra. A member of the House of Representatives called Australian TV shows 'cheap and nasty.' Leaping to the defence was prominent politician Billy Sneddon. His response was:

> *In Melbourne especially, programs are of a very high standard indeed. Those associated with television are to be congratulated on their skill...The live show 'In Melbourne Tonight' has a totally Australian cast and features a personality called Graham, who recently returned from overseas.*
>
> *He returned to TV last Saturday night and I would be surprised if a single television receiver in the whole of Melbourne was not tuned into his show. He has proved himself capable of attracting and holding the public interest through high grade entertainment.*
>
> *I may mention that he is assisted by a most attractive person known as 'Panda.'*
>
> *Anyone who criticises the standard of our TV programs, in Melbourne at any rate, is humbugging...TV Week 1959*

This national attention only served to increase the importance of live variety in television.

Channel 9 had acquired the rights to air the four star movie, *High Noon*, starring Grace Kelly and Academy Award winner Gary Cooper. From the publicity department, Warrick Purser (or was it Michael Schildberger?) engaged the amiable GTV-9 personality and commercial presenter Hal Todd and me for a splurge of publicity. Dressed in western gear, complete with guns and holsters we rode on horseback down Collins, Swanston and Flinders Streets at high noon on the very day the movie was to be aired. I'm not sure of Hal's equestrian skills, but mine were indeed limited, especially astride a frisky horse in peak hour traffic. The horse owners drove their

With Hal Todd (left) promoting the movie 'High Noon'

automobile close behind us in the event something unforeseen happened, like the horses bolting for instance. 'How could they have helped?' we thought. Determined, we rode on with Hal's words etched in my memory, 'My bottom is pinched so tightly to this saddle, nothing the horse can do will dislodge me!' Often involved in stunts for Channel 9 and *IMT*, one night Norm had me make my entrance from the lighting grid high in the ceiling of the main studio. Ascending via an extension ladder I perched on the grid among the hot spotlights waiting for my introduction. Then it happened. My spike heeled shoe got caught in the maze of equipment, making descent impossible. This was all going on live to air. A hydraulic platform was brought into the studio and Geoff Corke climbed aboard while the lift elevated him to it's full height where he reached up and extricated me from the gods.

Another time an above-ground swimming pool was installed outside the studios, to be featured in daytime live programming. Norm and I were asked to participate as passengers in a small boat, floating in the pool while the do's and don'ts of small craft were discussed. We climbed into the boat from the edge of the pool. Someone gave it a mighty shove, sending it skimming across the water, upending it and pitching us into the pool soaking us

Bert Newton and Panda share the spotlight on 'IMT'

Laughing it up on 'IMT' with Graham Kennedy and a contestant

through. Geoff once again came to my rescue. Plunging into the pool, he plucked me from the water, playfully offering mouth to mouth resuscitation, while Norm wrung out his wallet.

Outside the safety net of the Channel 9 studios, we were all vulnerable to the onslaught of the unknown masses. Personal appearances were twofold. Some, we were engaged to do for a fee set down by mutual agreement and the balance of appearances were for charity events where we donated our time to raise funds for the sick and needy. In those days security was almost non-existent and Graham and I accompanied one another to many such engagements, all of which attracted hordes of people. It was comforting having each others company in these unfamiliar circumstances and surroundings. Several times Graham personally invited me to partner him to television balls and the theatre, where in most instances we were protection for each other. Another time we found ourselves coupled together as dinner guests at Marion and Colin Bednall's Toorak home just around the corner from my apartment. Graham was a charming escort, ever attentive and caring, exceptionally well mannered, impeccably groomed, a stimulating conversationalist and good company.

It had come to my attention that an isolated columnist, writing under a pseudonym, was consistently down-grading everything I did, or said. This

Graham Kennedy and Panda with the Darrods wheel on 'IMT'

Graham Kennedy and Panda clowning around on 'IMT'

writer was particularly venomous and it wasn't too long before one of his colleagues became so aggravated by his regular written assault, that in confidence the writer's name was divulged to me. The miscreant was the boyfriend of a model whose ambition far exceeded her talent and in spite of his one man crusade, her niche in the television industry had been as conspicuous as a mosquito bite on an elephant. The couple would have been surprised to learn that their cloak of secrecy was uncovered and that the model's continuing facade of friendly behaviour towards me was in vain.

Robin was attending the South Yarra State School and doing remarkably well academically. He still loved school, was well adjusted and a perfectly happy child. He enjoyed travelling on the pillion seat of my motor scooter, but loved it even more when I purchased my first automobile, a French Simca Aronde. He was fascinated by and payed more attention to, how the car operated than he did the scenery. His love of cars and their mechanical complexities, probably stemmed from his imaginative preschool playing with his collection of match box cars, when he used to interchange the small rubber tyres or any movable part from one car to another.

Francois had divorced me which brought down the final curtain on our relationship, leaving us with a distant but cordial association, however, the bond Robin and I shared became even stronger.

No matter how smoothly life progresses, something or someone is bound to throw a spanner in the works just to upset one's equilibrium. It was in January 1959, that a beaurocratic decision was made. The police gaming squad visited the studios of GTV-9 and informed management that the format of the wheel was illegal and had to be discontinued on *IMT*.

This ruling affected all competitions on radio and television including Bob Dyer's prestigious 'Pick a Box' quiz show. The manner in which prizes could be won was considered to be a game of chance and therefore a form of gambling.

Both Darrods and GTV-9 complied with the ruling immediately. The Darrods segment continued without the wheel. My fashion presentations, joke telling and ad-lib banter with Graham went on as usual. All avenues were investigated to ascertain what would satisfy the law. To allow viewers the opportunity to participate in the Darrods segment, Norm came up with the idea of me relating viewer's 'Tall Stories.' Occasionally, one of them would be put into sketch form with Graham and I enacting the characters therein. Intense negotiations between GTV~9 management and the Attorney General's office finally bore fruit. The wheel with its abundant prizes returned to *IMT* in March, after an absence of two months.

One evening, when Val Ruff was fulfiling a singing engagement, Geoff was at a loose end and feeling he might need company, I included him in an invitation with a handful of friends to a late-night-bite at my apartment. He had already promised to meet his friend Jimmy Allan (lead saxophonist with the GTV-9 orchestra) at the Musicians' Club. Geoff asked if Jimmy might be included in the invitation. I agreed without hesitation. A friend of Geoff's was a friend of mine.

My jokes for the show were often tried out on the gentlemen of the orchestra, who collectively were a pretty good barometer as to the standard required in the laugh

Representing Darrods at Flemington on Oaks Day

department. Jimmy was not a complete stranger, but to this point he was just an acquaintance and a sometimes contributor of jokes to my repertoire. He fitted in perfectly and adding his sense of humour to the already cheerful group, there was additional resounding laughter that night. We became good friends and working colleagues. Any time 1 was to perform songs, Jimmy ran through the musical routines with me until I knew them backwards. He was patient, encouraging and inspiring.

Born to Constance and George Allan, his father died when Jimmy was six years old. With his sister Lettie and brother John, he was raised by his widowed mother, a former nurse, who encouraged him in every endeavour, especially music. In spite of the loss of his father and much thanks to his mother, he enjoyed a happy childhood. He studied flute under the musical tutelage of Gordon Middleborough and progressed to advanced studies with the brilliant concert flautist John Amadio.

During the early 1940's, as a young teenage musician, Jimmy was a member of the *Aussie Dinkum* concert party which travelled around Victoria to various military camps, entertaining the troops. The concert's star comedian was Joff Ellen, who, together with his dancer wife Bernie formed a lifelong friendship with Jimmy. At seventeen, he enlisted in the Royal Australian Navy and served in action on the *HMAS Shropshire* attached to the U.S. seventh fleet in the Pacific. He was also a member of the Royal Australian Navy Band under the baton of Warrant Officer Harry Blaskett, (Ron Blaskett's uncle.)

At the end of World War 11, Jimmy received an honourable discharge from the Navy and pursued a full time career as a professional musician. Working everywhere from Dance Palais', Night Clubs, and the Circus, to the Tivoli's Katherine Dunham Dancers show, the Princess theatre's Musical Comedy *Kismet*, the ABC and 3DB Radio Orchestras, 3UZs Sports Parade, the State Theatre Orchestra with Stan Bourne (Shane Bourne's father) and live concerts including the Bob Clemens Jazz concerts at the Melbourne Town Hall with his own group, 'The Cool-Tones' (Jimmy, Ron Rosenberg, Bruce Clark, Stan Harris and Ron Terry).

Aside from his incomparable musical talent, he had a remarkable ability to recall in detail, a mountain of comedy material he'd absorbed over the years. He was in his element playing in the orchestra backing the famous comedians George Wallace, Tommy Trinder and Jackie Whalen at the Tivoli, and Bob Hope, Morey Amsterdam, Stan Freberg, Marty Allen, Rowan and Martin, Leo De Lyon, Mickey Katz and Abbot and Costello at Festival Hall.

When top American artists started appearing in concert in Australia, he worked with Frank Sinatra, Nat 'King' Cole, Liberace, Johnny Ray, Louis Armstrong, Bill Haley and the Comets, Billy Daniels, The Ink Spots, Betty Hutton, Gene Krupa and Ella Fitzgerald.

Jimmy was so helpful to me that I asked him to manage my affairs, which he agreed to do. So now I had a manager. It was a perfect situation, he could also escort me to the various venues and his managerial status circumvented any columnist linking us romantically.

TV Week's Rod Lever asked if it would be possible to fly me to Perth and do a story and photo spread with my mother. Fearing an invasion of mother's privacy, 1 accepted the assignment with some reservation, but after telephoning her to make the necessary arrangements and hearing how excited she was at the prospect of having me back, if only for the weekend, my uncertainties were allayed. We took off on a Saturday Flight from Melbourne to Perth.

The anticipation of seeing my family again for the first time since the death of my brother Ron five years earlier, made the long journey pass quickly.

While in Perth, Rod had other company business to attend to, so a central Hotel was essential. We were booked into luxury suites on St Georges Terrace, the same hotel as Lady Patty and Sir Robert Menzies were staying at the time. Everything provided was first class and having a car at our disposal, made it convenient to find our way to mother's house.

The festivities rivalled some of our Christmas gatherings. Val, her children Valda and Kim, Norm, his wife Ursula and their son Damien, all joined us for one of mother's delicious roast lamb luncheons, after which we were entertained by Norm 'tickling the ivories' with renditions of his favourite musical treats. The only immediate family member missing was Ian, who was living in country Victoria. The pride they had in my achievements was apparent, but in the family hierarchy, I was still the little sister. Like many family get togethers, teasing and stories of the past made for a wonderful time. As the day progressed, the *TV Week* photographer clicked away while Rod took copious notes for his story. The end result was another successful *TV Week* spread and provided me with a memorable weekend with my family.

As usual, departure was an emotional wrench and although the telephone, mail and Interflora always kept me in touch with mother, this weekend was to be the last time I would ever see her.

Back in Melbourne to open the New Year's Eve show, a seemingly simple stunt was to be performed. Someone decided Graham would ride pillion on my motor scooter as I drove it through a giant hoop covered with white paper, featuring a glittering New Year's Eve message. The property department provided only one covered hoop, so there was no rehearsal. Sitting on the scooter facing the wall of white paper which obscured us from the audience, I was not afraid. While the orchestra struck up the overture, Graham climbed aboard. I was cued to start the motor, then cued again to plunge through the paper covered hoop. With Graham hanging on to me like super glue, I accelerated and blindly we drove through the hoop. When the paper split asunder, suddenly we were faced with cameras, crew, cables, lights and an audience all coming towards us as the cameramen started heading for the hills. Applying the brakes just short of a camera, it was a scary moment, but undaunted, Graham leapt off the scooter to welcome the audience, as I rode out of the studio to deafening applause.

In January 1959, *TV Week* premiered their Logie Awards, the first television awards given in Australia. They were named by Graham after John Logie Baird, who demonstrated the first practical television system in 1926, using Paul Nipkow's 1884 mechanical scanning device. The awards represented excellence in Performance, Direction and Production.

Logie night – from left to right: Hugh O'Brien, Panda, Norm Spencer, Graham Kennedy, Rod Biddle and Joff Ellen

The announced winners were:

BEST MALE PERSONALITY:	Graham Kennedy
BEST FEMALE PERSONALITY:	Panda
BEST REGULAR LIVE PROGRAM:	'In Melbourne Tonight'
MOST POPULAR FILM DRAMA SERIES:	'Perry Mason'
MOST POPULAR FILM VARIETY SHOW:	'Perry Como Show'
BEST REGULAR CHILDREN'S SHOW:	'The Happy Show'
SPECIAL AWARD FOR AN OUTSTANDING CHILDREN'S SHOW:	'Swallows Juniors'
SPECIAL AWARD FOR LIVE DRAMA PRODUCTION:	William Sterling
SPECIAL AWARD FOR TECHNICAL DIRECTION:	Ian Jones 'Hit Parade'
SPECIAL AWARD FOR OUTSTANDING PERFORMANCES:	Bill Collins 'Sunny Side Up'
SPECIAL AWARD FOR OUTSTANDING SPORTS:	ABC Sporting Department

The magazine reported:

'TV Week readers overwhelmingly voted Graham Kennedy and Panda as the outstanding television stars of 1958.'

To have begun life in rural Western Australia, in what could best be described as underprivileged conditions and working my way up via vaudeville, musical comedy and modelling, into television was no mean feat and now presented with the very first female Logie Award, in fact the only female award for 1958, seemed like a miracle. When mentioning these feelings to my friend Evie Hayes, she said,

'Enjoy it honey, you paid your dues!'

The beautiful and much admired English Actress Googie Withers honoured us by making the presentation live on *IMT*. To commemorate this historical television event, *TV Week* featured a colour portrait of Graham and me on their cover titled 'Stars of The Year.' It's moments like these, that one pinches oneself to see it it's real. It was a humbling experience.

26

BUSY

he glamorous side of television was *on camera*, but not apparent was the amount of time devoted to *off camera* activities helping to promote GTV-9's and my image.

Of course there were regular fittings for the nightly fashion changes, as well as rehearsals for musical routines, occasional sketches, intermittent personal appearances, gathering anecdotes for my *TV Week* column and photo shoots to announce station activities, such as the cover of *Listener In-TV* featuring Graham and me. It was to launch the upcoming annual telethon appeal, aiding the Yooralla Crippled Children's Hospital.

At journalist Robert Fent's request, a quiet luncheon at the Savoy Plaza Hotel was arranged for me and English stage and television star, Sabrina, who was in Melbourne for a theatrical season at the Tivoli Theatre. Robert explained there would be just the three of us. Instead, Sabrina was accompanied by an entourage including her mother Mrs Sykes and theatre representative Betty Stewart. It was a pleasant, combined interview-luncheon. Robert got his exclusive story and we all laughed when he displayed his notes divulging that I partook of a light garden salad, while sabrina tucked away half a roast chicken followed by strawberries and ice-cream, yet still retained her hour-glass figure. Afterwards, as we were descending the stairs from the dining room into the foyer, Robert discovered the publicist had leaked information of our presence and there was a crowd of autograph seekers awaiting our emergence. Instead of preparing for our next appointments, we spent an hour signing autographs.

As well as being a favourite venue for press conferences, the Savoy Plaza Hotel's dining room transformed into a cabaret at night featuring regulars Charles and Beryl White. The floor shows starred top international artists such as England's Alma Kogan and Dickie Valentine, Australia's Rolph Harris and America's Jane Powell, Vaughn Monroe, Al Martino, Sarah Vaughan and Helen Traubel, America's leading Wagnerian soprano (an unusual choice for a cabaret setting).

As a columnist, one of my assignments was to attend a press conference to meet, greet and put forth questions to Gregory Peck, who was in Australia making Stanley Kramer's movie *On The Beach*, with Ava Gardner and Fred Astaire. Fellow columnist Don Bennetts from HSV-7 and I, joined journalists representing local, national and international newspapers and magazines in firing a barrage of questions. Gregory responded with the dignity and intellect befitting a star of his magnitude. He was a fascinating and interesting man. This was a great opportunity to observe an international press conference adding another notch in my tree of knowledge.

At this point in time, Norm programmed additional material for me to perform on *IMT*. English Revue writer Peter Myers was in Sydney producing a very funny theatrical presentation *For Amusement Only*. Amongst its stars were pals, Toni Lamond, Frank Sheldon, Tikki Taylor and John Newman. Because of his extraordinary talent, he was engaged by GTV~9 to daily write four witty verses on topical issues and phone them in to *IMT* for me to learn, rehearse with Arthur Young and sing them to a calypso rhythm that same night. The audience responded favourably to my rendition of Peter's very funny verses.

When Bob Dyer came down to Melbourne from Sydney, GTV-9 presented a series of lavish national shows

Interviewing Gregory Peck for the movie 'On The Beach'

starring him, using the new technological breakthrough *video tape*. Bob secured the sponsorship of British Petroleum (BP) who supplied the financial backing necessary to produce these high priced productions. Graham, Joff and I were showcased in a scintillating, funny send-up of television panel shows. Also cast were, French singer Michele Matey, Paul Dalton and many of the Nine network's top entertainers. This was on Saturday night prime time and lived up to the advertised name 'Super Show.'

The reviews were complimentary. International and controversial actor of stage and motion pictures and sometime television critic Frank Thring could be crushingly cruel and at times would scathingly cut the best of us down to size with the poisonous drip of his pen. This show however, he gave the 'thumbs up,' giving credit to us for an entertaining show and likened some repartee between Bob Dyer and myself to the Hope and Crosby road shows. Whether or not one agreed with his comments, his column was on the required weekly reading list and caused lively debate around the studio corridors.

Having been a guest in Frank's home, I found him to be a character larger than life itself. Most hospitable, extremely witty and very, very funny. Anyone who knew him could never forget him. His vitriolic criticism was a source of much discussion.

B.P. Super show comedy sketch rehearsal.
Left to right: Graham Kennedy, Bob Dyer, Panda and Joff Ellen

GTV-9 and the press discontinued using my last name and 1 became known simply as 'Panda.' *Listener In-TV* and *TV Week*, editors Perc Dunstone and Rod Lever both agreed that the single word 'Panda' impacted more effectively on their headlines and billboards.

Settling down with a good book, listening to the full spectrum of music, solving crossword puzzles, attending the theatre and other live entertainment were a must on my recreational list, as were motion picture dramas, comedies, musicals and science fiction, all of which were valuable fodder for my brain. Not all, but most movies were viewed in the darkness of a Drive-in theatre which offered the advantage of anonymity.

Graham was the recipient of my tales of science fiction movies, as I gave him a glowing description of their story lines on *IMT*.

'*Tarantula* was about a scientist's experiment which went horribly wrong,' I explained. 'His formula exceeded all expectations, causing abnormal growth, resulting in a building-size tarantula threatening anything and everything in its path. The leading characters, portraying a young couple falling in love, were standing by huge desert boulders in the moonlight.

It was very romantic, but just as they were about to kiss, out of nowhere appeared a great big hairy…'

'Wait a minute!' Graham interrupted with a double take. 'Panda, are we still talking about the movie?' (A roar of laughter from the audience),

'Yes!' I continued, 'the gigantic hairy Tarantula leg thrust itself over the top of the outcrop of rocks, blocking the lover's path…' Graham grasped the moment and with his mugging and clowning, turned my review into a comedic triumph. Graham laughed, I laughed, the crew laughed and the audience laughed. The next day *IMT* received a film clip from the drive-in theatre management with their permission to air it on the show and the laughter started all over again. We were also presented with a life-time gold pass to the drive-in theatres. Amongst other science fiction reviews I presented were the 3-D monster movie *Creature from the Black Lagoon*, and Warner Brothers box office smash hit *Them!* Graham and I had people flocking to the drive-ins in droves.

When HSV-7's Late Show Comedian Joey Porter met his untimely death, a benefit was held for his bereft family, which brought together the cream of theatre and television entertainers to honour this much loved performer. The concert was held on a Sunday night at the West Melbourne Stadium seating 6,000, the largest auditorium in Melbourne at the time.

The luminaries appearing included *The Diamond Horseshoe* Tivoli star

Will Mahoney, England's Jimmy Wheeler, top billing in the up-coming Tivoli production of *Star-light Roof*, and the hard working and highly prized *Tivoli Ballet*. Headliner Johnny Lockwood flew in from the Sydney Tivoli's *Tropical Holiday*. There were comedy instrumentalists Guus Brox and Myrna, juggler Rudy Horn from the Ed Sullivan show in New York and Richard Walker and Helen Roberts from Her Majesty's Theatre production of *My Fair Lady*. From GTV-9 were Graham Kennedy, Joff Ellen and me in one of Joff's hilariously funny stand up sketches, Bert Newton, Evie Hayes, Frank Rich and other *IMT* regulars. HSV-7's personnel included John D'Arcy formerly of the *Hit Parade* and at that time host of *The Late Show*, chief announcer, Geoff Raymond, Shirley Broadway, Roy Lyons, Jackie Clancy and the featured band of Lou Toppano who rounded off this star studded night.

The auditorium was full to capacity, raising a goodly sum of money and every performer did their *primo* material, running the show more than three hours. Spectaculars of this magnitude were financially out of the question for an entrepreneur to stage and could only be presented by the generosity of personal contribution, the hallmark of show business performers. This was a gala night and we were all happy to donate our time as a tribute to the much loved Joey Porter.

Jimmy's band on the Bert Newton Teenage show (GTV9).
Left to right: Roy Hosking, Joe Hudson, Jimmy, Jack Westmore and Don Moore

My manager Jimmy became immersed in the art of orchestrating and arranging music. The myriad of different tones and colours achievable through creative writing held a fascination for him, so it was a logical step to explore further this innovative facet of music. Channel 9's Musical Director, Arthur Young tutored and fostered his endeavours in this complex area, spreading his wings in the field of music. Others who unselfishly shared with Jimmy their expertise in arranging music were guitarist Bruce Clark and pianist Ron Rosenberg (former members of his jazz group 'The Cool Tones').

One of Jimmy's earliest orchestrations was *The Chums Song*, arranged for Graham and me. It was played on *IMT* for many moons. Norm immediately saw his potential and appointed Jimmy bandleader for GTV-9's *The Bert Newton Teenage Show*. Jimmy and I had become each other's confidant, trusting unconditionally and constant companions.

October 1959, Hanna Pan from Pan Public Relations organised a photo shoot at Lennon's Broadbeach Hotel near Surfer's Paradise in Queensland on one of my free weekends. It was two days of heavenly relaxation in the sun. Saturday night we were guests at the hotel's floorshow where one of the former Kiwi's stars Red Moore was performing. Most memorable was his handling of a very inebriated heckler in the audience. When the heckler continued on with a tirade of indecipherable comments, Red said:

'There's at least one alcoholic who isn't anonymous!' and continued without interruption for the rest of his act.

Sunday morning we were up bright and early completing the two day photo shoot, then it was on a plane, back to Melbourne and *IMT*.

27

OUTSIDE BROADCASTS

GTV-9 was making its presence felt in the regional areas of Victoria, with a series of outside broadcasts of *IMT* in cities like Bendigo, Ballarat and Yallourn.

At the conclusion of *IMT*, we all took to our cars and drove to the scheduled country destination. At Ballarat, after catching just a few hours sleep, we were at the race track for a televised meeting with 'Ace' race caller Bert Bryant and commentator Eric Welsh. Graham and I presented the winner of the Ballarat Miners' Turf Club's main event with a special GTV-9 trophy. My commentary on the fashions and interviews with lady punters rounded off my role in the afternoon broadcast.

Knowing little, if anything about betting on horses, the principle of track odds was explained to me. When I asked the bookmaker if he would pay a hundred pounds if the horse won. He said,

'Panda! If you bet a pound on that particular horse and it wins, I'll pay you three hundred pounds!'

The bet was wagered and of course the horse ran last. Joff Ellen sidled up to me and said,

'Last week I saw that horse pulling a milk cart!' From the race track, we hastened back to our temporary studio for rehearsals and the show that night. The country folk embraced us affectionately and we in turn entertained them as only the cast of *IMT* could. The show contained the full company from Melbourne, including Graham and me, special guest Bob Dyer, Joff Ellen, Bert Newton, Bill McCormick, Dorothy Baker, Elaine McKenna, Joy Fountain, Barry McQueen, Bob Horsfall, Hal Todd, the Horrie Dargie Quintet and Ron Blaskett.

At Bendigo, in conjunction with the telecast, *TV Week* ran a photo competition for the local camera enthusiasts who were encouraged to take candid photographs of me and send them in to *TV Week*, where the winner would receive a valuable portable Radiogram. From the moment of leaving the hotel and throughout the entire day I was followed everywhere by groups of camera buffs. Not being caught unawares required great cunning, but the thanks received for each photograph captured, compensated for enduring the intense scrutiny.

The journey to Yallourn, site of Victoria's famous open cut coal mine, was slow and dangerous due to the almost impenetrable fog we encountered. Bumper to bumper, each car followed the other like a caravan of camels in a sand storm. On this occasion, the regular *IMT* cast was enhanced by the addition of talented Toni Lamond and Frank Sheldon.

Another telecast was done from the Puckapunyal army camp near Seymour, where Graham had undergone his military training and where Joff Ellen entertained the troops many times during World War II. Incorporating their local knowledge of the area, they had the young soldiers howling with laughter with wonderful old vaudevillian lines like:

> '*My dressingroom's got the best view in the barracks.*'
>
> '*How's that?*'
>
> '*It overlooks Panda's!*'

Outside broadcasts of Geoff Corke's Saturday morning breakfast shows were televised in the summertime from Sorrento beach on the Mornington Peninsula, (Bert Newton later replaced Geoff). The show provided a festive atmosphere for the area holiday makers. Early Saturday morning found chief engineer Rod Biddle at the base studio in Bendigo Street, Richmond, while Norm was ready in the outside broadcast (O.B.) van at Sorrento. With his crew standing by, as we positioned ourselves for a morning of action packed television from the beach, the show got underway with music from the Orchestra and songs from various members of GTV-9's stable of singing stars. There were interviews, games and competitions involving the audience, plus speed boat racing and demonstrations of water skiing. The whole area was populated by family holiday makers staying in vacation homes and camp grounds along the shoreline and exuberant onlookers stretched down the beach as far as the eye could see.

A daring broadcast was done from Graham's 'sick bed' at his mother's home. One couldn't imagine what disruption the household experienced that night with the huge O.B. van parked in the driveway, large connecting cables running through the house and the 1950's oversize TV camera cramped in Graham's bedroom. We even presented the Darrods segment from his bedside. Throughout all of this turmoil, Graham's mother could not have been more obliging, calmly providing refreshments to the cast and crew.

At one time, prior to dates being set for the Sorrento broadcasts, I had accepted an invitation to judge a beauty pageant on a Saturday afternoon at Yea, a country town 66 miles north of Melbourne. Acting as my manager, Jimmy was to drive me to the engagement. Sorrento was 60 miles south of Melbourne, so we had an anticipated 126 mile journey ahead of us. After the band played the finale to the show and Jimmy had packed his musical instruments, we left the beach and undaunted, set off in his white Porsche open sports car, in scorching heat, on what must have been the hottest day of the year.

Our instructions were to meet an official under the first large gum tree on the left after we turned off the main highway to Yea and when we made the turn, sure enough, the gentleman was waiting. He escorted us to his home, where I changed into suitable attire. Leaving Jimmy's car at the house and boarding the official's automobile, we started out across a wide field when a loud bang reverberated through the air. A rear tyre had blown out and instead of stopping and changing it, the official drove on gliding, sliding and wafting over the field of long grass in a hair-raising ride that would have challenged anything at Disneyland.

At the pageant site, a tent with rows of chairs had been set up for officials and all four tent flaps were elevated to catch any breath of air that might pass our way. The tray of an enormous feed truck, unprotected from the fierce rays of the sun, represented the stage where the judging would take place. At this time, I overheard a conversation between two teen-age boys swatting bush flies as they discussed the beauty pageant:

> 'Is your sheila in the contest?' one boy asked. His mate responded,
> 'Yeah, she's in it, but she's got no hope of winning!'

During the judging, I wondered which of the contestants had such a supportive beau.

With the winner crowned and the pageant over, Jimmy asked the obliging official if there was a shorter route back to Melbourne and given some detailed instructions, we took off on a winding mountainous road, more suited as a 'yak track'. It was a shorter route, but turned out to be very slow motoring. The steep slopes, hazardous bends and birds flying head first into the windscreen made for an uneasy journey home. The episode gave cause for careful consideration of future long distance engagements.

Back in 1957 when Graham mentioned my age, it was stated as being 25. Now two years later it remained the same and had become an annual twenty-fifth birthday celebration. This particular year, one of our sponsors 'Four and Twenty Pies' baked a giant meat pie bigger than a large serving platter as a substitute cake. Beautifully decorated, it was to be a surprise with Graham presenting it to me on the show.

In the property area outside the studio, where sets and props were stored, there was what was known as a cage, containing sponsors products and other valuables which were locked up for safe keeping. This is where they secreted the pie, out of my view, to ensure a genuine surprise. Unbeknown to the property master, the studio cat had been accidentally locked in the cage along with the pie. While I made my entrance on the show, fractured panic was going on in the cage. The cat had eaten a hearty meal from the pie leaving a gaping hole in the crust. What to do? Someone ran to the canteen, hi-jacked a regular 'Four and Twenty Pie' and raced back to the cage where someone's stroke of genius managed to repair the damage, disguising the leftovers of the cat's banquet.

Finally the moment of presentation arrived. As the band struck up *Happy Birthday*, Graham placed the enormous pie in front of me and everyone cheered. Not aware of what had happened, I demanded a knife for the ceremonial cutting. Graham was totally informed of the cat's feasting, saying it would be a pity to cut the pie now, but to save it for the party later. I was not to be put off and insisted Graham taste my birthday pie. With plenty of encouragement from the audience and much mugging from Graham, he finally succumbed to my pleas and gingerly bit into a slice of the contaminated pie, while the cat looked on slyly from the prop bay and the cast and crew simply fell to pieces. Although sensing something was wrong, it wasn't until I left the set that the whole story unfolded. That's show business!

28

STALKERS

ow wonderful it is to be loved and admired by so many people. So it is when one becomes famous. The undying faithfulness of one's supporters is quite overwhelming. Riding high on a rainbow of success, I had arrived as a celebrity. My show business background had paid off, rocketing me to television stardom. I loved doing what I was doing and the longer I did it, the better at it I got. However, this fame was in someway a handicap. Privacy had become a luxury and there emerged a murky, dark side to fame.

About to enter my apartment one night after the show, I was surprised to encounter other apartment residents who had stayed up late to warn me of a prowler sighted in the garden. Thanking them for their concern, I hurried to the phone and called the police.

As it happened, letters addressed to me by an unknown person had been arriving at both channel nine and my apartment threatening me and my well being. The dialogue contained in the letters indicated the writer was of questionable character. The handwriting was identical to some other mail of a more favourable nature. The case was handed over to the C.I.B. who came to my aid, collecting the evidence and setting an investigation in motion. Concerned that harm could come to me, the matter was treated most seriously and they offered a police escort if ever I felt the need for one.

After an intensive investigation the C.I.B. solved the case, only to discover the perpetrator was a woman who allegedly had a split personality. She was sentenced to psychiatric care. In spite of the anguish she caused me, through her solicitor, I offered best wishes for her recovery. With thanks, he said my gesture would be beneficial to her recuperation. The judge ordered the press to suppress her identity and as the victim of this unpleasant ordeal, perhaps he should have paid me the same courtesy, but alas he did not and at my expense, certain sections of the press had a field day which in turn invited more unstable characters to stalk me. Cracks in the woodwork had opened up and a sequence of incidents preceded a most disturbing period. Letters and telephone calls to GTV-9 were followed by personal visits to the station by a somewhat disturbed man attempting to make personal contact with me. Although GTV-9's security was minimal he was held at bay and those informed of the intruder made sure he could not reach me.

Determined, the man next called at Norm Spencer's home to pronounce his deep desire to meet me and to plead for Norm's intervention on his behalf. In no uncertain terms, Norm ordered him off his property, advising him that action would be taken if he did not immediately desist with his advances to either GTV-9, Norm or me. Unconcerned by Norm's admonition, he persisted and strange almost incoherent letters continued arriving at both GTV-9 and my apartment.

His next appearance was on my doorstep. Fortunately, friends who were visiting at the time, escorted him off the premises warning him never to return. Unperturbed, he continued stalking me until the tone of his correspondence became chilling to the point where police intervention was inevitable. In an illogical act, he made an appointment in writing, to meet me at my apartment at a specific time. When he rang the doorbell, he was promptly arrested by waiting police. Incidents like these occurred from time to time and were dealt with immediately by GTV-9's now updated security.

Driving along Toorak Road, a newsagent's billboard jumped out at me. It read: MY LIFE WITH PANDA. To say I was surprised, is an understatement. Journalist John Burrowes was a good friend and had written many articles about me. However, without my knowledge, he had been commissioned to interview Francois about our former life together in a two part series for *Listener-TV*. Most disturbing were photographs of our son Robin. I'd always been especially careful about keeping Robin's low profile intact so that his natural development would not be disrupted by my perceived image. For Francois and John to have breached this trust was a gross misjudgment. Of course Francois was oblivious to, and did not understand, the possible consequences of publicly revealing Robin's identity. Luckily, John did not include a current photograph of him, so identifying Robin was not a simple task for any stranger, but I still wore a worry-hat for many months afterwards.

29

WORLD TOUR

GTV-9 negotiated a new contract with me, increasing my salary and adding a bonus. On signing the contract for another year, Norm stated in a press release:

Panda's got talent, make no mistake about that, and what's more, she's still to show her best on TV. Meanwhile Panda is delighted to be with us for another year, and by the look of her ever growing fan mail, so are many viewers. If her letter bag is any indication to her popularity, Panda has more appeal today than she had a year ago. Pulling in nearly 1000 letters a week, probably the most on Melbourne TV, her mail graph shows an increase in recent months.

The bounteous bonus which came with the new contract was extremely generous. Qantas had just inaugurated an 'Around the World Service' with the newly commissioned Boeing 707 Jet liner and GTV-9 had organised a fact-finding business tour for me, as their way of saying thank you for my past years of service. Thrilled doesn't adequately describe my feelings at the time.

Having worked five nights a week since my start on *IMT*, plus the Specials and Saturday night movie hosting, the executives at GTV-9 felt I was deserving. It was like a dream. All of these wonderful things were happening to me and believing was difficult to comprehend.

Letters from Colin and Norm were forwarded to their counterparts in London, New York and Los Angeles announcing my impending tour. The list of top executives was pretty impressive. London's Lew Grade from Associated Television Limited, New York's Tom McManus of MCA TV Limited and Robert Fitzgerald from MCA TV Limited in Hollywood. Each of them responded with positive enthusiasm and awaited my itinerary.

Nigel Dick, Colin, Norm and Graham each gave me valuable advice on overseas travel. 'Don't pack too much clothing!' 'The minute you arrive in each city, confirm your next flight out!' 'Tip ten percent for cab fares, restaurant and beauty parlour bills!' 'Are you sure you'll have enough money?' and so forth.

GTV-9 even provided some spending money. There was much to do. Passport, visas, vaccinations, health certificate, traveller's cheques, wardrobe, luggage and hundreds of little details to attend to. The press were calling for information on where I would be staying, who I would be meeting and what were my plans in general. The itinerary had not been completed, so the questions remained unanswered for the time being. *Truth* newspaper went ahead with a story anyway. When seeing their billboard and full front page story I was shaken. The headline read:

PANDA'S ROMANCE
FLYING TO MEET TENNIS ACE.

Apparently the story came about because I was wearing a large platinum and diamond ring on the third finger, left hand. Graham drew attention to it by making references on the show like,

'Is your hand getting heavy?' 'Watch out the batteries don't go flat!' The press, ever alert, tracked me down for more details as to it's origin. At the time, it was a very personal matter and I was not willing to discuss the ring publicly.

An inquisitive reporter from *Truth* tried to put two and two together. Back in February 1958, American *Davis Cup* tennis player Barry MacKay was being escorted around the Nine studios by Geoff Corke. We were introduced and as the conversation got under way, Barry asked if I would partner him to the *Davis Cup Ball*. Agreeing to do so, we attended the function with the rest of the Davis Cup Team players and their partners. Barry returned to the United States and that was the end of it, except we did fleetingly meet again with Geoff at Channel nine the next time he was in town for the Davis Cup, where Jimmy, Geoff, Barry and I exchanged stories over a cup of coffee. The article was mostly harmless nonsense. However, when the reporter telephoned Barry's parents in the United States, they were not amused.

The wearing of the ring really did cause quite a stir. Firstly, everyone thought Graham was the donor. 1959 *TV Week* published an amusing article by Jack 'The Ace' Ayling, somewhat reminiscent of the style of Mickey Spillane. In part he said:

> *This story begins the night a character named Graham and a doll they call Panda do their act before the TV cameras and give out to one and all the impression they are about to become hitched.*
>
> *...But while all this might sound so much hotch potch to the guys who wander in and out of TV circles this doll called Panda throws them all into a head spin when she manages somehow to drag up her left hand and there on the third finger rests a rock that some say had to be hauled by tractor from the diamond mines. We open by saying that if Graham and Panda are about to see marriage man we wish to offer our congratulations. In fact we say we hope they live together for a long time as some guys have been known to do. Graham and Panda however, do not fall for this little trap and they decline our best wishes saying we may keep them for some later date at some other joint. Well we say this is all very puzzling and we would like to know what Panda is doing running around town dazzling the eyes of the side walkers and generally bumping up the business of opticians who get quite an income from patching up what they call the effects of glare.*
>
> *...we are satisfied that this guy Graham and peaches and cream Panda are, what the guys say, good pals.*
>
> *As they say at Flemington, the odds about them ever marrying would be one million to one AGAINST!*

Jack was quite a character and a popular contributor to publications of the day. With a good sense of humour, he was always welcome at the interview table.

The mystery of the ring was never officially divulged. It was designed and made especially for me by a distinguished Flinders Lane jeweller, who handcrafted his version of a Waratah centred with a diamond. I loved it and that's all that mattered.

Saying farewell to Robin before leaving for the airport and happy in the knowledge that my friend Joy Fountain would substitute for me on *IMT*, finally I was on my way around the world. Jimmy drove me to Essendon Airport where a crowd of friends, colleagues and acquaintances awaited my arrival, including Norm and Joff. Graham was there and gave me change in American currency left over from his previous trip and a *Saint Christopher* key ring which I have still. GTV-9's coverage of the departure was handled by cameraman Tony Hope, photographer Chris Whitehorn and publicity's' Albert Porges. Then I was on my way to Sydney to catch the 707 Qantas flight around the world.

30

LONDON

oday, a jumbo jet's direct flight from Sydney to London takes about twenty-three hours. However, in 1959, a complex route including several landings and take-offs was necessary. Extended delays at fuelling stops added hours to the travelling time. Not aware of what was ahead and climbing the steps to the 707 jet into the VIP first class section, the excitement was almost too much to bear. The plane left Sydney on its way to Darwin for re-fuelling. Here, the pilot obtained permission and invited me, as a VIP, to sit in the jet's control room for take-off. What a thrill! Strapped in a seat behind the pilot and co-pilot and opposite the flight engineer, the crew could be heard busily conversing as they did the compulsory check list of all the complicated equipment. Donning earphones, I listened to the control tower's instructions and watched closely as we roared down the runway, the pilot lifting the nose of the jet headed for Singapore.

On landing in Singapore, reality hit. The departure was delayed and we spent two hours in a non-airconditioned terminal. The need for warm clothing was a little premature. Dressed in a three piece woollen suit in preparation for the expected cold weather in London, I literally sizzled in Singapore's sticky, sultry heat and was glad to get out of there.

The plane jetted on, touching down in Bangkok, Calcutta and Karachi. The Karachi airport was being rebuilt and our arrival was very very close to the closure time for the day's construction. If re-fuelling could not be completed in time for the plane to be off the runway by 8.00 a.m. we would be forced to remain there until 7.00 p.m. when the airport once again became operative. Spending a day at any airport was most unappealing. The passengers were very happy when the plane was airborne and we were off to the next touch-downs in Beirut, Behrain and Cairo.

Cairo airport was huge. There were planes from many major world airlines, including the Soviet Union and The United Nations. The use of cameras was banned, all passengers were restricted to a specific area and armed soldiers patrolled the complex, making everyone feel a little uneasy.

Rome was the last touch-down before finally landing in London. Wendy Hansen, former chief receptionist at GTV-9 and now living in London, was there to meet me. At the hotel there were flowers from Jimmy and telegrams from friends, GTV-9 and *TV WEEK*.

My stay in London was limited and Wendy had much to show me in the shortest possible time. Colin's business friend, theatrical entrepreneur Lew Grade (years later dubbed Lord Lew Grade) was Deputy Managing Director of Associated Television Limited (ATV). He was in the south of France for the Christmas break, but had thoughtfully left instructions with his very obliging secretary Pamela Grey to take care of anything I needed. Lew had already obtained some almost impossible to get tickets for me to see two major theatre productions, *Irma La Douce* at the Lyric Theatre and *The World of Susie Wong* at the Prince of Wales Theatre.

Starring Elizabeth Seal and Keith Mitchell, *Irma La Douce* was a musical of unusual style. Originally a French show with lyrics and book by Alexandre Breffort and music by Marguerite Monnot. The English adaption was by Julian More, David Heneker and Monty Norman.

The story is about an impoverished Parisian student, Nestor, who falls in love with a gullible prostitute, Irma. In order to maintain a monogamous relationship with her, he disguises himself as a wealthy man who can singularly provide for her. To financially accomplish this, he has to work incredibly hard and becomes jealous of his other self (the wealthy man), so kills him off, is convicted of the fictitious crime and sentenced to Devil's Island. He escapes, manages to prove his innocence and reunites with his beloved Irma. It's cleverly written, funny and most entertaining. The hit song *Our Language of Love* came from this delightful and most successful musical, which in 1963 was produced into a non musical movie starring Shirley MacLaine and Jack Lemmon.

In London theatres during intermission, tea and biscuits were served to patrons in their seats, or if one preferred, cocktails were available in the foyer. Cigarette smoking was also tolerated in the theatre.

After *Irma La Douce* on Christmas Eve, Wendy introduced me to some fellow Australians and we had a late-night-bite at an Espresso bar. They were all homesick and couldn't get enough news about Australia. On leaving the café we ate hot roasted chestnuts cooked over an open fire by a street vendor and in the crisp frosty air, listened to carollers under a giant brilliantly lit Christmas tree.

Celebrating with a hearty English feast on Christmas day, we relaxed in readiness for Wendy's grand tour of London sights the next day.

We walked from the hotel down Oxford Street to Regent Street into Picadilly Circus, along Coventry Street, past The Prince of Wales theatre to the Haymarket. Past Her Majesty's Theatre, down Pall Mall to Trafalgar Square. Here, like all tourists, we fed the multitude of pigeons, then off to Whitehall, past the horse guards to where the trooping of the colours is performed. We stood on the steps at 10 Downing Street, walked on by the House of Parliament, Big Ben, St Margaret's Church where most of the socialite weddings take place, visited Westminster Abbey, inspecting the tombs therein, of poets and past Royal figures. On to Great St George Street, into Birdcage Walk, St James park, houses of the regiments of the Queen's Guard, then to Buckingham Palace, the Queen Victoria monument, along the Mall past Clarence House and St James Palace up to Admiralty Arch, back to Trafalger Square. Finally we gave our feet a rest and caught the tube train from Picadilly Circus to Madame Tussard's Wax Works.

The weather was unbelievably cold. At the first opportunity, I went on a shopping spree at Harrods Department Store, purchasing a warm, heavily lined top-coat and a cloche hat.

During my visit to London, on Colin's instructions I was to catch up with Sir Arthur Warner and interview him on GTV-9's newly acquired small portable tape recorder. Sir Arthur was leader of the Upper House in Victoria, Minister for Transport, probably the most important man in Australian Electronics and founder of GTV-9. A keen yachtsman, this was the first Christmas holiday season he had not sailed in the Sydney to Hobart yacht race, as he and Lady Warner were on a visit to England and Europe. He was exactly what one would expect of a man of his distinction. First and foremost a gentleman, courteous and a most engaging conversationalist.

The very charming Mr Goldberg from Raoul Merton shoes called and invited me to join him and his family for cocktails at the Grosvenor Hotel. He gave me an address in Los Angeles where, if I so desired, I could obtain shoes with his compliments.

Molly Douglas, representing *TV Times*, telephoned for an interview and unfolded her plans for an inspirational story and photo shoot. As it turned out, her itinerary was almost a duplication of Wendy's marathon tour, so we did the whole thing again. Next morning, following this whirlwind trip to London, I was on my way to New York.

31

NEW YORK

he plane took us over the Isle of Man and Northern Ireland and was approaching the east coast of North America, when bad weather in New York caused the plane to be diverted to Goose Airport (Goose Bay) Labrador, in Canada, where we touched down in temperatures of twenty-nine degrees below freezing. The pilot announced we would be plane bound because of the extreme cold. Everything was white. There was ice in every direction and the bay was frozen over.

Saying good-bye to Goose Bay, we were finally approaching our destination. The weather was still questionable for landing, so the plane was put in a holding pattern over New York. For a while it was touch and go as to whether we would be diverted to Boston, Massachusetts, or Montreal, Canada. Finally a clearance was given and we landed at Eidelwild Airport (now JFK Airport) New York.

Checking in at the Waldorf Astoria, there were greetings from home, flowers from Jimmy and messages galore. Correspondent George McCadden, New York representative of *The News Limited of Australia*, was to cover my New York visit for *TV Week*. He telephoned almost at the same time as I checked into my room and asked me to join him and his wife Hazel for dinner at the famous New York restaurant 'Top Of Sixes' on the 49th floor of the new Tishman building. I had contracted a virus before leaving London and by now was feeling its severe debilitating effects. After dinner, George and Hazel, a warm and caring couple, were most understanding when I excused myself for an early night.

Next morning, as in London, there were many phone calls to make. My first was to Tom McManus, vice president of the mammoth *Music Corporation of America Limited* (MCA). Meeting him in his Madison Avenue office, he introduced me to the casting director of the 'Jack Paar Show' on which I was to appear if still in New York when Jack returned from his tropical vacation. It was not to be. Unfortunately I had to decline the offer as the wheels were turning and exhaustive arrangements had already been set in motion for my round of appointments in Hollywood. Before leaving his office, Tom extended an invitation to join him, his wife Mary-Jane and a business associate for lunch the following day.

George McCadden accompanied me to a four hour rehearsal of the 'Perry Como Show' at the historic *Ziegfeld Theatre* where I met the adorable Perry. Relaxed and natural, he was an utterly delightful person who questioned me in detail about Australia. He displayed great pleasure about his show being received with such enthusiasm in a country so far from the United States and appreciatively accepted his Logie award which I presented to him on behalf of *TV Week*.

In the history of American television, Perry Como would most likely go down as the most popular singing star. He started out as a barber, then changed direction and became a singer with the Ted Weems Orchestra. From there he went to network radio, where his recording career escalated. Three of his biggest hits in the 1940's were, *Till The End Of Time, Prisoner Of Love,* and *If I Loved You*. Of course he made many other hit recordings in the ensuing years. His radio show, *The Chesterfield Supper Club*, was successfully adapted to television, starting out as three fifteen minute shows a week, but shortly afterwards became a one hour a week top rating primetime variety show running for eight years. Following this success he reduced his work load and concentrated on doing only a few specials each year. He was the recipient of four Emmy Awards from 1954 to 1959 for best singer, best Master of Ceremonies, best male personality and best actor in a musical or variety show.

The beautiful Maureen O'Hara was Perry's special guest and I was pleased when she too agreed to a taped interview on my portable recorder. The interview was a breeze. Born in Ireland, she won many drama awards and was established as a major motion picture star following her role in *How Green Was My Valley*. She liked all of her leading men and was especially partial to working with John Wayne. How lucky I was to have met this outstanding actress and gracious lady.

Perry's station-break announcer Frank Gallop, an integral part of the show, was another charmer. We sat in the stalls, where he had me enthralled with his endless supply of show-biz anecdotes.

After dining with the McCaddens, we returned to the Ziegfeld Theatre as Perry's guests for the broadcast of his glittering show all in living colour.

Back stage with Perry at the 'Perry Como Show' in New York

Lunch next day with my wonderful new friends held yet another surprise. Tom McManus' wife, Mary-Jane, had been one of the original cast of Hollywood's 'Little Rascals' movie series of the 1930's. Just a small child at the time, she, like the rest of the cast became a household name internationally. What a small world!

During the luncheon, it was obvious that I was not well and a wretched virus was taking its toll. My friends insisted I visit their dear friend and physician Dr Henry Sampson. Henry was extremely sympathetic and kind to and advised me that in addition to the virus, I had a mild touch of asthma. Giving me the appropriate asthma and viral medications, he ordered me back to the Waldorf, and bed.

About 9:00 a.m. December 31st the telephone woke me; it was Graham calling from Melbourne, during *IMT*'s New Year's Eve telecast.

On the set of the 'Perry Como Show' with Maureen O'Hara

Live to air, we chatted about New York and my activities, causing the show to run overtime so that *IMT's* New Year countdown started a little after midnight. No one seemed concerned and when Graham signed off, Norm handed the phone to Jimmy so that we could exchange New Year's greetings.

Tom and Mary-Jane had big plans for New Year's Eve. They had Henry pick me up at the Waldorf and visit them at their Manhattan apartment. From there, the four of us joined their friends Maria and Ed Ellenger from National Geographic at the elegant Laurent restaurant for dinner. Seated at a round table covered with a crisp white cotton cloth, the waiter placed a snow white table napkin on each of our laps and handed out the menus. Cocktails were served and as we perused the menu, I was encouraged to order anything my heart desired. Well! There were some delicacies I'd only heard of in the movies. My eyes fixed on an entree 'Pheasant under glass.' After telling my hosts I'd not tasted pheasant before, they said, 'Then that's what you'll have!'

It was obscenely expensive and gave cause to wonder what could possibly be done to a pheasant to cost that much. Finally the presentation was made and as my fork pierced the juicy, tender flesh of the bird and I raised it to my mouth, my taste buds took a vacation. The virus had left them totally numb and at ten dollars a bite, I looked across at my doting hosts and said,

Mmmm... Delicious!

Later that evening, we went to the Manhattan apartment of Thana Skouris, niece of motion picture magnate Spiros Skouris, head of Twentieth Century Fox Corporation. Here we rang in the New Year with some of Thana's friends including Ann Byington, socialite divorcee Bobo Rockefeller and Broadway actor George Grizzard. George was embarking on his first Hollywood venture into motion pictures and we exchanged notes on our Hollywood itineraries.

Next day, although the virus was still causing me problems and a day in bed was beckoning, I wasn't about to miss out on the New Year's Day activities with my new found friends. It was a gala social gathering at the 'El Morocco' nightclub for the annual 'Eggnog and Cocktail Party' to raise funds for 'Boys' Towns in Italy.' Spiros Skouris' sister in law Mrs George Skouris was chairwoman of the event. Some of the celebrities I rubbed shoulders with were, Spiros Skouris, film producer Darryl F. Zanuck, artist Salvador Dali, musician Lionel Hampton and once again I caught up with Bob Hope. The outing concluded with dinner at the famous Italian restaurant called Maria's and a night cap at Thana's apartment.

Next morning when I opened my mouth to confirm times with George for a taped interview and photo shoot with Hugh O'Brien, there emerged only a faint whisper. My voice had almost disappeared. What a disaster! Requesting some salt from room service, I made a hot salt gargle and managed to croak out an audible husky sound, so felt the interview would probably be alright.

Breakfast interview in New York with Hugh O'Brien

George and a photographer accompanied me to a swank Sutton Place apartment Hugh was occupying while in New York. A butler answered the door and ushered us into an impressive dwelling filled with Spanish antiques. Hugh invited us to join him for breakfast. Sitting at an ancient Spanish table, I produced the portable tape recorder and started firing questions about his life and career.

He was proud of his enlistment and service in the Marine corps in World War II in which he became a drill instructor at the tender age of eighteen. He entered the acting profession at the close of the war, appearing in several television series including *The Loretta Young Show*, and finally secured the title role in the television drama, *The Life and Legend of Wyatt Earp*. The series ran for six years. He was currently in New York during a hiatus from Wyatt Earp to star in the stage show *Destry Rides Again* at the Imperial Theatre and generously invited me to be his guest at the dress rehearsal a couple of days later.

That evening Henry escorted me to dinner at Sardis restaurant, famous as a meeting place of Broadway stars who wined and dined there after their performances. The walls of the restaurant featured sketches of well known Broadway actors and actresses, lending an air of theatrical mysticism. It was rumoured that when the establishment closed at night, ghosts of past actors and actresses could be seen and heard laughing and boasting of their triumphs.

After dinner we went on to a Broadway show *The Music Man*, at the Majestic Theatre. Words couldn't describe how excited I was. I would have pinched myself to see if it were true, but was so numb from the virus, I wouldn't have felt it anyway. The show was exhilarating. Musical highlights *Trouble, Goodnight My Someone* and the rousing *Seventy-six Trombones* were part of this extraordinary musical with the book, music and lyrics by Meredith Willson.

The following day was my last full day in New York, so Henry drove me on a sight seeing tour of the city, visiting the Empire State building, where we rode about three different elevators to reach the top. At its sky high gift shop I purchased school souvenirs for Robin. We next visited Harlem, China Town, The Bowery, Broadway, Central Park, the New and Old Museums, the hospital where Henry had privileges and the Metropolitan Opera House. Admittedly it was a whirlwind tour, but time was limited.

We picked up Tom and Mary-Jane to visit real estate magnate Ed Ellinger Senior and his wife. Maria and Ed, their son and daughter in law, were staying with them for the holiday season. Here we were served cocktails in a magnificent apartment furnished with beautiful art treasures. After bidding our elegant hosts adieu, the six of us sealed the day dining at the gourmet French restaurant, 'Henry IV'.

My last few hours in New York were spent doing photo shoots at 'Rockefeller Center,' 'Radio City Music Hall,' and with Hugh O'Brien in his Imperial Theatre dressing room during the dress rehearsal of *Destry Rides Again*. I couldn't stay for the rehearsal as there was packing to do and a plane to catch, but promised Hugh a water skiing date when he visited Australia to present his own show at the Princess Theatre in Melbourne.

George and Hazel McCadden called around to take me to the Airport, but before we left there were cocktails to be had with Ann Byington and Thana Skouris in the Waldorf's 'Peacock Alley' where Australian pianist Ray Hartley was entertaining. Hugging Ann and Thana goodbye, it was off to the Airport and up and away to San Francisco.

With just one day in San Francisco, there was little time to see or do very much so I enjoyed a complete day of rest at the historic St Francis Hotel, in preparation for a heavy schedule of appointments in Los Angeles.

32

HOLLYWOOD

On arrival in Los Angeles, the hostess asked me to remain on board until all passengers had disembarked, as members of the media were waiting. Not sure of what to expect, when allowed to exit, I looked down the stairs of the plane onto the tarmac and was taken aback. A crowd of VIPs from Warner Brothers Studio, Music Corporation of America (MCA), Qantas and *TV Week* were there to greet me. Blinding spot lights were turned on, cameras were rolling and flash bulbs were popping as I stepped onto the welcoming red carpet. This was the land of Hollywood!

When they were all done with their filming, photographing and interviews, the welcoming VIPs escorted me to the Beverley Hilton Hotel in Beverley Hills. When the Hurrahs were over, Mishel Green, veteran Hollywood special representative for *News Week of Australia*, treated me to dinner at the Laua restaurant where we met up with the proprietor Steve Crane (ex-husband of Lana Turner) and dined on exotic south seas cuisine. Over dinner, Mishel gave me valuable advice on the Hollywood scene.

A good night's sleep was behind me and a limousine delivered me to the MCA offices, where top executive Bob Fitzgerald showed me around, introducing all and sundry. We spent a great deal of time working out an itinerary for studio photo shoots and interviews, then dined at the 'Tail O' The Cock' restaurant.

Next day, at Review Studios, Bob had prearranged a luncheon with *Leave It To Beaver* child stars Jerry Mathers and Tony Dow. Jerry was possibly the most loved television child star of the fifties and sixties. Before landing the 'Beaver Cleaver' role he had played in many episodes of other shows, including the *Ed Wynn Show, Lux Video Theatre*, and Alfred Hitchcock's *The Trouble With Harry*. During lunch Jerry talked about acting roles and hobbies. His favourite hobby was a gun collection. Considering that guns were not toys, I thought it was a strange hobby for a child.

Tony Dow on the other hand had little experience in acting. He came to the role of Beaver's older brother Wally via a brilliant athletic background. He was a star Junior Olympics diving champion. Tony was a good looking boy and the heartthrob of millions of teeny boppers.

After lunch a grand and interesting tour of *Review Studios* was offered. There were meetings and photo shoots with such famous Hollywood identities as Darren McGaven. He was shooting an episode of the popular adventure series *River Boat*, in which he played Grey Holden to his partner Burt Reynolds' Ben Fraser. Darren's spirited personality matched his friendliness, as he introduced me to almost everybody on the set including actor Tony Lambert who played Joshua.

We visited the set of *The Juggler* a made for Television costume drama. Here, Tony Curtis and Patricia Medina were dressed in period costumes for their individual roles. Although deeply engrossed in their parts, they took time out for a brief interview and photo shoot.

Another day at the *Review Studios*, Public Relations Director Neil Ames, took me around the main action packed movie sets. He introduced me to Director, Alfred Hitchcock who was checking out the stage of a famous movie theatre set, already featured in several past motion pictures. It was a real theatre with plush audience seating and full stage facilities.

Continuing on, I interviewed *Johnny Staccato* star John Cassavetes, a genuinely nice person. He was a much in demand actor, having appeared in more than one hundred television dramas at that time, including several episodes of *Alfred Hitchcock Presents*. His Johnny Staccato portrayal was that of a part time detective and jazz pianist. During the interview he spoke affectionately of his beautiful wife, actress Gena Rowlands and told me of his plans to move forward into the area of directing. Two of his greatest motion picture successes yet to come were *The Dirty Dozen* and *Rosemary's Baby*. Both won him much acclaim.

During lunch-break Neil and I sat at a table surrounded by a room full of famous actors. Amongst them were Richard Widmark, Edmond O'Brien, Wagon Train's Ward Bond (one of John Wayne's best friends), Gregory Peck and the one and only Cary Grant. When Cary walked into the restaurant, the entire room lit up with his presence. Tall, handsome and charismatic, it was not surprising that he was held in such esteem. I was interested to learn that he started out in show business as a member of an acrobatic troupe in vaudeville, progressed to Broadway, finally landing a contract with Paramount Studios. The rest is history.

Completing the interviews for the day, I hurried back to the Beverly Hilton to shower and change for a get-together with one of GTV-9's representatives, Australian ventriloquist Clifford Guest and his wife Dana at their Beverly Hills residence. Later that evening we went to the famous 'Ben Blue's' night club. A brilliant comedian, with an outstanding supporting cast, Ben had the audience eating out of the palm of his hand while performing his classic comedy sketches. He appeared in many movies and was a regular on television's *The Frank Sinatra Show*, and *Saturday Night Review* in the 1950's. Sitting at our table, he spoke nostalgically of his Australian tour with the Tivoli circuit and his desire for a return visit. We left the club with our sides aching from the after effects of continuous laughter.

Bob Fitzgerald arranged for me to sit in on a dress rehearsal of *The Dinah Shore Show*, telecast in living colour. From 1951 until January 1960, Dinah hosted her own music and variety television shows and had already won three Emmy awards, was voted 'Woman of the Year,' 'Mother of the year,' and one of the 'Ten most admired women in the world.' Dinah's show, like the *Perry Como Show*, was televised in beautiful colour. Black and white was still being

On Hollywood set of 'The Juggler' with (left to right) Elisha Cooke, Panda, Patricia Medina and Tony Curtis

prominently aired and in Australia, all television was aired in black and white. In fact, in the United States, a 'C' in *TV Guide*, denoted shows aired in colour, as opposed to today's program guides where colour dominates the airwaves and 'B&W' denotes black and white. A complete reversal of the early days of colour television.

Also in the studio, was the great pianist, composer and conductor Andre Previn. Interviewing him was inspiring. He was gentle natured, friendly and most cooperative and proudly displayed a lavish musical score he was working on.

By the time Sunday came around I was ready for a rest. Cliff and Dana had me over and we sat back, relaxed and watched the cream of television.

On Monday morning a limousine arrived to take me to the production offices of *The Oscar Levant Show*, on which I was to make my Hollywood debut. Oscar was an internationally celebrated concert pianist, composer, recording artist and movie actor.

He was renowned for interpreting the works of George Gershwin, of whom he was a good friend. When heard on radio, his stinging, uncanny wit soon gathered a following and this led him to feature roles in movies like, *The Barkley's of Broadway*, *The Band Wagon*, *Rhapsody in Blue*, *An American in Paris* and others. In Hollywood he also composed music for motion pictures and authored three books, *Memoirs of an Amnesiac*, *A Smattering of Ignorance*, and *The Importance of being Oscar*. Now with his own television talk show, he was more popular than ever. Possibly the most controversial television show in America at that time, Oscar's no nonsense approach to interviewing, had all sorts of famous people apprehensive about appearing with him. Even though the warning was issued that if he didn't like me, he might simply cut me off and go to a commercial, I was not deterred.

Returning that evening for the show, I sat with motion picture actor Vincent Price who preceded me on the program. He talked to me about his nickname 'Master of Menace' and was curious about my role on IMT. Vincent was passionate about connoisseur cooking and fine art. With academic degrees to his credit, he was considered an authority on both subjects. His overwhelming success as a dramatic actor was Hollywood lore. Later he turned his talents to a wide variety of character roles and was especially noted for those of Edgar Allan Poe.

When Oscar said goodnight to Vincent, my turn came around. He introduced me by saying,

'Here's a TV actress from Australia. I don't know who she is but let's meet her.' He was not only funny, but kind, considerate and very hospitable.

Not at all like I had been told to expect. He asked about the progress of Australian television which was in its infancy and about the success of movie star Danny Kaye's recent tour down under, in which Clifford Guest was one of Danny's supporting acts. When commenting on my admiration of his music, he asked,

'How would anyone in Australia know about Oscar Levant?'

'By your movies, recordings, books and newspaper headlines!' I responded. He pricked up his ears at the mention of news headlines (which regarding him, were often controversial) and said, 'Don't pay any attention to them!' and smiled. I commented on his pixie like smile which he mugged again for the audience and they roared their approval. Everything went so well that he closed the interview with, 'Thank you for being here, you are a most charming guest.' How could I not be flattered?

I was hoping to catch up with former regular *IMT* singer and friend Diana Trask while in Hollywood, but she was appearing at the *Cloister Inn* in Chicago at the time so our paths didn't cross. Diana was a smash hit on the American television series *Sing Along With Mitch* (Mitch Miller) and later became even more successful as a regular on the *Grand Ole Opry*. Other Australian singers to hit the big time in the United States were Lana Cantrell and later in the 1970's, Helen Reddy. Each of these girls, with their remarkable talent, had a huge following in the United States.

Climbing into a Warner Brothers limousine, I was driven to their studios where executive Carl Schaefer accompanied me to the set of *77 Sunset Strip*, for a meeting with my former modelling colleague actress Victoria Shaw and her husband, actor Roger Smith who played Jeff Spencer in the series. Here I interviewed the two of them. Discussing Roger's career I learned he was discovered by James Cagney, who indirectly helped him win a contract with Warner Brothers. We spoke of Victoria's role opposite Tyrone Power in the movie, *The Eddy Duchin Story*, as well as her guest starring roles in television dramas. Victoria said she would have to be careful not to pick up my Australian accent or her dialogue coach would have to start from scratch again. Also that day, another of the series' stars Efrem Zimbalist Jr. who played Stuart Bailey, came on to the set and introduced me to Louis Quinn who played Rosco. Efrem was a gentleman and in spite of a severe virus he was willing to be interviewed.

On the set of Maverick, I met and interviewed Jack Kelly. He played Bart, one of the Maverick brothers, to Janes Garner's Bret. His role was described as a wry, frontier hustler and his character was smattered with charm, which was obviously drawn from his own personality. He was from an acting family. His sister was actress Nancy Kelly. As a child he had a wealth of experience on the stage and radio. Jack appeared in numerous movies and television dramas in the 1950's before signing on the dotted line for the co-starring role in Maverick. Inquiring about my next port of call and learning I would be visiting Honolulu, he gave me a card with a hand written personal message to Bob Herrick at the Hawaiian Village Hotel and told me to call Bob if I needed anything at all. It didn't matter to Jack that my reservation was at the Reef Hotel, he simply offered his hospitality, saying, 'Reservations can sometimes go awry.' An important appointment was to meet Sanford Cummings, Vice President of ABC-TV network studios, where he proudly displayed the company's impressive plans for the studios future expansions to cope with the anticipated massive output of their many top rating series, some of which would filter through to GTV-9.

In Hollywood with Clifford Guest (left) and Jack Kelly (Maverick)

I invited Cliff to join me next day for an interview with Roger Moore. Cliff and Roger were pals from way back and it gave them an opportunity to catch up with one another. Roger greeted us warmly on the set of *The Alaskans*, an adventure series, in which his character was that of Silky Harris. This was only January 1960, so there would be many other series and movies ahead for Roger, including the famous James Bond.

Another day, another interview. Neil Ames ushered me onto the set of *Wagon Train* for a filmed interview with Robert Horton. Dressed in buckskin to play trail scout Flint McCullough, Robert sat with me and discussed his climb up the ladder of success. After a stint in the coast guard during World War II, he played in stock theatre and New York based television dramas including the romantic *King's Row*. When cast in *Wagon Train* he became one of television's most popular identities.

On the same set I met one of motion picture's famous character actors, Peter Lorre, whose best and memorable role was possibly that of Joel Cairo, opposite Humphrey Bogart and Sydney Greenstreet in *The Maltese Falcon*. Currently, he was playing a part in this particular episode of *Wagon Train*. His sense of humour had the most serious stoney faced staff members smiling.

As a farewell gesture, on my last night in Hollywood, Cliff and Dana took me to the Moulin Rouge night club and later suggested that if I was daring enough we would stop off at a strip joint to experience another side of Hollywood. I agreed and indeed it was a memorable night. The following day they toured me around the popular attractions before wending our way to the airport. A grand and glittering Hollywood visit was over and I was in flight again.

The long trip from Los Angeles, via a San Francisco Qantas connection to Honolulu without sleep made my very early morning arrival there awkward and disappointing. My reservation at the Reef Hotel was not recorded by the desk clerk, who advised, that if I cared to wait around in the Hotel lobby until late afternoon, a room might become available. Might become available? An eight hour wait? This was not the island paradise I'd read about. I was exhausted and badly needed sleep. Just as I was about to go to a pay Phone and call Qantas to get me on the first flight out of there, I remembered Jack Kelly's introduction to Bob Herrick at the Hawaiian Village Hotel. On telephoning Bob and explaining my connection with Jack and the intolerable situation at the Reef Hotel, he couldn't have been nicer. Within minutes, a courtesy car picked me up and delivered me to the Hawaiian Village Hotel, where a large airy room with a panoramic view of the ocean awaited me. I was treated like a queen and could not have thanked Jack Kelly enough for his introduction to Bob.

Dick McMillan from the Hawaiian Tourist Bureau had been a guest at my apartment where I entertained his troupe of Hawaiian dancers during their *IMT* engagements. After a few hours sleep I telephoned and informed him of the change from the Reef Hotel to the Hawaiian Village. Only there for a couple of days, he and his wife entertained me at their home and showed me a first class tour of Honolulu including dinner at *Don the Beachcomber* and to see and hear recording star Don Ho in a cabaret setting.

Behind the scenes in Hollywood. Left to right: Clifford Guest, Panda and Roger Moore

Dick also introduced journalist Bob Krauss of the Honolulu Advertiser who interviewed me for his column *In One Ear*. Dick told him of my joke telling on *IMT*. He asked for an example so I related one of my old jokes which he repeated in his column.

An early morning departure from the Honolulu Airport, brought about a surprise reunion with Mike Douglas, a member of *The Diamonds*, popular American singing group. On a return visit to Australia for a concert tour and appearances on *IMT*, he preceded his colleagues to tie up some business ends. A friend of Jimmy (who coached Mike on flute), we were able to make arrangements to sit together on the flight to Sydney.

The trip back also gave cause for reflection. Staying in New York, where my health was at a very low ebb, validated my belief in people. Those beautiful, total strangers, who were all prominent members of New York society, not only embraced me as a friend but showed a compassionate kindness that I couldn't have imagined.

Hollywood lived up to the expectations of its world wide image, but my unrestricted access to some of its biggest stars was somewhat unexpected, as was the stars unequivocal cooperation for their individual interviews and photo shoots. Along with the comforting letters and flowers from Jimmy at each of my hotels, Cliff and Dana came through as good friends, not allowing me to become homesick for a moment, in fact, everyone treated me so considerately that I was leaving the United States with a sense of loss.

At GTV-9 studios with US singing group 'The Diamonds'

33

HOME AGAIN

I was overjoyed to be back on Australian terra firma. Jimmy flew into Sydney to meet me, then it was back to Melbourne. Dear friends Norm and Joff took time out from the studio to pick us up from Melbourne's Essendon Airport.

There was a happy reunion with Robin, who bombarded me with endless questions about every place visited and was delighted with the assortment of souvenirs I showered upon him.

A party at Norm's Sandringham home became a dual celebration combining Norm's birthday and my welcome home. Graham, Joff, Rosie Sturgess and husband Peter McMahon, Joy Fountain, Horrie Dargie and his wife, Elaine McKenna and other *IMT* members partied on into the wee small hours. It was good to be back.

During my absence Graham also enjoyed a vacation, so on returning to *IMT*, we were both fresh and rested. Now in February 1960, on the first *IMT*, Graham and I received our second Logie Awards. Hugh O'Brien had arrived in Australia to appear in his own show at the Princess Theatre and was on hand at GTV-9 to make the Logie Award presentations on *IMT*. *Listener In-TV* reported in part:

> *...The most important event for IMT addicts was the return of Graham and Panda on Monday night. An occasion enlarged by the appearance in a presentation ceremony of visiting American Western Star Hugh O'Brian, better known as Wyatt Earp. The session followed the smooth IMT pattern without elaborate welcome fanfare. The regular stars were not impeded in re-establishing contact with their fans ... Kennedy snapped into one of his most scintillating moods, but it was Panda who stole the show. It's no easy matter after around the world glamour trip to walk into the home studio again without some loss of identity, but Panda contrived to remain exactly herself...*

While Hugh was in Melbourne, I kept my promise of a water skiing date with him. Jimmy picked us up and we motored to the Sorrento weekend home of our good friends Ron and Gwen D'albora. From the comfort of Ron's motor boat, we watched Hugh's skills on water skis as he skimmed over the shimmering water for most of the afternoon.

34

1960 Surprises

TV-9 kept moving forward. Graham was keen to have his own weekly one hour National variety show and GTV-9 backed him all the way. In the beginning, it would be aired in Melbourne, Sydney, Adelaide and Brisbane. Graham's appearances on *IMT* were reduced to Monday and Tuesday nights allowing him preparation time for his new Friday night show, which would be followed by 30 minutes of *IMT*. Substitute hosts for *IMT* on Wednesday and Thursday nights were Barry McQueen and Bert Newton respectively.

Bert Newton's success at GTV-9 was well established. Back in 1959, Bert's Saturday afternoon teen-age show further extended his audience appeal.

Norm appointed Jimmy Musical Director for the show, which boasted the best teen-age talent available, including one of Television's hottest teen heartthrobs Col Joy. So now the timing for Bert to host a regular *IMT* was spot on and the acquisition of ABV-2's Barry McQueen, with his wry sense of humour, further diversified the appeal of *IMT*. After a short period of time Barry switched to GTV-9's revived breakfast show which had been suspended for many months.

My position was unchanged except that in addition to five nights a week on *IMT* in my usual segment, I would be appearing weekly on *The Graham Kennedy Show* presenting live commercials with Graham. At that time, live commercials were an important part of the show's appeal.

The Graham Kennedy Show was first televised in Melbourne on Friday February 12 at 9:30 p.m. The same show was then sent interstate on video tape and was shown the next day (Saturday) in Adelaide at 9:30 p.m., Sydney aired it Tuesday at 10:00 p.m., and Brisbane, the following Saturday at 9:30 p.m.

Sydney's ATN-7 had a thirteen week contract, but did not renew it due to unfavourable ratings. Not to be discouraged, GTV-9 sold the show to TCN-9, where a great deal of promotion went into it's successful launch. Norm jetted Graham and me to TCN-9, where for three days we made personal appearances and short films to promote the show's debut on that channel. As chaperone, producer Tom Miller kept us on a roll of tight appointments. We returned to Melbourne confident of the show's future success.

TCN-9 first aired the show at 10:00 p.m., on May 2, 1960. Gradually it's popularity and ratings began to climb and like *IMT* before it, *The Graham Kennedy Show* was also on it's way into television history.

Visiting American comedian Paul Gilbert, father of Melissa (Little House on the Prairie) Gilbert, was booked to appear. He'd seen me on the Oscar Levant Show in the United States and requested that I appear with him in his award winning sketch. With Norm's approval, we immediately went into rehearsal. I played the lady of the house, while Paul's role was that of a media addicted quiz contestant. The sketch was fast paced, packed with laughs and no one had more fun than us.

The studio doors at GTV-9 were swinging back and forth with the coming and going of some extraordinary talent. Producer Tom Miller, who also headed *Talent Promotions of Australia* (TPA), engaged a high standard of imported acts for the show's future episodes. The contractual deals between GTV-9, the major hotel circuits and airlines to import talent, ensured a plentiful supply of fresh faces to complement those of us seen weekly on the show.

Some of the most prestigious names appeared. US recording artists *The Diamonds*, Pat Boone, Nancy Wilson, Earl Grant, Jeri Southern and Al Morgan. Philipino recording and cabaret artist Pilita; Japan's top television and recording star Peggy Hayama. Cream of the Jazz world: Drummer Buddy Rich, saxophonist Benny Carter and the *Oscar Peterson Trio*. Tap dancer

Arthur Duncan who went on to become a regular on the *Lawrence Welk Show*, Louis Quinn from the high rating *77 Sunset Strip*, Comedian Garry Morton who later produced TV shows in America for his wife Lucille Ball and Movie Actor and Comedian Buddy Lester, with whom Jimmy and I cemented a lifelong friendship.

Some of the most loved acts were the American Comedy duo *Delo and Daly* (Ken Delo and Jonathan Daly). Also from the United States was Tommy Hanlon Jnr., who made Australia his home and hosted the successful afternoon television show *It Could be You*. Another American comedian to blitz the afternoon show ratings was Larry K. Nixon, who first appeared on GTV-9, then moved to HSV-7 to present *Lady For a Day*.

In the beginning, amongst the Australian talent represented were the Horrie Dargie Quintet, Evie Hayes, Annette Klooger, Johnny Marco, Elaine McKenna and *IMT* announcers, Geoff Corke, Pete Smith, Hal Todd, Jack Little and Phillip Brady. There were also Arthur Young and the GTV-9 Orchestra and ballet, plus regulars Joff Ellen, Rosie Sturgess, Bert Newton and myself.

Comedy writers were engaged to deliver a never ending supply of sketches, taxing their fertile imaginations to the limit. Writers who come to mind were Hugh Stuckey, Freddy Parsons, Mike McColl-Jones and much respected actor-comedian-writer Johnny Ladd.

My television exposure was expanding. The overseas trip had given me the opportunity to see first hand how the television industry created product in other parts of the world. My successful appearance on the Oscar Levant Show in Hollywood, plus the compliments that followed, inspired a belief in myself that no matter what came my way in the future, I would be able to work through any obstacles and deliver a performance worthy of the occasion.

Norm continued to carefully select additional material and had me singing songs to various cast members including Graham, Joff, Ron Blaskett and Gerry Gee, Jack Bowkett from *The Tunetwisters* and *The Four Debs*. Some of the songs like *Smarty*, *If I Only Had a Brain*, *Little White Duck*, *Ma! (He's Making Eyes At Me)*, and *Oh Johnny*, with their cute lyrics were winners. Later I advanced to show songs such as, *Just Blew In From The Windy City*, accompanied by the GTV-9 Ballet. I also performed a version of Sammy Cahn and James Van Heusen's Academy Award winning hit *High Hopes*, with vocal backing by *The Four Debs* (Kath Danaher, Judy Pomeroy and Pauline and Betty Lys). Learning the new material, inclusive of an occasional dance routine, revived the happy memories of my theatrical days with the Tivoli and J.C. Williamson. An amateur song writer, I presented one of my songs *The Bogie Man* to Norm, who liked it enough to have Horrie Dargie harmonize it and set a routine for his quintet, which they performed with a full orchestral background. I was thrilled and considered myself very lucky to have this talented singing group introduce my song to television.

35

TWIN LAKES

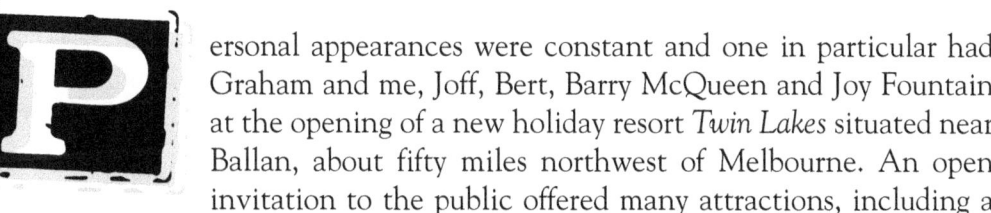ersonal appearances were constant and one in particular had Graham and me, Joff, Bert, Barry McQueen and Joy Fountain at the opening of a new holiday resort *Twin Lakes* situated near Ballan, about fifty miles northwest of Melbourne. An open invitation to the public offered many attractions, including a water ski exhibition, water ballet show, jet speed boat rides and for lucky fishermen, an angling competition with a winning prize of one hundred pounds.

Thousands of good-time seekers found their way to the *Twin Lakes* opening. It was a beautiful day, with a carnival atmosphere. There were bountiful picnic baskets, the laughter of children filled the air, as they delighted in the many rides and each of the aquatic events was well patronised. We were not at all aware of the pending danger. While Graham and I signed hundreds of autographs, the crowd became a little too enthusiastic, pressing closer and closer until the situation became potentially hazardous.

Jimmy's Porsche was the nearest car to the stage, so a quick decision was made. Jimmy, John and the promoters managed to squeeze us through the crowd and into the car. Graham scrambled into the back seat and I climbed into the passengers side, while Jimmy from the drivers seat, locked the doors and started the motor. We felt the car rocking as the crowd pressed against it's sides. John helped close the soft hood over our heads, but it offered little protection. Cautiously, we inched our way along, distancing ourselves from the crushing crowd to where we eventually found John and Val waiting with Graham's car and we were able to make our getaway. So as not to get caught up in the ensuing homeward bound traffic jam, the five of us stopped off at a hotel to regain our composure, lingering over a drink and a bite to eat, until the bumper to bumper traffic cleared.

Joff had not been particularly well during the previous week and when I met up with him following the *Twin Lakes* event and asked how he had recovered so quickly, he said:

> *Whenever I'm not feeling well I go to the doctor. After all he has to live. Then I get a prescription and go to the chemist. After all the chemist has to live. Then I go home and throw the medicine away because I've got to live too!*

36

LETTERS

ost newspaper and magazine publications employed a resident critic to provide an alternative opinion and to pass personal judgment on us and the shows we appeared in. To respond to unfavourable criticism irrespective of it's validity or unfairness would only give the critic (usually anonymous) fodder for further criticism, so it was customary to remain silent.

Fortunately, the publications also provided a healthy forum for viewers to have their say. The format of these columns was consistent, although the names of the columns varied from one publication to the next. Apart from the traditional *Letters to the Editor*, others used antonyms, like *Listener In-TV's*, *Axes and Orchids*.

When discussing topics on television, one had to be ever so careful not to offend viewer's sensitivities. They were resolute in their opinions and sometimes responded with amusing letters, like one particular viewer who put pen to paper after hearing Graham and me discuss how much it cost to feed my dog. The letter stated:

> I have had a TV set since the beginning of television and have heard some remarkable things on the air, but one remark heard last week left me speechless.

> *I'm getting on in years now and have often wondered what I would like to do when I finally give up work. Boy oh boy! Now I know. My one ambition now is to take the place of Panda's dog, and have six pounds per week spent on me just for my meat alone. Who wants the pension when one can get six quids worth of tucker at Panda's!*
>
> *Remember Panda, should anything happen to your dog, I asked first.*

Another viewer was indignant about a critic's acrimonious view of me. She accused the critic of having a befuddled brain, a tough hide and suffering from sour grapes because of the salary difference between us. Then she spoke glowingly, showering me with accolades, adding that

> *It would be a good thing for so called "Widgies" to try and emulate her…*

Her post script read:

> *All I've said about Panda goes double for Graham, so heaven help you if you ever turn on GK. I'd really go to town on you then, because we love him.*

My good friend, singer Annette Klooger, also shared with me an amusing viewer anecdote:

> *When will someone pay Panda's fare to darkest Africa so she can take as many pictures of animals as she likes and give viewers a spell … And perhaps it would be a good idea to take Annette Klooger and her mournful singing along too…*

Occasionally, cartoonists were assigned to punch up the humour of viewer's letters with comical illustrations and witty dialogue. Accompanying the above letter, a cartoonist portrayed Annette and me on Safari in Africa featuring a large python upstaging us.

37

END DARRODS

Speculation over my continuance as the representative of Darrods, 'the style store in the heart of Bourke Street' made sporadic news in the gossip columns but had no impact on my position. Finally, in April 1960, GTV-9 and Darrods came to a parting of the ways and the final decision had nothing to do with me. From its inception, Darrods had been responsible for the prizes on the wheel and everything was satisfactory until we did a live edition of *IMT* from Ballarat.

According to reports, a young honeymooning Albury couple had their car and savings stolen. Agreeing to a request, Darrods allowed the bride to join our regular contestants for a chance at winning a prize on the wheel. Because of their extenuating circumstances, everyone was hoping for the best result as she spun the wheel around. Whether it was fate or good fortune, she won a car. On the face of it, it was the best result for all concerned. However, behind the scenes, Darrods refused to pay for the car, claiming it had not been won strictly in accordance with the rules of the quiz. The final outcome was that GTV-9 paid for the car and after almost three years, Darrods sponsorship came to an end and I would no longer wear their slogan 'Darrods the style store in the heart of Bourke Street.'

The importance of the segment was such that GTV9's sales department headed by Nigel Dick, took over and it continued nightly on *IMT* with prizes totalling many thousands of dollars. Included were a block of land, car, fibre-glass boat with out-board motor, TV set and an untold number of other valuable prizes. For the first time, alternative sponsors could buy advertising time during the segment which was good news for the sales department. A big plus for me was that the *Myer Emporium*, who were wonderfully cooperative, sponsored my nightly fashion statements and the viewers approval was instant.

38

Magic

raham had several comedy bits which periodically were repeated when he felt the time was right. Sometimes he donned a girl's blonde wig and mimed a recording of Helen Kane's version of *I Wanna Be Loved By You*. Another favourite was a good old vaudeville bit. He would feign physical distress and call out,

'Resuscitation! Resuscitation!' whereupon I would recite something like,
'A curious bird is the Pelican!
Its beak can hold more than its belly can…'
'Not recitation!' interrupted Graham, throwing his arms in the air, 'Resuscitation!' Each of these *bits* were guaranteed laughs. One night, on the way to the studio, I had come in contact with an allergen and by show time, was afflicted with asthma, which induced laboured breathing. Graham was not aware of my predicament and started in with his comedy piece. In the middle of his animated collapse, he uttered his opening line:

'Resuscitation! Resuscitation!' Trying to respond, my voice was not forthcoming and I rushed from the set gasping for breath. Live to air television once again proved that the potential to leave oneself vulnerable was ever present.

My distress was later explained to the audience, who in turn filled the GTV-9 mail room with hundreds of letters of support from fellow asthmatics and sympathizers. Some even sent a dose of their precious life saving medication, whilst others recommended various remedies. There is no accounting for the kindness, goodwill and generosity of strangers. Luckily, my asthma attacks and fainting episodes were infrequent and kept under wraps.

IMT's third anniversary show had come and gone with a big bang. We home grown heroes of GTV-9 had had our big day and we all counted our blessings. Blasting off into a fourth year was just as exhilarating as the first. The learning process was forever ongoing and we continued to develop our diverse talents.

In Melbourne, the seventh Australian convention of interstate and overseas magicians was being held. A good friend Alf Gertler, known to viewers as *Bernard The Magician*, asked me to appear with him in a brand new levitation illusion on *IMT*. I was placed in a trance and positioned on a slender, twelve inches wide, body length wooden pallet. With me on board, Graham and Bert each took an end of the pallet, then rested it on the backs of two chairs. After a cloth was draped over my body, Alf performed his magical incantation and the chairs were then removed, leaving me rigidly suspended in mid-air. At rehearsal everything went like clockwork, but on the show, the old bug-a-boo Murphy's Law, reared it's ugly head.

Bernard the Magician (Alf Gertler) working his magic on me on 'IMT'

Instead of the two chairs being removed simultaneously, one was moved prematurely. The pallet became unsteady and I started to slip off, head first. In a split second the trance was interrupted and the illusion in danger of becoming a disaster. Just as quickly, Alf adroitly compensated for the slip. Repeating his incantation and reinstating the trance, he brought the illusion to it's successful climax.

By mid 1960, GTV-9 had earned a deserving and respected standing in the Australian television industry, so it was not surprising that a strong rumour circulating caused disquiet amongst its large staff. As it turned out, the rumour proved to be true. Sir Arthur Warner, Chairman of General Television Corporation Ltd. (GTV-9), had negotiated a deal with Sir Frank Packer, owner of Television Corporation Limited (TCN-9) Sydney, to take over GTV-9. Sir Frank was also managing director of Consolidated Press Limited of Sydney, which amongst others published the *Daily Telegraph* (Sydney) and the *Australian Women's Weekly*.

Approximately a week later, more shock waves surged through the studios when Norm Spencer announced his resignation as Program Manager and accepted a similar but more lucrative offer from HSV-7. *Truth* newspaper reported Norm as saying:

> *Channel 7 approached me a couple of times to join them. They approached me again this week and I agreed to sign...*
>
> *I would like to take Graham Kennedy and Panda with me but I have not discussed a move with them yet.*

Norm's departure from Channel 9 was deeply felt by all. He would be missed from our daily working lives, but certainly not socially.

There were big moves ahead at HSV-7. Management had extravagant plans for Norm and a new venue for his proposed variety shows but did not disclose either of them at that time. GTV-9's children's show host Happy Hammond also resigned and joined Channel 7.

At nine, any complacency about tenure was gone and rumours of staff cutbacks and possible cancellations of shows were rife. With Tom Miller as executive producer, Colin Bednall acted promptly, appointing Rod Kinnear as Norm's successor, Ian Holmes assistant program manager and Ron Davis to fill the *IMT* senior director's chair. Colin assured one and all that the policies which had made the station successful would remain in place and the current top ratings guaranteed that no changes were imminent. He reassured those of us under contract to nine that all contracts would be honoured and positions would be safeguarded.

Around this time Graham was indignant about the press accusing we TV identities of exploiting our position on television by charging excessive fees for personal appearances. He felt obliged to respond on *IMT*, referring to the many charitable causes to which we unselfishly gave of our time. *Talent Promotions of Australia* published a list of fees paid to top GTV-9 personalities. On a sliding scale of fees, Graham and I were on top, followed closely by Joff, then Bert, the Horrie Dargie quintet and so on. For 1960, these fees were quite agreeable. They were set down by GTV-9 and *Talent Promotions of Australia*, preventing our over-exposure at alternative engagements.

One does not have to be in television to know how exhausting a day in the city can be, running from one appointment to the next. At the end of one of these days, after showering and feeling refreshed, I set out for the studio about 6:00 p.m., ordered a meal from a nearby cafe and began memorising the lyrics to a routine for an upcoming show. A member of the studio staff approached and said that Tom Miller and Ron Davis were both looking for me. Leaving the meal in mid bite, I started searching the offices, studios and corridors for Tom and Ron. About ten minutes later, there they were in a doorway. In a calm and almost nonchalant manner, they told me to prepare to be the hostess of *IMT* that same night. It was Graham's night off and substitute compere Bert had been stricken with gastric flu. Having previously hosted *The Panda Show* the powers that be decided I was the obvious choice to host *IMT* at such short notice. A little overawed, but delighted with this honour, I had only about two hours before the show went to air. As well as the general grooming sequence, there was an assortment of scripts to be addressed and introductions, tags and jokes to be memorised. Tom and Ron were confidently relaxed, giving me Geoff Corke, Hal Todd and Jack Little to bounce off. The show went like a dream, there wasn't a glitch and the switchboard lit up with viewers congratulations.

TV Week 1960 quoted director Ron Davis as saying:

> *Things looked black when Bert suddenly became ill, but the IMT team once again pulled together. They proved they can rally together in all sorts of circumstances. I want to thank Panda, Jack Little, Hal Todd and Geoff Corke for their efforts. As a girl confronted very late with a major TV task, Panda did a great job.*

Channel 9 was ever vigilant of its personalities safety and did everything necessary to protect us. However, it was not fail safe and I had an ongoing problem of unwanted callers. A generous viewer delivered to the studio a two months old German Shepherd puppy for my protection. Although dubious about accepting the puppy, Jimmy agreed to take charge of exercising the dog twice daily and making sure I would have a controllable well trained dog. Now *Plato* had entered my life and proved to be a great source of comfort and company.

It was not at all unusual for the press to hint at possible romances, even if there was little validity to their suppositions. At one time Joy Fountain was romantically linked to Bert Newton; A young *pre-Seekers* Advertising Executive Athol Guy to GTV-9 dancer, Pauline Whalley; teenage singer Helen Reddy to musician, Kenny Weate; and even Francois to another GTV-9 dancer Valmai Ennor.

Although quite accustomed to romance rumours about me and whosoever, alarm bells went off when the press began probing into my relationship with Jimmy. They had not forgotten the diamond ring episode and periodically, more or less as routine, hunted me down to re-examine it and it's source. Since the last rumour confrontation, things had changed. Jimmy asked me to marry him and I said, 'Yes!' It was our secret until we finally agreed to a September wedding. The first person to hear the news was Robin. He and Jimmy were firm friends by this time and he was very happy about the union.

We had a clandestine meeting with Graham, Norm, Joff and HSV-7 friend Don Bennetts. Here we unfolded our plans. Graham agreed to be best man, whilst Norm would give me away and Norm's daughter Diane and Joff's daughter Cheryl were to be bridesmaids. We asked Don to fill the shoes of groomsman and for his father the Rev. R.H. Bennetts to perform the wedding ceremony in his Frankston, Methodist Church.

When Colin was informed of our plans, the wheels were set in motion. It was August 24 and GTV-9's continuous on-air promotion advised viewers to watch for Graham's very special announcement on *IMT*.

Journalist John Burrowes kept pursuing us, suggesting big news was about to break and that *Listener In-TV* already had a story layout and the presses were ready to roll.

Once the news was announced, it was like I was sucked into a vortex and that the print media had exploded. The Billboards, headlines and magazine covers spewed out the news:

PANDA TO WED. TV'S BEST KEPT SECRET.

WEDDING BELLS FOR PANDA. READ HER OWN STORY.

PANDA: 'I'LL WED MY MANAGER.'

PANDA'S NEXT HUSBAND.

PANDA'S CHOICE FOR HER NEW HUSBAND.

TV WEDDING OF THE YEAR.

TV'S ROMANCE OF THE YEAR.

PANDA TELLS TANYA. (Tanya Halesworth Ch-2 hostess)

ALL STAR CAST FOR PANDA'S WEDDING.

It was never ending. The interviews, photographs and unusual attention given to a simple wedding announcement was extraordinary. I was staggered by the exposure. Surely this couldn't be happening?

39

WEDDING PLANS

There's no doubt about it, it was one of television's best kept secrets and did indeed surprise colleagues and viewers alike, ending rumours once and for all that Graham and I were in love. Of course we never were.

Planning a small wedding didn't seem too daunting until it came to our notice that GTV-9 executives had gotten their heads together and come up with a plan.

Jimmy and I were summoned to a meeting with Colin. Here, he disclosed their lavish plans to televise the wedding *live-to-air* providing we were agreeable. it was to be the first time an Australian wedding ceremony would be televised live, in it's entirety.

We looked at each other in astonishment. Colin assured us that the intrusion of television cameras would not detract from the dignity of the ceremony, which would be treated with the utmost reverence according the occasion and that GTV-9 would assist us with any plans for such an extravagant affair.

After advising the rest of the wedding party, all agreed the outcome would be something special. The date was set for Saturday September 24, 1960. Don's father, the Rev. R.H. Bennetts, declared his Frankston Church too small to cater to the expected large congregation and gained permission from his colleague the Rev. Waites to perform the wedding ceremony at the spacious Auburn Methodist Church.

Don made all of the arrangements concerning the Church, including a 32 voice choir. Because of his television experience, he was extremely helpful in the interaction between the technicalities of both the religious aspect and a complex television program.

Don also assumed the responsibility of coordinating the mens' fashions. Graham, Don, Norm and Jimmy, conferred with Collins Street society tailor George Michael. Between them they agreed to black silk mohair suits, featuring continental jackets with half cuffs on both the sleeves and slim-cut trousers. Norm balked at the slim-cut trousers and opted for the regular style. Accessories included specially designed pointy-toed shoes, American style shirts, silver cufflinks, matching tie tacks and grey silk ties. For my going away outfit, I was also measured and fitted for an ensemble sheath dress and jacket made from fine wool, in a tiny pink and white houndstooth weave.

Following this I hastened into Myer's exclusive couturier, to have them design a wedding gown. Bolts of gorgeous fabrics and suggested styles were placed before me. The final choice of fabric was imported white French lace, delicately hand painted with pale pink wild roses and white painted leaves. The exquisite fabric was beautifully crafted and perfect for the occasion. The gown's design was classically simple, featuring a fitted bodice with demure scalloped neckline, long sleeves and a subtly flared, below the knee skirt with scalloped hemline. Accessories included elegant shoes embroidered with the same fabric. Also hand made, were large French silk roses formed into a dainty hat, skillfully structured to frame my face. Having settled on the gown and accessories, the designer swore everybody involved to complete secrecy.

The telecast was a major challenge for GTV-9's Chief Engineer Rod Biddle, who was set for a possible whopping sized headache. Television coverage of the wedding would include, arrival at the Church of the guests and wedding party, the entire ceremony inside the Church, followed by our departure. The crew would then race to Como Park for coverage of a drive through appearance of the wedding entourage in limousines, to benefit a Brotherhood of St Laurence charity affair. Here we would finally take our leave and continue on to the reception, while the camera crew headed for the Melbourne Cricket Ground to cover the last quarter of the Grand Final football match between Melbourne and Collingwood. For 1960, without the benefit of today's technology, this was to be a monumental challenge.

There were many days of planning with his talented crew for this hectic agenda. Directors, technical directors, sound and lighting technicians, camera crews and hundreds of complicated details went into this elaborate plan. We were delighted to learn that Eric Pearce had been engaged to provide the commentary.

The huge outside broadcast van, TV cameras, microphones and lighting would have to be set up in and outside the Church and at the other two locations. The major question was, 'Can it all be accomplished?' There was never a doubt. HSV-7 would also feature the wedding in their evening programming and 3UZ's Tom Jones would present a description on his *Newsbeat* program on Sunday morning at 9:30 a.m. and again at 12:40 p.m., so their equipment also had to be accommodated.

We distributed hundreds of wedding invitations through the mail. There were additional invitations requested by the press for admittance to the Church and reception. Channel 9 executive Nigel Dick, helped us organise the reception at *The Embers* in South Yarra, flowers at each of the venues, a three tiered wedding cake, limousines and other fine details. The headlines continued:

PANDA GETS VIP WEDDING COVER.

BIG SHOW BUSINESS WEDDING FOR PANDA.

PANDA NAMES THE DAY.

PANDA THE VERY FULL STORY.

PANDA AND JIMMY: THEIR STORY.

WHY I LOVE PANDA BY JIMMY ALLAN.

WHY I LOVE JIMMY BY PANDA.

Friend Evie Hayes asked me to be her special guest at an American style bridal shower held in my honour at her South Yarra home. She sent out invitations which read:

There's going to be a shower

for a certain special miss

who's headed for the altar

and the state of wedded bliss.

The guests were many including Norm, Joff and Colin's wives, Amy, Bernie and Marion. Joy was there, so

With Evie Hayes, showing off Evie's pets

too were Elaine McKenna, Rosa Nicholls, TV presenters Judy Ann Ford, Laurel Young, Lesley Webster and other mutual friends. Some of our favourite lady journalists came with their note books and photographers to capture this American flavoured bridal shower.

Evie's home was transformed into a pink fantasy. Pink tulle was draped around the tables in all it's prettiness. Table centerpieces, a Swan and a Panda, were delicately sculpted in butter. Parasol frames swathed in pink, decorated the entrance. Pink tulle cascaded from the chandeliers. Pink champagne was scattered with petals of pink blossom. There were pink heart shaped iced cakes. Even the heart shaped bread for the sandwiches was tinted pink. Puffed up balls of tulle wafted in the warm breeze from the windows. Evie's pets, Patches and Timothy, her cat and dog, wore pink bows in their fur.

If ever I was made to feel special, Evie succeeded on this wonderful day. She excelled in entertaining and this was one of her finest efforts.

And still the headlines continued:

ALL PINK TEA FOR PANDA.

PINK PARTY FOR PANDA.

PANDA'S PINK PARTY.

PANDA'S PARTY.

PANDA'S SPENDING SPREE.

Left to right: Joy Fountain, Panda and Elaine McKenna at Evie Hayes' Shower Tea

Nearing our wedding date, we were in the studio parking lot with Plato on a leash, when Phil Burns, one of GTV-9's sound technicians, approached and told us how much he loved German Shepherds. He volunteered to take care of Plato while we were honeymooning. It was a perfect situation. A spacious yard, securely fenced and a handler who really doted on him.

Hundreds of cards, letters and even small gifts arrived for me at the studio, all of which were loving and sincere. one in particular was very touching, it was anonymous and read:

Dear Panda,

I wish I could send you a lovely present but being a pensioner you will understand how difficult it is to balance one's budget. Just want to wish you all the happiness in the world, you deserve it. I am sure you will both be very happy 1 think you have made a wise choice in Jimmy he has a very kind face. I hope the clover brings you lots of good health and luck to both of you.

A sincere fan.

The letter and its contents, a four leaf clover, I have still.

40

WEDDING DAY

he print media were ever present now. Certain sections of the press were following Jimmy and me wherever we went, even staking out my apartment. It was frustrating and very disquieting.

We were thankful when the wedding day finally came around and everything that had to be done was behind us. Jimmy stayed with the Spencers overnight at Sandringham, so that it would be easy for Don, on his way from Frankston, to pick him up and drive to Graham's home in St Kilda, where they would dress and leave together by limousine for the Church. Amy Spencer picked up and took care of Robin, along with her son Dennis and joined Joff, Bernie and their son Russell for the proceedings.

I was fortunate to have the assistance of Tom Miller's secretary Jeanette Berry at the apartment to take care of those coming and going. She answered the constantly ringing telephone, took delivery of flowers, ushered in the photo journalists who wanted pre-wedding photographs for their early editions and also the team of hairdressers, Marie, Terry and Diane DuCane. She fussed over Norm and the bridesmaids Cheryl and Diane, who looked adorable in their white hail spot muslin dresses and finally before she left for the Church, helped me into my gown.

Except for Norm, at last everyone had left the apartment. It was so peaceful and quiet, one could hear a pin drop. The storm clouds had been gathering all morning. Suddenly the peace and quiet was abruptly shattered. A major electrical storm had erupted which increased both Norm's and my nervousness. A tempest of thunder, lightning and a downpour likened to 'The Rains Of Ranchipur' threatened to wreak havoc on our day of days.

Suggesting that Norm should help himself to a drink, I leaned over the television set, picked up a copy of *TV Week* which one of the visitors had left open at Saturday's program guide and staring back at me, it read:

1.45   9. PANDA'S WEDDING SPECIAL.

GTV-9's cameras will be situated inside and outside the Auburn Methodist Church to bring you a direct telecast of the 'TV Wedding of 1960.' After the ceremony, the mobile unit will rush to Como Park where Panda and Jimmy will make an appearance at a Charity Fete.

(1 1/4. Hrs.)

It hadn't occurred to me that it would be listed in the program guide, but there it was. In fact it was in all of the program guides. The TV set was staring us in the face, but neither gave a thought to turning it on to watch the arrival of guests at the Church. The thunder and lightning gave a final defiant burst, but the rain persisted.

In the meantime Jimmy, Graham and Don were preparing to leave for the Church. The limousine was waiting and the chauffeur carrying a large umbrella, escorted them one at a time to the vehicle. Jimmy and Graham managed to reach the spacious rear interior of the car with only their shoes spattered with raindrops, but just as Don was leaving the house, a huge black cloud overhead opened up and rain poured down, creating a deluge. His head and jacket remained dry under the umbrella, but the lower half of his silk mohair trousers took on the full brunt of the downpour. Don refused to sit on the seat and instead, while holding the creases of his slacks in place, stood hunched over in the limousine, all the way to the Church. In the vestry, before the service, he had dried out completely, with creases still intact. Don's antics helped minimise the nervousness each of them was experiencing. However, waiting for my arrival, they began pacing back and forth, but the tension was soon broken when Jimmy and Don heard Graham utter, 'I feel as if I'm going to do a National Show'. Jimmy would rather be anywhere but in the limelight and for that reason was glad to be behind the scene in the Church's vestry.

The doorbell rang. It was our chauffeur. Not about to walk through large puddles of water in beautiful hand embroidered shoes, I rustled through the wardrobe and changed into a pair of white court shoes, carrying the precious bridal slippers in one hand and a bouquet of white tulips in the other. The rain had eased a little as I stepped out of the apartment. Waiting under the large verandah next to the staircase were a number of thoughtful tenants proffering a huge golf umbrella for protection en route to the limousine. Once inside the vehicle, I slipped back into the embroidered shoes. Norm made it without incident and we were on our way.

Approaching the Church, there were hordes of people in raincoats holding umbrellas. Traffic police and other police officers were holding back the crowd. They even had a loud-speaker in use. As we drew near, the scene became hushed. One could see the journalists jostling for position and taking notes. Photographers aimed their cameras in our direction. At a discreet distance was Rod Biddle's outside crew with their TV cameras, lights and microphones. The crowd craned their necks for a good view, cheering and calling out, 'Panda! Look this way.' 'Panda! Look over here,' And so forth. Flash bulbs popped and home movie cameras rolled as the crowd entered into the spirit of the moment. Reaching the vestibule, we were confronted by another wave of photographers and journalists.

As the strains of Richard Wagner's *Bridal March* from *Lohengrin* filled the Church, with bridesmaids Cheryl and Diane in tow, I took Norm's arm and we walked down the aisle to where Jimmy, Graham, Don and his father stood in front of the altar.

Don's father, the Rev. Bennetts, delivered a beautiful service. Jimmy and I exchanged wedding rings, kissed before the

Behind the scenes on our Wedding Day

altar and when we retired to the vestry for the signing and witnessing of the marriage certificate, the thirty-two voice choir lifted their voices in song for the congregation's pleasure. Our bridal party then emerged from the vestry to the inspirational melody of Mendelssohn's *Wedding March*. We made our way through the capacity packed Church to the outside cheering throng. The limousine whisked us away while the television crew hightailed it to Como Park. Waiting for them to set up, Colin had invited the entire bridal party to call in on him and partake of a glass of champagne, after which we motored through the receptive crowd at Como Park and on to the lush reception at The Embers.

Here it was clear that our guests were in high spirits. Sitting at the bridal table, the usual traditional speeches, toasts and telegrams were delivered with great hilarity. We cut the cake and sipped champagne. My old colleague Athol Shmith took Jimmy and me into another drawing room for photographs just for ourselves. We then slipped away to my apartment, changed into going away clothes, returned to say goodbye and in great secrecy set out for Surfer's Paradise. The headlines continued in our absence:

PANDA WED TODAY.

CROWDS WAIT IN RAIN TO SEE PANDA.

PANDA ... CHURCH SCENES.

PANDA'S MARRIAGE.

WHAT A WEDDING AND WHAT A DAY.

THE WONDERFUL WEDDING OF PANDA.

THE TV WEDDING OF THE YEAR.

THE REAL STORY OF PANDA'S WEDDING.

PANDA'S WEDDING...

A picture souvenir inside 1960 *TV Week*'s 8 page lift out photo spread was quite an achievement. Their editorial best describes what went on behind the scenes:

> *THIS SPECIAL ISSUE OF TV WEEK contains a center 8 page pull-out souvenir supplement of the biggest event in TV this year -the wedding of Panda to Jimmy Allan at Auburn Methodist Church last Saturday afternoon.*
>
> *TV WEEK team of six reporters and photographers, together with a big sub editing and printing staff, worked through the weekend to prepare this special feature.*
>
> *While Panda's wedding and reception took place, cars were racing between the Church, 'The Embers' and our office relaying photographic film and reports of the event.*
>
> *We took hundreds of photographs, from which we have selected the best for publication.*
>
> *High-speed coverage of an event like this normally would be impossible with a magazine of the format and large circulation of TV WEEK, but our staff was willing to work overtime to ensure our readers receive the best possible coverage.*
>
> *The usual teletype section and Cyril Pearl column are missing this week to enable us to publish the Panda supplement inside. They will be back next week.*

In Surfer's Paradise, a self contained apartment overlooking the ocean, provided privacy from the hustle and bustle of everyone and everything. Here we stretched out on the hot white sand every day drinking in the sunshine, peace and quiet.

Lunching at a Surfer's Paradise hotel garden barbecue, it appeared we were about to spend our honeymoon with the Collingwood football team, who were also getting away from it all following their disappointing loss on the 24th. They invited us to a party and here we were spotted by a reporter, who begged us on behalf of *Listener In-TV* to do a honeymoon photo spread. So as not to be continually pursued by them, we agreed on the condition that it was final and that we be left alone.

Friend Annette Klooger was appearing at the Broadbeach Hotel, so we surprised her one evening by showing up for dinner in the Cabaret room. On her night off she joined us at the drive-in theatre. As we sat together enjoying the movie, gradually a fog rolled in, almost obliterating the screen, whereupon management made an announcement over the speakers,

'If everyone will kindly turn on their motors, the fog will lift and the movie will continue.'

The patrons obliged, but instead of the fog dispersing, the exhaust fumes only added to the problem, reducing visibility to zero and the movie had to be abandoned.

Following days of golfing, boating, fishing, swimming, watching water ski ballets and even sharing a go-cart track with an ex-European King and his entourage of aides and security personnel, finally the honeymoon was over. Returning our complimentary Simca automobile to the dealer in Brisbane, we boarded a plane for Melbourne and home.

41

IMT Return

ack from our honeymoon, we noted Phil's genuine attachment to Plato. Jimmy had moved into the apartment, so my need for security no longer existed. Phil dearly wanted to keep Plato and as it was a better life style than apartment living for a large dog, we agreed to leave him in Phil's loving care.

The apartment was now ours instead of mine. Wedding gifts stacked in the guest room had to be opened and acknowledged, as well as those collected from Don's home in Frankston, where he and his parents had stored those which had been delivered to the reception. It was all very overwhelming. Robin was pleased to see us and enjoyed his Surfer's Paradise souvenirs.

On the very day we arrived home, my first phone call came from Evie. After exchanging the usual pleasantries, she became quite serious and informed me that there was some dissatisfaction with a couple of GTV-9 personalities who were resentful of the unprecedented publicity I had generated since the wedding announcement in August. She warned me to be prepared for a possible confrontation. During her illustrious career she too had to cope with these situations and was concerned about the repercussions that might befall me. We talked about the print media making their own decisions as to what they publish, but somehow this obvious fact had been distorted and it seemed I was being held personally responsible for the complainants lack of publicity. Evie wanted me to be cognisant of these facts before going into the studio.

It was somewhat puzzling to understand how I could be placed in this position. GTV-9 had made their own executive decision to televise the wedding. The publicity that followed was generated by viewer interest and GTV-9, the newspapers and magazines all gained financially. The publicity also benefited the *image* of GTV-9, *In Melbourne Tonight*, and the *Graham Kennedy Show*. The purpose of headlines is to sell newspapers and magazines, not to promote the careers of television personalities. Anyone who thinks otherwise is extremely naive. Consequently, the studio placed all on camera personnel on notice that any contact with the press was to be handled exclusively by the Channel 9 publicity department and no interviews could be granted without their consent. In the long run, this effort to control what and whom the press featured proved futile. The editors decided what stories and which personalities would best serve them commercially and this in part was influenced by their subscribers.

I was also taken aback when informed that my nights were reduced to the same number as Graham. I would continue on the *Graham Kennedy Show* and share the *IMT's* with both Graham and Bert. However, GTV-9 was obliged to pay my full contractual salary.

Another phone call came through, this time from an *Age* newspaper journalist. A most respected man, he was someone I had not previously met. He requested a private meeting of a personal nature at my apartment and although it seemed very mysterious, an afternoon appointment was set up. He was on time and following introductions and the offering of refreshments, chills crept up my spine as he unfolded the substance of a request by an editor from an opposition publication. He named the person, who was known to us both and related that the editor's request was, 'to help remove Panda from television' via an editorial vendetta. I was shocked by this disclosure, but apparently not as much as my informer who was an honourable journalist with impeccable credentials. The request made to him violated his code of ethics and on principle, he felt I had a right to know who was behind this dastardly act. He advised that it is not the position of the press to remove anybody from television and that I should not be distracted by this unprofessional behaviour, adding that I was simply a victim of celebrity. His timely advice was well taken and appreciated.

Things returned to normal pretty quickly, with Jimmy playing in the *IMT* orchestra and me back in the groove of my usual role. In addition, Tom had programmed *The Horse In Striped Pajamas* to sing with Joff's daughter Cheryl, so we set about learning and rehearsing the song. It felt good to be back with the *IMT* gang.

Comedians were coming and going through the doors of television with varying success. Earlier in the year, because his style of comedy was different, English stand-up comedian Jackie Clancy was a big hit on television until he told a risque joke. If my memory serves me well, it was about a father spanking his small son on the bottom, whereupon the son examined his rear end in the mirror and exclaimed:

'Now look what you've done, you've cracked it!' It seems pretty tame by today's standards, where some misguided comedians substitute foul language for humour.

Jackie also appeared on Channel 9, but his greatest triumph was a top rating 3UZ radio show with Bill Acfield. 3UZ was responsible for nurturing outstanding talent, amongst whom were Graham Kennedy, Happy Hammond, Noel Ferrier, Mary Hardy and the inimitable Don Lund.

Listener In-TV journalist John Burrowes invited us to a book opening. John's good friend, champion cyclist Russell Mockridge, had been writing his autobiography in collaboration with John, when Russell met with his untimely death in a road accident. John and Russell's widow Irene, together completed the book and this was it's launching day. Jimmy and I attended the bitter sweet occasion and John later sent a personal note:

> *Dear Jimmy and Panda,*
>
> *The most welcome sight I've seen since Kyle* looked up at me for the first time on September 21, 1959, was your two welcome, smiling, and very appreciated faces on Friday night at the reception. Russell would, like me, have been very proud, very honoured, for what you have done.*
>
> *I just had to put this on record. You'll understand.*
>
> *See you soon. John B.*
>
> *** John's son.**

Wedding bells were in the air. Popular comedian Jonathan Daly (of Delo and Daly fame), enjoyed a great deal of success at GTV-9 and we were all delighted when he and former colleague of mine, model and TV presenter Marlene Duff, met, fell in love, were married in Hollywood and made their home in Santa Barbara. At the same time, Joy was planning to take off for the United States in the new year for a reunion with her brother Jim.

Negotiations for my future services had been put forth by outside interests and now, for the first time since joining *IMT*, I gave serious consideration to leaving GTV-9 and moving on to one of the new lucrative and exciting prospects available, which would expand my artistic interests and longevity. To walk away from the comfortable life of the past three and a half years was no easy decision, so deferring the final resolution until year's end seemed the most sensible path to follow.

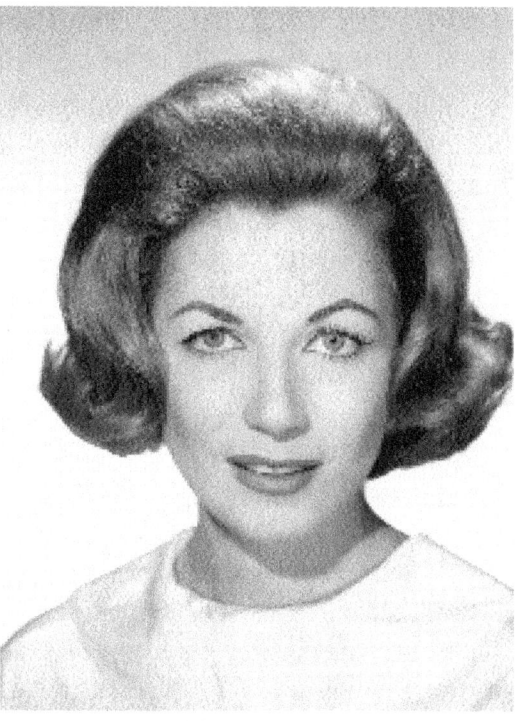

Publicity photograph

Bearing this in mind, an alarming situation came to the fore. When preparing to leave for the studio one Friday afternoon, irregular heartbeats once again pounded my chest, accompanied by the usual unpleasant side effects and I fainted. Luckily Jimmy was at home. This time the unconsciousness was rather prolonged so the doctor was summoned. He ordered a couple of days bed rest to be followed by intensive medical tests. The results were inconclusive except for a questionable heart rhythm and a positive reading of mild anaemia. As always I bounced back quickly and thought nothing of it, except that the press pounced on the situation and billboards like PANDA COLLAPSES, hit the streets. These were not the kind of headlines one needed when contemplating new contractual offers, so rumours of any illness had to be quashed immediately. This was done swiftly and luckily soon forgotten.

December was upon us. Deborah Garland did an end of year feature story about Jimmy's and my future dream home for *Woman's Day*, after which we turned our attention to preparations for Christmas. We had invited several guests to call at the apartment on Christmas day for a little egg-nog and turkey. When stepping out of bed that morning, with all the identifiable symptoms as before, I fainted again. The doctor called around and during his examination, Jimmy could be heard calling from the kitchen:

'Now the stuffing is in the turkey, how do I sew it up?' The doctor told him to wait a minute or two and when he'd finished attending to me, joined Jimmy and proceeded to show him how to suture a turkey without leaving a scar. There was a lot of laughter emanating from the kitchen during this surgical lesson and on completion, the two of them toasted their mastery with a sip of Harveys Bristol Cream.

Following the special New Year's Eve show the cast and most of the crew slipped away on vacation. We, on the other hand, stayed close to home as negotiations for my future role in television were ongoing. The Wilsons and d'Alboras at Sorrento and the Spencers at Rosebud entertained us and at other times we ventured into Melbourne's movie houses and caught up on some of the season's winners. one in particular was Alfred Hitchcock's *Psycho*. In 1961, *Psycho* was probably one of the most talked about thriller movies of all time. It was showing at the Barclay theatre in Russell Street and here, at an intermediate session, we bumped into Graham and his friends Val and Jonn Wesley. This was the first time we'd seen Graham since he called at the apartment on Christmas day, so we all sat together in the dress circle. Although tempted, I resisted telling Graham about my future plans, as it was neither the right time nor the place.

In the meantime, Deborah Garland did another cover and story of me with *Woman's Day* cookery editor Margaret Fulton, featuring a recipe layout.

The previous September, HSV-7's manager, Keith Cairns had formerly announced Seven's acquisition of the 2500-seat, Fitzroy Regent Theatre. It would be transformed into an International television studio with completion in January. Well it was now mid-January and Norm telephoned to say that Channel 7 was offering me a contract to join them and be part of the new shows emanating from their now almost completed *Teletheatre*. It was a very lucrative offer and was not a total surprise as we had talked about the possibility of a move to HSV-7. A meeting with Norm and the executives at Channel 7 headed by Keith Cairns was arranged.

On January 30, 1961 I called into Colin's office at Channel 9 and submitted my resignation, asking to be released from my contract which had some months of validity still. Colin was very surprised and asked if I could be persuaded to stay. We talked about success and the possibilities of disappointment if things didn't work out the way they were planned. We were both a little nostalgic about the breaking away from the *IMT* family.

However, my decision was final and irreversible. At the conclusion of this meeting he advised that I was not to appear on Channel 9 until further notice, which included *IMT* and the *Graham Kennedy Show*. The release from my contract was refused.

Gathering a few belongings from the dressing room and placing them in the car, I was surprised to see Graham arriving in the car park at such an early hour. One could only assume he had been notified of the situation. After unfolding the story of my resignation, Graham said he was sorry to hear the news but wished me well.

Now it was up to Keith and Colin to sort out the contractual release. Until that time, it would be a waiting game. To sit quietly at home was not to be. That night as soon as Graham announced on *IMT* that I would be leaving GTV-9 and joining HSV-7 the phone rang nonstop and so did the headlines.

PANDA SWITCH - TV SHOCK

PANDA'S NEW LOOK

NEW JOB FOR PANDA

PANDA TO LEAVE GTV-9

PANDA WILL JOIN HSV-7

WHY PANDA QUIT

Almost everyone had something to say. *The Herald* quoted Norm,

> ...Panda will be cast in an entirely new role and will have much more scope when she joins HSV-7 ... he was overjoyed to have her back again.

The Sun reported:

> ... In the surprise television announcement of the year, Mr Keith Cairns, HSV-7 manager, said yesterday:

> We are delighted to have the services of Panda, an outstanding personality who has been developed by TV. Panda will be associated with the very intense development of our new live TV shows from our new studio in Fitzroy.

The Age stated in part:

> *Her 'dumb blonde' act, and her bright personality, quickly gained a following for her. Between them, Graham Kennedy and Panda laid viewers 'in the aisles,' stacking rating on rating until they were the personalities most worshiped in Melbourne TV.*
>
> *Each helped the other to popularity. ...Panda and Graham were the in-front-of-the camera personalities who 'made' In Melbourne Tonight, and in turn, spread Channel 9's reputation far and wide ... There's no mystery that Panda's strength lay in her comedy sketch timing and in the modelling with which she entered television.*
>
> *This column which has been one of Panda's severest (though fair, I hope) critics, wishes her well in her new appointment ... Panda a model come TV personality of unknown vintage has been responsible for the sale of more TV sets in Melbourne than anyone else, except perhaps Graham Kennedy.*

There was a great deal of brouhaha over the move to Seven and I was caught in the midst of it all.

42

SIGNING WITH CHANNEL 7

A couple of weeks later, Colin released me from the GTV-9 contract and I started at HSV-7 in mid February. Due to technical difficulties, the teletheatre was yet to open it's doors for production.

Direct from Bobby Limb's variety show, comedian Buster Fiddess was to be partnered with me as HSV-7's new comedy team assisted by Englishman Len Lowe, whose portfolio of scripts would become our bag of laughs. Up to this point the show's format was still in the talking stages and the waiting was excruciatingly slow.

When band leader Lou Toppano and HSV-7 parted company, Norm contracted Jimmy, appointing him musical Director. His duties would be to handle all musical commitments including that of conductor, musical arranger, be responsible for forming the new 12 piece HSV-7 orchestra and engaging arrangers and copyists in preparation for the teletheatre opening. He would also be Musical Director of *Sunnyside Up*. Of course this move caused more headlines:

JIMMY JOINS PANDA AT HSV.

JIMMY ALLAN JOINS HSV-7 - AND PANDA.

JIMMY TO JOIN PANDA.

In March, I was presented with my third Logie Award. Those of us nominated were flown to Sydney and received our awards at a star studded glittering ceremony at the Chevron Hilton Hotel. Some of those sharing the podium with me were, Bruce Gyngell, Brian Henderson, Graham and Bert. All proceeds from the affair went to the National Heart Foundation. It was a fabulous night.

Everything at the Teletheatre had at last started to come together. As well as teaming with Buster in comedy routines, one of my responsibilities was to make sure that as much publicity as possible went to the promotion of the upcoming shows. Len was less than forthcoming with his comedy material and although it was possible to grab a headline in the press, it was almost impossible to lay ones hands on a script. When the scripts did arrive, there was little substance in them for me.

Left to right: Panda, Harold Knights (Golf Pro), Buster Fiddess, Peter Colville, Vic Gordon and Len Lowe

Meanwhile, *Listener In-TV* featured me on their cover with radio 3DB's chief announcer John Eden and a child from the Children's Hospital to promote the annual charity appeal. It would be telecast on Channel 7 and broadcast over 3DB's airwaves on Good Friday. Almost everyone at HSV-7, 3DB, *The Herald*, *Sun* and *Sporting Globe*, along with hundreds of volunteers, took part in this huge fund raiser.

Channel 9 also telecast an annual marathon fund raiser for The Yooralla Crippled Childrens' Hospital appeal, in which I happily participated when working at Nine.

In April 1961, I was honoured to have appeared on the covers of *TV Times*, *TV Week* and front page of *The Herald*.

A lavish teletheatre opening was set for Easter Sunday night, April 2 at 8:00 p.m. The show was headlined by Bing Crosby's brother, singer, band leader and movie star Bob Crosby. It was billed as the most expensive extravaganza seen on Melbourne TV. There were 600 invited guests at the full dress rehearsal in the afternoon and another 600 at the 'on air' show that evening. As well as the comedy team of Buster and me, also on the bill were pianist Winifred Atwell, singer Darryl Stewart, British comedy duo Hope and Keen, singers Lorraine Davey and Gaynor Bunning. The star guest of honour was the brilliant comedian Jimmy Edwards.

Panda, Bob Crosby and Norm Spencer

The show received both good and mediocre reviews. *Truth's* critic Veritas summed up the comedy routines with:

> The sketches were drawn out and contained about as many laughs as a symphony concert. One thing Channel 7 will not have to sack the script writers. There weren't any.

My disappointment at having so little to do in the sketches was magnified when I discovered, in one critic's column, that the scripts were re-cycled from a past HSV7 variety show *Bandwagon*. Due to working five nights a week on *IMT*, I'd never laid eyes on this show and was not aware we were performing re-hashed scripts. However, *TV Week* commented that our comedy team went together like 'bacon and eggs,' so all was not lost. The only consolation was that unlike theatre, one night's television programming was over and done with and was already yesterday's news. So now it could only be onward and upward.

Norm's love of live television once again found an avenue of expression. He introduced *Top Of The Town*, a weekly live variety show hosted by one of Channel 7's popular personalities Brian Naylor and later by English comedian Geofrey Lenner. The show was expected to be in for a long run. Buster and I headed the comedy team and visiting overseas and local artists spiced up the program each week. Even though there were many grand moments, the teletheatre had frustrating teething problems with sound and staging, which dogged the best efforts of the dedicated crew, resulting in over budget production costs and causing those who held the purse strings to pull tightly on the monetary reins.

Norm and Keith met with me regarding joining 3DB personality Charles Skase in his radio program *Music-Go-Round*, three times a week on Mondays, Wednesdays and Thursdays from 4:15 p.m. to 5:00 p.m. It didn't seem too demanding so I agreed. After all there would be more revenue in the kitty and it didn't interfere with my HSV-7 schedule. 3DB's Curtis Crawford was at the contract signing and I was now in the radio game. The program was referred to as a 'middle of the road' show, with pleasant chit-chat and music. Charles was one of Australia's leading baritones and we often played a track or two from his albums. My role was to supply show business news, beauty tips and topical conversation.

Charles asked me to make an appearance at a fete for his son's school. Here I met a young rascal named Christopher (Charles' son), a very pleasant child with plenty of get up and go. At that time, who could have guessed his future in the corporate world.

I'd learned long ago that stepping outside one's home into a working environment produced

Radio 3DB's Charles Skase and Panda

an increased level of criticism. However, when one is elevated to the position of a high profile television celebrity, the degree of praise and criticism that follows, reaches a height to which nothing in your life can prepare you.

Reading the written word about oneself, whether it be pro or con, can be either satisfying or disconcerting, so it was always with reservation that one scanned any story pertaining to one's life, career or privacy.

Perc Dunstone, Editor of *Listener In-TV*, engaged eminent journalist Ian McFarling to write a three part series about me. I was unsure of it's content as he was writing from a neutral position. Ian had just returned from an extended assignment in the United States and was aware of the television scene over there, but was not quite used to our version of the electronic media.

Panda and Jeffrey Lenner. 'Top Of The Town'

We had never met and knew little, if anything about each other. Ian was quiet but inquisitive and spent days following me around as he formulated ideas for his articles. He sourced some information from Norm, Peter Fox, Athol Shmith's sister Verna, Buster and others. On completion, the headlines read:

PANDA'S CRUCIAL YEAR.

FOR PANDA 1961 IS CRUCIAL.

WHO IS PANDA? WHAT IS SHE?

He dealt with day to day activities at the studio, my background and future and was curious about the obvious success. In part he said of one show he witnessed,

> *Bob Crosby, for years was one of the biggest names in show business here or anywhere else ... but strangely there was someone else up on the stage who kept attracting more attention. It was the first time I had come to close quarters with this particular phenomenon and for a time I found it puzzling. The person was Panda ...*
>
> *Panda's dry humour goes back to well before she burst into TV. Peter Fox head of a model agency which once handled Panda's modelling jobs, said ... 'It was in the days when some of her friends called her by the nickname of Pandemonium...'*
>
> *Panda, at the time, was one of Melbourne's leading models ... Photographers and fashion houses remember her as one of the easiest and most charming girls they have worked with.*

During my time on *IMT*, sometimes the press would refer to my role as a 'dumb blonde act', for want of a better title. About this he commented:

> *Is she really as dumb as that? Is it a pose?*
>
> *...there isn't another person who has either worked with her or merely watched her who will agree. It was a deliberately cultivated pose...once it was seen what a hit she made on TV with her own brand of idiocy, it was decided to play it for what it was worth.*
>
> *When we saw it there we cultivated it...We latched on to it very early.*
>
> *Panda is given a lot of credit for it. The fact that she made so much out of a 'nothing' spot is, according to both admirers and detractors, a measure of her shrewdness and talent.*
>
> *She's no idiot, she's no dumb blonde, says Buster Fiddess...It can take a clever person to play dumb.*
>
> *The fact remains that Panda has had one of the most remarkable successes in the history of Australian show business...*

After four years in television and hundreds of articles later, I found it curious that there was still so much interest in my comings and goings. After a while, one becomes detached from these stories and views them as though they are talking about someone else.

Norm introduced more specials like *The Guy Mitchell Show*. Guy was an American major recording artist in the early to mid 50s and had his own television show in The United States. He also played detective George Romack in the TV series *Whispering Smith*. Discovered by Arthur Godfrey's Talent Scouts in 1949, he became an International star.

Another luminary we worked side by side with at the teletheatre was Raymond Burr in his own *Special*. At that time Ray had twice won Emmy awards for his role in the original *Perry Mason* television series. After serving

Signing with Channel 7

in the U.S. Navy during world war two, he switched to motion picture acting. Known for his charismatic performances, his most memorable roles would have to be *A Place In The Sun* and Alfred Hitchcock's *Rear Window*. Ray was an especially likable very professional person. 'Friendly' could have been his second name and we all loved working with him. Ray and I shared *Woman's Day* and *Listener In-TV* covers during his visit and the American Show Business Bible *Variety* gave glowing reports of his *Special*.

Jimmy and I spent much of our spare time looking for a block of land on which to build a home. At long last we found just the right location, on the side of a North Balwyn hill. Buster introduced us to a reliable builder and we set about drawing up plans for a two story house with an end of year completion date. I may have lived in many homes up to this time, but had never owned one. It was a very exciting prospect.

Entertainers have always been known for giving their time to raise funds for charity. This work does not go unrewarded. A memorable occasion took place when, working at GTV9, a group of us including the Horrie Dargie Quintet took a small concert party to the Iron Lung ward of the Fairfield Hospital. The tops of patients heads were all that could be seen until you looked into their faces reflected in a small mirror attached to the Iron Lung. It was then that their expressions of delight helped us understand the joy they received from our presence. That was more than enough reward.

Another precious moment occurred when just prior to our marriage, Jimmy and I were invited to the Yooralla Crippled Children's Hospital. We were totally surprised when they presented us with a beautiful wedding gift. The gift was purchased with money raised from a collection that patients had taken up. It was an emotional moment and tears filled our eyes and it took a minute or two until we regained enough composure to thank them. They were so happy for us, they wanted to share their joy. I never lost sight of the fact that those on the receiving end of charity are truly appreciative of the donors.

Robin continued to make excellent grades at school and like most young boys he aspired to be good at sports. He asked Jimmy and I to join Francois as spectators at a football match in South Yarra between his school and an opposing team. It was great fun watching the thirty-six boys running all over the field, chasing after the ball. There was perhaps more enthusiasm than football skills, but an enormous amount of pleasure.

His interest in football never waned and he became an avid Footscray follower. As a special gift for his birthday, I telephoned Ted Whitten (the

Footscray captain at that time) to procure the autographs of the entire team on a new football. Ted was most obliging and on one of their training nights, Jimmy delivered the football to the Footscray club-house where the whole team autographed it for us. On his birthday, he was more than thrilled to receive the autographed football, however, when we next saw this treasure there was not a signature to be found. The ball had been kicked around so much that the ink had worn off. Considering his tender age, it proved that kicking a football around is a whole lot more exhilarating than having it sit on a shelf covered in autographs.

Buster Fiddess and Panda. 'Top Of The Town'

Evie Hayes, 'The Hostess With The Mostest', invited Jimmy and I to join in a birthday celebration for husband Will on a yacht on the beautiful waters of Geelong. Old pals from GTV-9 Geoff Corke and wife Val Ruff, Dorothy Moore from *Bye Bye Birdie*, and Roger Carroll from the *Winifred Atwell* show were also aboard. Exchanging memories with each other was a highlight of the day. At one point Will handed me a baited fishing line to see which of us could catch the first fish. Throwing the line over the side, I quickly felt a firm tug and reeling it in, discovered a pretty white fish wriggling crazily on the hook. About to reach out and unhook it, Will roared, 'Don't touch it! It's a new born shark!' He immediately took over, firmly gripping the body of the shark and quickly disposing of the head with it's razorsharp teeth. He used the remainder of the flesh as bait from which he caught several whiting and flathead. After a basket lunch Evie produced a large birthday cake. Will blew out the candles and declared, 'Anyone caught counting the candles will have to walk the plank!'

Another birthday was that of friend Diana Trask who'd returned to Melbourne from the United States after her success on the *Mitch Miller Show*. For her twenty-first birthday, her parents held a party in her honour. Jimmy and I were pleased to see her again and we happily mingled with her guests amongst whom were Eric Pearce, Rod Kinnear, Bert Newton, Graham Kennedy, radio personalities 3AW's Geoff Manion and Norm Banks and 3KZ's Ron Cadee and Stan Rofe. Diana had not been spoiled by her International success.

Following media criticism that I was not being given enough material to perform in the show, Norm called Jimmy and me to a meeting where he announced:

'It's time Panda strutted her stuff.' He gave us two sheet music copies of *The Roaring Twenties* (theme from the TV series of the same name), instructing Jimmy to write a rousing arrangement and for me to learn the lyrics. He then called his choreographer Betty Meddings to set a show stopping routine with ballet accompaniment. Wardrobe mistress Pat Norman, fitted me out with an original 1920s black dress. It was encrusted all over with bugle beads, was quite heavy, but looked just great. On the night of the show, with the enthusiastic support of the ballet urging me on, the song and dance routine was received with a standing ovation and with much improved comedy material than in past shows, I was on cloud nine. The reviews were all favourable and to quote *TV Week 1961*:

'Panda came to life, and probably has never done better work.' It was Norm's turn to thumb his nose at his detractors by successfully showcasing another of my talents.

Along with the press raves and viewer reaction to this performance, the big brass at Channel 7 were also impressed. When Norm decided I was to have my own show, the executives were one hundred percent behind him. Norm plucked HSV-7 sports editor Mike Williamson from his usual role and made him my side-kick. I would be working on the Monday night show full time, with additional guest appearances on *Top Of The Town*. Sad to say, the 3DB radio show had to be abandoned due to conflicting times. Radio was a great experience, and there were no regrets.

My new show, titled *Merry-Go-Round*, was packed with diversified segments like party games, new faces, and the Wheel of Fortune with huge prizes to be won.

There would be guest stars, regular entertainers including Gordon and Colville, Vikki Hammond, Frank Wilson, Lorraine Davey, Peter Langdon and the Four Clefs. Betty Meddings and Jack Manuel shared the ballet's choreography and Jimmy conducted the HSV-7 Orchestra.

I went into action immediately by subscribing to the script writer's bible, Robert Orben's *Current Comedy*, extracting comedy ideas and working them into material for Mike and I to perform. For script rehearsals, we met at my apartment for lunch and learned the routines. Mike was especially cooperative and worked very hard and professionally at anything that came his way. We were both supporters of the Victorian Football League's Melbourne Football Club and had often worked together at their annual

Doing the Charlston on 'Top Of The Town'

Panda and Jimmy at rehearsal for 'Top Of The Town'

concerts so we were not strangers. Mike was to be a great asset, lending his vast experience to interviews with some of the sporting world's heroes.

Conferences with my personal dress designer Nancy Bartlett to select fabrics and designs, produced at my expense, many attractive gowns for this glamorous fast moving show.

It was the start of a happy and productive period. Commercial television had not until this time even considered a woman as host of a regular prime time variety show. While at GTV-9, I had been given my own special *PANDA* show and also hosted *IMT*. Now *Merry-Go-Round* was launched as a regular Monday night variety show. This was another first and heralded a new era for women in commercial television.

Another invitation arrived from the Spastic Children's Society appeal. They were preparing an art display of television personalities' paintings, etchings and drawings, to be shown in Melbourne and Sydney and later auctioned off. My effort was a drawing of a sardine can containing shapes representative of showgirls. I titled it, *Canned Chorus Girls Without Cloves*. However, when it was reproduced in the media, they had taken my play on words 'Cloves' and substituted the word 'Gloves.' Confusing? Yes! But it worked and helped raise funds for the Spastic Children.

In September *TV Times* featured Mike and I on their cover with an accompanying story and HSV-7 surprised Jimmy and me on *Merry-Go-Round* with a silver cutlery service for our first wedding anniversary. With our wonderful friends, a sumptuous affair was held at a city hotel where Jimmy slipped a diamond and platinum eternity ring onto the third finger of my left hand.

Panda and Jack Manuel at rehearsal for 'Top Of The Town'

Merry-Go-Round was going great guns. Ratings were so good Channel 9 re-shuffled their *IMT* format. They put Toni Lamond in the chair on Mondays opposite my show. Of course we were just pawns in the commercially volatile stakes. I was happy that in television's fifth year of male dominated variety hosting, we girls had found our niche.

An interview with Scottish singer Andy Stewart was scheduled for me to do on the next *Merry-Go-Round*. Everybody was familiar with his hit song *Scottish Soldier* which was on top of the charts, but no one could supply me with details of his biography. I telephoned several sources and gathered enough information to do an hour with him. With plenty of ammunition the interview lasted about ten minutes and was favourably received by both viewers and reviewers. The next day, Andy sent a huge bouquet of flowers, thanking me for the best interview he'd ever had.

Amongst others I interviewed Scotsman Alistair McHarg, Irishman Jimmy O'Dea, 'King of the Leprechauns' from Walt Disney's film *Darby O'Gill and The Little People* and eighteen year old American pop star Bobby Vee who was to sing in concert at Festival Hall with the Everly Brothers and Mark Wynter. Bobby came directly from the *Dick Clark*, *Dinah Shore* and *Perry Como* shows in the United States. He brought a new arrangement of his *Baby Face* medley, which had been written and copied for him in the United States. He was devastated when, at rehearsal, many mistakes in the copying of the parts were discovered, so calling for a break, Jimmy worked on eliminating all of the problems and the much relieved Bobby gave a shining rendition of his medley.

Merry-Go-Round. Left to right: Vic Gordon, Peter Colville, Panda and Mike Williamson

His troubles were a reminder of my guest appearance on Brisbane's Channel-7 *Late Show*. The successful Roaring Twenties routine on *Top Of The Town* prompted an invitation for me to appear in a special live 'Twenties' show to do the same song and dance. Jimmy modified the arrangement to suit a smaller orchestra. However, the studio musicians had been replaced by a group who specialised in 'Twenties' music. Unfortunately the band's music reading skills were non-existent and the embarrassed conductor sent me away while he tried to teach them the routine so they could play it by ear. Show time and there I was. No production, no ballet and a band scuffling to remember a rather complex routine. Typical of show business people, everyone at Brisbane's Channel-7 was very helpful and understanding. The band did their very best and we managed to get through it all without disappointing the audience. There probably isn't a performer who cannot relate to a similar situation in their career.

A theme night on *Merry-Go-Round* was sponsored by a washing machine company. To compliment the sponsor, Jimmy and I worked on a parody of Operatic Arias to present if you like, a Soap opera.

Incorporating Mike, Peter, Lorraine and me, we lifted our non-operatic voices to the rafters in a rollicking operatic riot and brought down the house. One reviewer liked it so much, he asked for it to be repeated on another show.

The non-commercial ABC's Corrine Kirby had entered the arena on Monday nights and the press were comparing us three girls with our male counterparts. When *TV Times* acknowledged that Norm appointed me the first woman compere, he spoke loudly and clearly when asked if women were good at ad-libbing, fast thinking, or handling embarrassing situations, he commented:

> *As for thinking faster and ad-libbing, that too depends on the person and not their sex.*
>
> *Embarrassing situations? Panda can handle these better than anyone I know - man or woman. But that doesn't prove that women are better than men.*
>
> *She's just good at it. That's all.*

The parody of operatic arias was too successful to be ignored, so we decided to do another. This time an impression of one of Australia's famous duos of voice and flute, Glenda Raymond and John Amadio. Jimmy arranged the music and with him playing flute, the two of us performed (with tongue in cheek) a special version of *The Lass With The Delicate Air*. The audience laughed in all the right places so we must have done something right.

With Scottish singing sensation, Andy Stewart

Panda and international pop star Bobby Vee

Jimmy was conducting the Orchestra for three shows; *Merry-Go-Round, Top Of The Town,* and *Sunnyside Up.* Our busy schedules left us little time to visit our almost completed new house. The builder gave us the move in date of early December and the excitement was picking up pace. On moving day, Mike was a real dear. We gave him the key and he went out to the house, delivering a car load of clothing and patiently waited for the delivery of our new appliances, refrigerator, washing machine, drying cabinet etc. That night he brought his wife Greta over and joined us for dinner. It was a relaxing conclusion to an exhausting day.

Trying to maintain some kind of privacy was impossible. John Burrowes telephoned to say he had located our new home and that *Listener In-TV* was going to photograph it and run a story with or without our co-operation. We figured if we agreed, at least we would have some control over the story and a promise they would not publish the address. It was frustrating. Privacy was definitely our most treasured need. Until one does not have any, one cannot imagine what it is like. Alas, it is a penalty of fame.

In our new home, we had the space, secure fencing and ability to handle the daily care necessary for good 'doggie' parenting. At every opportunity we visited kennels looking for a puppy. We fell in love with a three month old, liver and white coloured, German Short haired Pointer and 'Caspar' came into our lives.

Merry-Go-Round was swamped with sponsors and we were on top of everything, music, dance, comedy, games, glamour and fun. Songs like *All I Do Is Dream Of You, I'm Just Wild About Harry, Toy Balloons*, and plenty of other uplifting song and dance routines were right up my alley. Our *New Faces* segment, the forerunner of similar shows to follow, turned out to be an absolute winner.

Panda and Jimmy perform 'The Lass With The Delicate Air'

A Soap Opera. Left to right: Vic Gordon, Lorraine Davey, Peter Langdon, Panda and Mike Williamson

43

PRINCESS

Christmas and New Year had kissed us goodbye and at the end of January Channel 7's staff were roused out of their complacency with the news that *Top Of The Town* and *Merry-Go-Round* would finish. According to the sales department, *Merry-Go-Round* had been a most sought after commodity and all of our 1961 sponsors were looking forward to another season with us. However, this was not to be.

Horrie Dargie, Arthur Young and sales representative John Tilbrook, created a production company called DYT (Dargie, Young and Tilbrook) and had engaged Jonathan Daly to host a talk show based on America's Jack Paar/Johnny Carson format. The shows would replace *Top Of The Town* and *Merry-Go-Round*. Jimmy was retained as musical director for the three nights a week show, so his schedule was unchanged, conducting four live shows inclusive of *Sunnyside Up*.

When hearing the disappointing news about *Merry-Go-Round*, Norm raised my spirits by announcing that I would be cast in the children's show, 'The Happy Show', five evenings a week, to lift it's ratings which had hit rock bottom. Happy Hammond was visiting the United States and in his absence, Norm starred me as 'Princess Panda' in the children's variety show and assigned the lovable Vic Gordon as comedy relief. He was dubbed 'Funny-face,' consistent with his rubbery faced expressions.

Ecstatic beyond measure, it was a role I had asked Norm to consider at GTV-9 after my return from the 1959 world tour, but at that time he wanted me to remain working in *IMT*. Now everything had turned full circle and my wish was granted. The headlines spewed out again:

PANDA SWITCHED.

PANDA'S HAPPY SHOW.

PANDA IS STILL A FORCE.

PANDA FOR CHILDRENS SHOW.

PANDA'S FUTURE? SURPRISE TWIST.

Publicity photograph – Princess Panda

Princess Panda with the Olivettes

Princess Panda. Publicity photograph

Shortly after, Toni Lamond lost her role as hostess of Monday's *IMT* and was replaced by Bert Newton. Like me, I know Toni was equally proud of her achievements as hostess of prime time television and the respect for us both went up several notches.

My entree into children's television seemed to surprise most of the TV pundits, who questioned my ability to accomplish anything that didn't fall within the parameters of adult television entertainment.

I felt none of the doubts that pervaded certain sections of the press. My credentials of four and a half years as a high profile television entertainer, a loving mother who taught my child to read and write by the time he was four years old and my personal tutoring of children's classes at the Bambi Shmith Model College were each a triumph in every sense of the word. Having these hands-on experiences, I was probably better equipped to handle this new mission than any of my predecessors in children's television.

Norm's detractors didn't know where he was going with this new assignment. Norm on the other hand knew exactly what he was doing. I was about to venture into a new dimension of television, a stimulating challenge.

My new position was once again doing what I did in *Merry-Go-Round*. Hosting, comedy, singing, dancing and interviews, as well as question and joke time with the children's audience.

Norm appointed Doug McKenzie producer and the supporting cast included: John D'Arcy (Big John); Roy Lyons (Cousin Roy); and Anne Watt (Lovely Anne). Bob Horsfall (Robbie Bob) would be joining the show at a later date. There was also Olive Wallace's children's dancing troupe 'The Olivettes,' music by versatile organist Shirley Radford and drummer Stan Harris. The show hit top ratings immediately and when Happy returned from the United States he walked into a very exciting children's show.

It's new found success was the talk of television's sales departments and sponsors were backing up to buy commercial spots. Some time later, theme shows were introduced: *The Beach, Wild West, Circus, The Australian Bush, Winter Wonderland* and *Party Time*. Each day we presented one or the other of diversified guests like football hero Ron Barassi, 'Parer The Magician' and his rabbit 'Frosty,' a veterinarian with 'Peter's Pet Time,' from Melbourne's Zoo, a zoologist, handling exotic animals and new talent like child singer-guitarist Peter Doyle. Then there were multiple musical renditions from us cast members. Something for everyone.

Vic's comedy was hilarious and I loved working in the sketches with him. Roy played his straight man and I was often included in the routines. In one sketch, Vic had me tap dancing in hobnailed boots. The children screamed with delight at their Princess, in full dress and tiara, clod-hopping around the set. Vic was a totally unselfish comedian. He was not envious of anyone and happily shared his knowledge, not only of comedy, but of the theatre. His sense of humour was infectious and he, unlike some comedians, genuinely laughed at other people's jokes. He had a wonderful disposition and was loved by all of us. At rehearsal, Vic, Roy and I exchanged jokes every day and to say it was a joy to go to work is an understatement.

There was never a cross word spoken by any member of the cast. John was a stalwart at

With football hero Ron Barassi during IMT

Panda with Happy Hammond

Channel 7 and a versatile performer. King of the puns, he practiced them on anyone who came within earshot. He would also do anything asked of him, a most co-operative, likable and distinctive individual.

Anne, a dear person, had a surprising sense of humour and often joined in the merriment at rehearsals. A former *Swallows Junior*, she had a sweet singing voice and was a big fan of Judith Durham and *The Seekers*.

Roy was an experienced comedy straight man with a clear sense of what was right and wrong in that department and like John and Anne was ever synergetic. He too carried a tune well, especially in the country and western vernacular.

Happy, I knew and worked with at GTV-9 so there were no surprises or ego trips with him. A seasoned performer in every sense of the word, we were well adapted to each other.

When Bob joined the show, we were lucky to add his song and dance talents to our cast and like Happy, I knew him from our GTV-9 days.

As 'King Corky,' my pal Geoff Corke was also presenting a children's show at GTV-9, so now we were friendly rivals. Geoff's *Tarax Show* cast included Susan-Gaye Anderson, Ron Blaskett with his ventriloquist doll Gerry Gee and Ernie Carroll as "Professor Ratbaggy." Later Elaine McKenna, Patti McGrath and our dear friend Joff Ellen as "Joffa-Boy," joined the show.

The success of 'Princess Panda' was so overwhelming, that my HSV-7 mailbag bulged at the seams every day with stack upon stack of letters. The plaudits and popularity I had enjoyed in other areas of television could not compare with this astonishing new found success. I didn't think it possible to reach a higher pinnacle. Now, not only the viewing audience were applauding, but so too were the most formidable critics.

The headlines kept coming:

PRINCESS PANDA HAS 'CLICKED.'

PANDA HAS IT MADE.

PANDA'S BIG COMEBACK.

A reviewer from *TV Week* 1962 reported in part:

> *I really expected to see Panda fall flat on her photogenic face in the show, but I was wrong. She radiates the same amount of charm, the same friendly surprise at her own ability and her own immense appreciation of the art of good showmanship ... Panda has that wonderful ability to make other women like her. There is no cattiness in her make-up and her sisters know it. This endears her to the young and the old, the married and the unmarried and makes her a splendid compere ...*

Another charity concert, *The Show Of Shows* at Festival Hall to aid the St John of God home for mentally retarded children, 'Actors' Benevolent Fund' and 'Musicians' Relief Fund' brought a brigade of stars together again. This time Vic and I worked one of his brilliant comedy routines. Whilst delivering a monologue, I performed a magical illusion on stage, during which Vic entered from the audience continually interrupting me with a barrage of comedy material. The audience reception to this piece climaxed into prolonged belly laughs. Others on the bill were Frank Rich, Kevin Coulson, Geoff Corke, Frank Wilson, Kenric Hudson, Vikki Hammond, Syd Heylen, Honest John Gilbert, Graham Kennedy, Joff Ellen, Rosie Sturgess, Jonathan Daly, Bert Newton, Toni Lamond, Horrie Dargie Quintet, Tommy Hanlon Jnr., Buster Fiddess, Annette Klooger, Deidree Thurlowe and John Larson (stars of *The Desert Song*), the Victorian Symphony Orchestra featuring pianist Isador Goodman, Glenda Raymond and the Victorian Trumpet Trio.

Following this concert *TV Week* 1962 reported:

> *Panda again proved her versatility at the 'Show Of Shows' at Festival Hall, Sunday night, April 15.*
>
> *Panda and Vic 'Funny Face' Gordon did a comedy routine and really brought the house down.*

In the midst of all this flurry of accolades, for the first time in Channel 9's history they broke their policy of never buying back a star and made me an offer to return to their fold. At this point in time, HSV-7 had two top rating live variety shows, *Sunnyside Up* and our children's *Happy Show*, both of which greatly outrated their opposition. While negotiations were going on, the headlines boasted:

CHANNEL NINE BID FOR PANDA?

PANDA'S GTV-9 OFFER.

PANDA OFFER.

PANDA IS CONSIDERING GTV's OFFER.

GTV-9's BIG OFFER TO PANDA.

PANDA'S BIG COMEBACK.

It was most flattering, but my going to work each day was such a joy and with the entire cast radiating positive vibrations, walking away from this phenomenon would be a mistake, so I signed a new and more lucrative contract with HSV-7.

Listener In-TV reported:

> Less than three months ago even her kindest critics were saying Panda, the most-talked-about, most publicised woman on Australian television, had reached the end of the TV road. Last week, had she been spiteful, Panda had a golden opportunity to 'spit in the eye' of everyone who said she was finished as a TV star.
>
> Because of her wonderful success in HSV7's 'Happy Show,' Panda received an unprecedented 'come back to GTV-9' offer. She has turned it down, however, in favour of a new contract with HSV-7 which puts her right on top of the TV world.
>
> ...Panda wowed them with an enthusiasm that's rare in an adult. She avoided the mistake of talking down to her young audience and radiated such charm and warmth for children that they couldn't help liking her ... Fan mail and phone calls zoomed and more sponsors began asking how much it cost to advertise on the program ... Panda is now one of Australia's highest paid TV personalities.

The various regular segments I performed in the show were solid and done with confidence and professionalism. Everyone at Channel 7 and the show

Princess Panda on the set of 'The Happy Show'

supported me in every way and I couldn't have asked for more, so it was quite a shock to find myself suddenly victimised.

It happened that producer Doug McKenzie took some time off from the show and appointed a stand-in in his absence. Before leaving he prepared the necessary running sheets (programs) to be distributed to the cast and members of the technical staff at the daily production meetings.

At the very first meeting, Doug's stand-in eliminated me from all but one of my usual segments on the show, substituting himself. Challenging him, I explained what management expected under the terms of my new contract. Defiant, he would not change the program to reinstate my segments.

It appeared that the same situation which occurred in *Top Of The Town* was confronting me again. It was pointless pursuing the matter, so excusing myself, I left the meeting and headed for my dressing room. Upon reaching it, through sheer frustration and realising the impossibility of performing a show whilst in this unsettled state, I telephoned Keith Cairns in his manager's office and asked permission to be excused from the show. He sensed my distress and came immediately to the dressing room.

With much coaxing, he had me unfold the story as he scanned the running sheet. We also discussed the *Top Of The Town* script debacle, where I was almost written out of that show. Being primarily responsible for lifting

With Vic Gordon entertaining the children at HSV7

the children's show from the brink of cancellation to it's top rating position, I had earned the right not to be sidelined. Keith was obviously disturbed about this surprising turn of events and comforting me, told me to take the evening off while he took care of the matter.

My regular segments were restored and when Doug returned, his stand-in was conspicuous by his absence. No one ever mentioned the incident to me, however, there was a feeling of empathy in the air, an understanding we would continue to support one another under any circumstance.

With soaring ratings, the show was bought by Channel 7's sister station ATN-7 in Sydney and soon after, was also aired across the country. We had a national children's variety show, viewed throughout Australia. Now mother and the rest of the family were able to tune in five times a week.

Requests for audience tickets began piling up. Children from different states were begging to see the show. People I'd not heard from in years were requesting tickets on behalf of their family and friends. When the children did arrive, they queued up for hours to be sure they would get into the studio on time. The audience was divided into two sections. One for children (on camera), the other for the parents (off camera), where the latter could keep a watchful eye on their precious offspring. And precious they were. I can't recall any child deliberately misbehaving. They were having too much fun.

The tiered seating provided for the children was a perfect background for interviews. Each child could be seen clearly on camera and often were unpredictable, especially the pre-schoolers. It was not unusual for a little one to leave their seat, approach me on camera and live-to-air, speaking directly into the microphone say,

'Princess Panda, I want to do wee wee.' To which I would announce that Lovely Anne, Cousin Roy or some other cast member accompany them to their parent or guardian for toilet access. The show then continued as though nothing had happened. They talked about their families, pets, sang songs and told jokes and riddles. Each of them were as cute as any child could be. Sometimes the older children 'zapped' me with a smart-alec riddle, like the time a girl asked:

'What is six inches long, has a hole at one end and hair on the other?' Following a loud gasp from the parent's section, I said,

'I don't know!' She responded with, 'A toothbrush!'

'Lovely Anne' would hand out gifts to those I'd interviewed and during the show's finale, every child received something to take home with them, like party hats, packets of Twisties, chocolate Bertie Beetles, ice cream, cookies and other goodies.

When addressing the children, it was important to keep a cool head. One time, while standing amongst my charges interviewing a child, I sensed something was wrong with a small boy seated behind me. He did not look at all well. On camera, with microphone in one hand, I reached across with the other hand and held the boy whilst summoning Vic to his rescue. He was undergoing a seizure. Vic carried the ailing boy from the audience as I announced he was not feeling well and continued the segment. Later, inquiring of the parents as to his condition, they explained his medical status was that of epilepsy. It was very disappointing from their point of view, as the boy had longed to be a member of the audience and there he was, lying on a bench in a dressing room slipping in and out of consciousness, unaware of his surroundings.

At other times, distraught parents brought into the show their terminally ill youngsters suffering from leukemia or some other equally devastating disease. It was upsetting and one could not imagine how the parents were coping. Some parents were angry at the world, yet others accepted the inevitable. The sadness of those encounters I remember still.

The imagination of children is far reaching, like the time Jimmy had purchased some sausages from our favourite butcher. With them in hand he called at an adjoining store for another purchase. On returning home he realised he'd left the sausages on the counter of the second store so telephoned the proprietor asking him to set them aside, adding he would be back in a few minutes to collect them. The proprietor had earlier noticed the package on the counter, unwrapped it and wondered to whom it belonged and after Jimmy's telephone call, he told his wife and small daughter that the sausages belonged to 'Princess Panda.' His daughter scornfully replied,

'Princess Panda wouldn't eat sausages!' She must have thought that after Bertie Beetles, Twisties, and other children's show goodies, sausages were too far down the food chain to even be considered as part of a 'royal' diet. However, it did illustrate what power television advertising has on children.

Another time I was surrounded by youngsters requesting autographs. During the long wait for his turn, one small tike, in desperation of obtaining 'anyone's' autograph, turned to Jimmy and asked,

'Are you somebody?'

Producer Alf Spargo asked me to appear in a *Sunnyside Up* sketch with his star comedian Syd Heylen and comedy team Honest John Gilbert, Maurie Fields and Val Jellay. It was to be kept secret, as my role in the sketch was the tag and he didn't even want the crew to know. When the children's show finished, I drove to Fitzroy and sneaked into the teletheatre. Behind the scenes, I donned a baby dress and bonnet and once the sketch was in progress, climbed into a child's cot, was covered up with a blanket and wheeled onto the set, where on cue, I sat up and declared Syd my 'Daddy.' Once again the comedy magic of surprise, action and re-action bagged the laugh.

In early September, HSV-7 and their affiliate radio station 3DB were set to challenge GTV-9 and their affiliate radio station 3AK to a Sunday Australian Rules game at the South Melbourne football ground. Most of the personalities from each establishment were in attendance, some playing on the field and the rest in the grand stand as spectators.

When Jimmy and I arrived, on attempting to enter the premises, we were mobbed by a crushing crowd of fans where a serious situation soon developed. There was a force like a powerful oceanic wave swamping us, knocking me and some of the crowd to the ground. Jimmy managed to stay upright, hauling me and several children back onto our feet. With no security in sight, a dozen or so of Channel 7's personnel rescued us by dispersing the crowd. We were whisked away and secured in a safe area where first aid was administered to the grazes and bruises sustained. The crowd had simply become a little over zealous but it could have turned into a catastrophe. The incident set down new rules for future public appearances with a guarantee of safety for everyone.

It was reminiscent of one of my appearances at the Myer Emporium for a hosiery promotion timed to coincide with their television commercials. The venue was just inside the store's main Bourke Street entrance on the ground floor. When I appeared, the crowd swelled and the entrance became more and more congested until there was a gridlock with no pedestrian traffic able to move inside the store or past the front doors. Because there was obvious danger of injury to people and the possibility of mass panic, after only a brief appearance, the fire officers terminated the promotion and escorted me safely from the area. The crowd numbers had been underestimated, however we all learned from the experience.

In mid October, Jimmy and I were guests at a special dinner held in our honour. Wearing a lovely pale buttercup knee length lace gown, everything was proceeding well with glowing speeches and tributes, including a few good natured jibes, aimed at us both. In the midst of this happy occasion something went awry. I had been experiencing abdominal pain for days and without warning, suffered an abnormally severe haemorrhage. Jimmy covered my tracks, as I made a hasty retreat into the ladies room. Something was dreadfully wrong and all I could do was try to relax and hope that the problem would subside, but it didn't. Eventually Jimmy excused us, brought the car to the restaurant entrance and smuggled me into the night.

From that moment on, everything happened so fast, there was no time to catch one's breath and I found myself in hospital undergoing major surgery. Jumping on the bandwagon, the press delivered their headlines:

PANDA SERIOUSLY ILL.

PANDA FOR HOSPITAL.

PANDA IN HOSPITAL.

PANDA HAS OPERATION ET CETERA.

Under the scalpel, the incision revealed a large abdominal tumour. Instead of a straight forward procedure as had been anticipated, when the tumour was exposed to the air, it spread everywhere like static electricity, adhering to every part of the abdominal cavity it could reach. The surgeon, assisted by another of his colleagues then had a nightmare on his hands, carefully cutting the tumour away from all it had adhered to. Four hours later it was finally over and when I eventually recovered from the anaesthetic, the surgeon related the events of the operating theatre adding, 'We nearly lost you.' He explained that doctors are not without emotion. They too have deep feelings about their responsibility to the patient's life. They are always prepared for the unexpected.

When it happens though, they can become both mentally and physically challenged and in my particular case, totally drained.

At that moment in time, I cared not what had happened, just that it was good to be alive. The press followed with progress reports:

PANDA'S OPERATION 'SHE'LL BE ALRIGHT.'

PANDA IMPROVES AFTER OPERATION. PANDA ON THE MEND.

PANDA IS FINE ... AND SO ON.

From all over Australia, thousands of get well cards, letters and flowers kept arriving daily at the hospital and at Channel 7. In a wonderful gesture of kindness, Wally Webb of Webray television, had a brand new twenty-five inch TV set installed at the foot of the hospital bed for my personal use during the entire stay. There were no visitors and no phone calls. Jimmy was at my bedside every moment he could get away from his work. Gradually my health improved and I was released from hospital. The press saga continued:

PANDA LEAVES HOSPITAL.

PANDA RETURNS HOME.

PANDA 'I FEEL FINE.'

PANDA STILL SHAKY.

PANDA CAME HOME LAST WEEKEND.

After two weeks in hospital and during the three weeks convalescing, Channel 7 sent Happy, Vic and a film crew to do an interview at home for presentation on the children's show and the evening news that same day. I was impatient to return to the show.

When given the final O.K. to resume work, Channel 7 went into overdrive announcing my return and a huge publicity splurge was ongoing for days. Triple column sized advertisements went into *The Sun*, *The Herald*, and *Listener In-TV*, and a full page in *TV Week*. The advertisements read:

PANDA IS BACK TOMORROW.

Followed simply by,

SHE'S BACK.

and they were helped along by further press headlines:

I'LL BE BACK SOON. PANDA.

BIG WELCOME FOR PANDA.

WELCOME BACK TO PANDA.

PANDA BACK IN HAPPY SHOW.

John Newman (post J.C.W. and pre 'Tikki and John's') at this time was an executive with the Myer Emporium. He approached me with a suggestion that Myers produce a 'Princess Panda' doll for Christmas and we did just that. The dolls were dressed Princess style and came with a tiara and letter which read,

> '*Hello! I am your Princess Panda doll.*'
>
> *To my new mother:*
>
> *   *I have sleeping eyes.*
> *   *My hair can be washed and combed.*
> *   *You have seen me on television.*
> *   *I love you. Please look after me.*

It was introduced on the children's show in conjunction with Myers. Press promotion of my appearances in Myers' Toyland were splashed throughout *The Herald*. Thanks to John's imagination, creativity and organisation, it was one great big success.

1962 had drawn to a close and so too had Robin's school exams. A person of high attainment, his goal was a scholarship to enter High School. An 'A' student, at age thirteen and a half, he knew exactly where he was going. There was never a question of if he would do well, it was a matter of fact that he always did well. His quest was approached with great determination and finally, with the exams behind him, in December the Melbourne branch of the Office Of Education proposed to award Robin a Commonwealth Secondary Scholarship tenable at Melbourne High School, South Yarra. This was a proud moment for me. Then there was a follow-up letter from the Prime Minister's Department. We were all very excited to read:

> *I have considerable pleasure in informing you that a Commonwealth Secondary Scholarship has been awarded to your son Robin.*
>
> *Please convey to him my sincere congratulations. I hope that the scholarship will assist him to realise the promise revealed by his success in obtaining this award.*
>
> *Yours sincerely,*
>
> J.G. Gorton
>
> Minister-in-Charge

We hightailed it into the city and had great fun outfitting Robin in his school uniform, with all of the extras. He was in his element trying on shoes, jackets, slacks etc., and couldn't wait for admission day.

44

TULLE & TIARAS

efore our show resumed in the new year, HSV-7 presented a telethon to aid the Playgrounds and Recreation Association in a mid January television appeal. Including me, most of Channel 7's personalities made individual appearances. Famous American ventriloquist Edgar Bergen (Candice's father) accompanied by his dummies Mortimer Snerd and Charlie McCarthy entertained, as did Chips Rafferty and George Wallace Jnr. Sheila Bradley and Jeff Warren from *The King and I* and Patricia Moore, Kevin Coulson, Jill Perryman and Kevan Johnston from *Carnival* also gave of their talents.

Following this, we were back into the routine of the children's show and had been invited to participate in the annual *Moomba parade*. On an appropriately decorated float, we agreed to entertain the crowd while travelling along the entire route. This meant delving into our repertoire and coming up with just the right material. Fortunately, as the float was continually on the move, every so often a new audience was waiting and a tight abridged version of the show was repeated as required. A grand piano was positioned on the float for Shirley and a sound system blared out, as we warbled songs and cavorted with visual comedy, while the Olivettes preceded the float, dancing their way along the Moomba route. This was a normal TV show day, so timing our movements had to be precise. After paying our respects to the Lord Mayor and Lady Mayoress at the Melbourne Town Hall, the driver took the first available exit and headed for HSV-7's South Melbourne studios, where after a lightning rehearsal and costume change, we were on the air.

The events of the past few months had put our home furnishing plans on hold. Before moving into the house the flooring had been sanded, polished and permanently sealed throughout, establishing attractive living quarters. With just a piano and a few odd pieces of furniture, we embarked on the task of searching through every interior decorating book and magazine for inspiration on the best possibilities of dealing with a practically empty house. There were regular visits to furniture outlets where we observed the trendy styles, the more traditional and antique pieces on display.

By chance, we came across an excellent upholstery showroom in the Melbourne suburb of Hawthorn and when we ventured inside, discovered they also imported beautiful hand made chair frames. A talented young hand carving craftsman James Brown had a workshop at the rear of the premises and when the proprietor, Len Moody, introduced us to him, we fell in love with his creative skills.

Now we had a source for obtaining unique, custom made quality furniture. The cost was considerable and only one piece could be made at a time, so it was prudent for us to be patient. The first project was our bedroom. In one of my interior decorating books was a picture of a striking colonial canopy bed. Discussing the picture with Mr Brown, he artistically designed a bed based on my concept. We were more than thrilled with the result and asked him to make two matching bedside tables and a tallboy chest of drawers, each sitting on hand carved bases with elegantly curved legs. While these were being crafted, Mr Moody was masterfully producing a wing sofa and two matching lounge chairs, in addition to an Italian framed, velvet upholstered bedroom armchair. The attention to detail of these talented craftsmen was remarkable. Later we added two large leather fireside wing chairs. Additionally there were end tables, coffee tables, large combination bookcase-cocktail cabinet and hand carved high backed side chairs, all exhibiting Mr Brown's magic touch.

A lovely secretaire, handed down from Jimmy's mother, was revamped with a new hand carved base and legs. Each of the furnished rooms offered something different in wood texture. The kitchen setting was crafted from Queensland maple; the dining room suite, walnut; the living room, solid oak; and the bedroom, mahogany. Some moons later, we covered the polished floors with wall to wall wool carpeting, completing the picture. Graham was also decorating his handsome Frankston home, so we happily passed on to him the good news of our discovery of Mr Moody's establishment which he too put to good use.

The city of Geelong was to hold its two week long district festival in March and most of Channel 7's personalities would appear at the venue in outside broadcasts, including our children's *Happy Show, Sunnyside Up*, and *Daly at Night*. A breakfast production from Geelong's eastern beach was also programmed, so our two day telecast of four individual shows would be frought with high powered tension. Norm was especially proficient at outside broadcasts and as commander in chief, working with each show's producer, pulled the whole thing off with a minimum of problems. The main concern of the breakfast telecast was trying to get just the right angle to avoid the blinding glare of the morning sunlight in the camera lenses. Some pretty clever maneuvering by the camera crews saved the day. That same morning, after eating something which had upset his stomach, Vic was feeling a little 'green around the gills.' At one point during the telecast he excused himself and rushed to the toilet where he expected to throw up, except that he was intercepted by a youngster who said:

'Funny Face! Can I please have your autograph?' To put a retching experience on hold was quite a challenge, but he managed to do so, discovering in the process that being a public figure definitely has its drawbacks.

Also in March, I received a huge surprise in my mail box, from *TV Week*. It was an invitation which read:

> *Dear Panda,*
>
> *We would be very pleased if you would do us the honour of attending the Logie Awards presentations at the Chevron-Hilton in Sydney on Saturday night March 23. During the evening we would like you to accept an Award from our guest of honour, Tony Hancock.*
>
> *If you are able to attend, please give me a ring at 34 4111 so I may advise you of the special travel arrangements.*
>
> *Yours sincerely,*
>
> *Rod Lever.*

My last three Logie Awards were very special to me but this one was even more so as it was awarded for my role as Princess Panda. Best female personality the fourth time around was a very humbling experience. Some of the other winners were George Wallace, Graham Kennedy, Johnny O'Keefe, Bob Dyer, Chuck Faulkner, Happy Hammond, Tommy Hanlon Jnr., Bobby Limb and wife Dawn Lake, The Lorrae Desmond Show and the Joan Sutherland Spectacular. As it turned out, Tony Hancock was hospitalised and unable to attend, however, I did get to meet him when he later appeared on Channel 7.

Jimmy was very busy arranging music for another teletheatre production of the new 'Variety 7' show. Brisbane's popular comedian George Wallace and his comedy team Eddie Edwards and Carol Yule flew in from Queensland, while I, along with Happy, Vic, 1962 *Sun* Aria winner Maureen Howard, The Thin Men and other regulars including the Horrie Dargie Quintet and Organist Shirley Radford performed under Jimmy's musical direction. Norm was at the helm and another show was born. The reviews were favourable and *TV Week* commented:

> *Panda again proved her versatility in the opening of HSV-7's new variety show, 'Variety 7' last week. Working with Brisbane comic George Wallace, Panda was, as usual, excellent.*

Shortly after, I had to take time off from the children's show due to a bruised spine. There are an inestimable number of people who have experienced this disability and like me, regretted the misadventure which caused it. Mine was as simple as missing a step on a staircase. Easy to do, not so easy to recover from. The doctor referred me to a blind physiotherapist. It was either his nimble fingers or the follow up set of exercises he advised which enabled me to return to work within a couple of days and just in time to experience another first.

In 1947, Edwin Land invented the instant black-and-white picture camera known as the *Polaroid Land Camera* and by the 1960's many thousands had been sold in Australia. I had one of the original models and the novelty of being able to view a photograph in less than a minute of taking it, seemed miraculous. In those days, to preserve the picture, a special developer had to be smoothed over the photograph. A little messy when on location, but if one forgot to do so, rapid deterioration of the picture resulted.

Polaroid had long been a sponsor on Channel 7 and recently introduced a new colour film and camera as an alternative to their black and white. Though not yet commercially available here, they, in co-operation with *TV Week* snapped a photo of Vic, Happy and me during the show and reproduced it in *TV Week*, Australia wide. It was the first time a colour polaroid had ever been shot in a television studio and except for technical publications, *TV Week* was the first magazine in the world to use and develop the film in print and was hailed as one of their proudest achievements. The colour development took place in the camera itself and used up less than 60 seconds, as opposed to 90 minutes for regular colour film development. *Polaroid* advertised on our show and each day a lucky child was chosen and photographed to commemorate his or her visit to the studio. *Polaroid* and *TV Week*'s experiment was a much discussed success story.

I was offered a new contract by Channel 7 and once again the signing ceremony took place in Keith's office. There was an increase in salary plus additional concessions. The move from Channel 9 to Channel 7 had already cemented my standing in the television industry, providing an independence one could only dream of. Television contracts had to be earned, so naturally the successful negotiations not only bumped up my salary but my confidence as well.

The children's show ticketing took an unusual turn. Someone had either stolen or counterfeited a large batch of these little right of entry cards, causing chaos during mid year school holidays. Suddenly, instead of the normal number of children turning up at the Dorcas Street studio, we found the audience had almost doubled. Extra seating had to be squashed into place and the overflow of parents were forced to view the show from a television monitor in the foyer. Reservations had been made a year in advance and each ticket was carefully documented, so those involved with the distribution checked and double checked all sources of leakage from the office, but to no avail. Keeping in mind admission was free, we were afraid someone was out there profiteering. Was this an office slipup or a genuine forgery? The show's staff was put on extra alert, security was upgraded ensuring the situation would not be repeated and new tickets were allocated, putting an end to the mysterious caper which remains unsolved to this day.

During the Ball season, the entire staff, dressed in their gladrags, gathered together for the annual Channel 7 Ball held at the Kew City Hall. There was no doubt that there was an enigmatical air to it this time around. During the week prior to the event, there had been a great deal of whispering in corridors about the floor show. Rumour had it that the Georgian Dancers would provide the entertainment. No one could mentally place this troupe of dancers and curiosity grew as the Ball progressed. Halfway through the evening, as the musicians returned to the stage after a band break, the lights dimmed and following an announcement something like; 'Ladies and Gentlemen, for your entertainment we proudly present the

Georgian Dancers. The spotlight flashed on to a staircase at one end of the stage, whereupon eight conspicuously tall ballerinas swept down the stairs on to the ballroom floor to the romantic strains of Tchaikovsky's *Swan Lake*, to perform a dramatic version of the famous ballet. Stunned by their overpowering appearance, it wasn't until a few bars into the music that the audience realised they'd been hoodwinked. The dancers, all wearing identical wigs, false eyelashes, make-up and ballerina costumes were none other than male members of Channel 7's staff. Amongst others, the *corps de ballet* included Roy Lyons and Vic Gordon from the children's show; director, Alf Potter; costume designer, Ci Howe; sales representative, Peter Cooper; and producer, Doug McKenzie. They were awkwardly brilliant and had us rolling in the aisles. The whole production was put together by choreographer Betty Meddings, producer Ian Jones and our own Vic 'Funnyface' Gordon. It was the best kept secret of the season and they wowed everyone.

Since entering television I continued the trend of engaging a professional portrait photographer for my publicity photographs. Athol Shmith wore the crown as Melbourne's elite social photographer and just like my modelling days, we still enjoyed working together on photo shoots at his Collins Street studio.

Following my selection from the proofs, the photographs were distributed to the various media outlets, as well as the studio publicity department for the printing of fan cards. Paying for the photo shoots and prints myself gave me control of which photographs would go where and to whom, enabling each publication to have exclusive pictures for their files.

The distribution of fan photographs played a big part in the public relations of all television stations. Postcard size, they were printed in black and white and mailed out on request. Reasoning that HSV-7 was a subsidiary company of arguably the largest publisher of newspapers and magazines in Australia, including *The Herald, Sun, Weekly Times, Sporting Globe* and so forth and that this company already reproduced colour photographs in print on a regular basis, I suggested to HSV-7's publicity director, Dick Voumard, the idea of having colour fan photographs printed. Dick embraced the concept, researched it, had it approved by management and because of my brainchild, in 1963, HSV-7 introduced the very first colour fan photographs of TV personalities in Australia. In honour of my suggestion, Dick arranged for the initial distribution to be of me, also the children's show cast. The new colour prints created an avalanche of requests from viewers and within a short period of time, other networks in Australia followed suit. *TV Times* reported:

> ...*HSV-7's order for Princess Panda's Ean card runs into 80,000 copies a year.*

Given the cost of producing the pictures, envelopes, stamps and staff, there was a substantial sum expended on those little souvenirs. It's not surprising that since those days, networks request viewers send stamped, self-addressed envelopes in response to their giveaways and competitions.

Many celebrities brought their children in to see the show and they were usually introduced to the audience. *Sunnyside Up's* Val Jellay and Maurie Fields brought their little son Marty into the studio to celebrate his second birthday, sportscaster Ron Casey proudly introduced his young daughter, Happy's wife Rita, showed off their pre-school daughters, along with Roy, John and Bob's sons and daughters. Jonathan and Marlene Daly's infant daughter made her television debut on the show, as did many others. They all loved having their offspring on television, we loved having them and judging by the mail-room, so too did the approving viewing audience.

The producers of *Daly At Night* brought back from the USA, singer, straight man, Ken Delo to rejoin his comedy partner Jonathan Daly and put together a top class variety series, *Delo and Daly*, for HSV-7. With Norm Spencer as director, Joe Latona producer-choreographer, Hugh Stuckey's comedy writers and Jimmy's musical direction, it was predictably fast paced with the smooth, slick look of the American variety shows. Success was

'Delo and Daly Show'. Left to right: Ken Delo, Jonathon Daly and conductor Jimmy Allan

Panda barbequing with Joe Latona

instantaneous. Ken and Jonathan were a breath of fresh air, doing their own matchless comedy routines. Ken's engaging singing style later elevated him to world recognition in the Lawrence Welk Show. Other outstanding performers were the super stylish Joe Latona Dancers, a new singing group 'Take Five', singer-actress Vikki Hammond and an unlimited list of International guest stars. This dazzling show became the yardstick by which many variety show producers drew inspiration for years to come. Ann Hathaway, a member of the same 'Take Five' singing group, later married HSV-7 trombonist-arranger, Johnny Hawker. They joined forces as a vocal duo and enjoyed much success with hits like Cinderella Rockafella.

Jimmy was engaged as musical director for Ken Delo's Australian recording debut on the Astor label. The album turned out to be a best seller. By October, the Delo and Daly show had made a huge impact nationally. Ken and Jonathan were invited to appear in the Sydney Lord Mayor's Command Performance. Jimmy had become such a significant part of the Delo and Daly show, that they invited him to accompany them to the gala event and conduct their music.

About this time the Simca was becoming somewhat of a problem. Now five years old and although still running smoothly, shifting gears, especially into first, required the strength of an Olympic weight lifter. Most times, by bypassing first gear and starting the vehicle in second, the problem was temporarily solved, but it was obvious that a trade-in for a new car was inevitable.

Ken Delo (left) and Jimmy record an L.P. for Astor Records

On display, in the showroom window of Lane's Motors in Exhibition Street, was a gleaming white MGB with red upholstery and black hood and it surely captured my attention. Having driven Jimmy's Porsche convertible many times, been a passenger in Joy Fountain's MG-TF and test driven an MGA, the unmistakable mechanics of a sports car were not unfamiliar.

Jimmy recommended we take it on the road and if satisfied, then I should buy it. The ride was smoother than the other MG's I'd travelled in, so the decision was made and a deal was done. The excitement of picking up the new MGB was a thrill beyond compare. All I wanted to do was collect the keys and skedaddle.

However, when the company representative escorted me to the delivery room, where I expected a 'thanks and adieu,' he promptly went into his ritual. Despite my absolutely itching to get away, he painstakingly went over every inch of the car pointing out everything an MGB owner should know, such as the motor, rev counter, odometer, gasoline gauge, dip stick, how to disassemble the hood, correct tyre pressure, including the spare tyre in the trunk. He tooted the horn, flicked on the lights, turned on the radio, tried the windscreen wipers and added a long list of other familiar information. When he was about to demonstrate how to change a tyre, I stopped him, leapt behind the wheel and escaped into the city traffic on my way to HSV-7 for a production meeting. When pulling into the car park, distinguished photo-journalist Frank Howe, approached with his trusty camera and wasted no time in capturing a picture of me in my new sports car for the cover of *Listener In-TV*.

At the same time, *TV Times* featured me on their cover and introduced a five part weekly series of 'LOOK SMART' with Panda, inclusive of grooming tips, make-up, fashion, deportment, social graces and general information.

The MGB became an instrument of pleasurable adventures. Vacations were a welcome respite from a year in the public eye and to go some place where nobody recognised us was a luxury. Usually, we'd select a country town where there was no television and takeoff on a sight seeing tour of some region or another. At one time a visit to the heart of the Murrumbidgee irrigation area in the wine growing district of Griffith in New South Wales appealed to us, so with Caspar in the good hands of famous police dog trainers at the Mummery Kennels we set out through Shepparton, Jerilderie, Narrandera, Leeton and on to Griffith.

The motel reservation was made through a well known chain, but the accommodation was certainly not what we expected. The suite was very, very basic. With temperatures over 100 degrees farenheight, there was no air-conditioning, just an electric fan, radio and telephone. During our stay, we motored out to the sight of the proposed murrumbidgee television station which was about to undergo construction and paid a visit to a vineyard and winery. Our host persuaded us to partake of his finest Pinot Chardonnay and amongst other pertinent information, expounded his theory on its complexities, bouquet, intensity and balance. We left with a greater respect for the art of wine making and a broader vocabulary. The starkness of this country town struck a memorable note of my rural upbringing.

That night, after dinner at a local hotel, we adjourned to a table in the vicinity of the bar. During the short time we were there, a brawny, deeply tanned man approached the bar and ordered, 'the usual,' whereupon the barman opened two large bottles of beer (equivalent of eight glasses) and set them in front of the man who, drinking straight from the bottle swilled down the contents in about five minutes, then picked up his change and left without a word, (or a tip).

Next morning we prepared for the long drive home. The motel manager directed us to a place to purchase ice. As we drew near, it became obvious that what resembled a large backyard shed was in actual fact the ice dispenser. Two wiry young men dressed in shorts, singlets, wide brimmed hats and heavy boots politely told us to put two shillings in the honesty box and help ourselves.

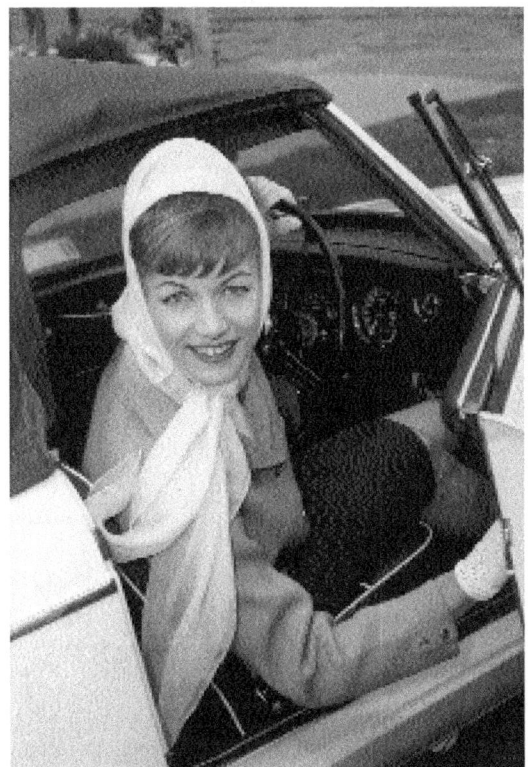

In my new MGB sports car

Walking through the entrance of this structure, staring us in the eyes were huge, commercial size blocks of ice, looking as though they had been carved from a glacier and here we were, with our urban mentality, expecting to find a neat little plastic bag of cubed ice to pour into our car-fridge. Sitting on top of one of the blocks was a professional ice pick. Jimmy looked at me, shrugged his shoulders and with ice pick in hand, started chip, chip, chipping away until a small block split asunder. He fitted it snugly into the car-fridge, unfortunately leaving little room for refreshments.

We planned journeying west to Hay, then south to Deniliquin, Echuca and home. Motoring to Hay with the top of the MGB down and our cooler on the back seat, we hadn't gone far before the block of ice began to melt and the vibration of the car caused it to become very noisy as it bounced, bumped and moved around making deafening sounds like screeching cockatoos. After suffering this torture for a while, we eventually stopped and muffled the noise by wrapping the ice in a towel. Managing to make it to Hay, the irritant was hastily disposed of and replaced with cubed ice for a more peaceful ride.

Some time during the trip, we took a detour and before long, found ourselves bogged up to the axles on a sandy road. At the time, the temperature was about 110 degrees farenheight and the sun was beating down on us like a furnace. Using a plastic picnic plate, Jimmy managed to dig down to solid ground and after carefully laying scrub branches behind the rear wheels, he backed the car in the direction from whence we'd come and returned to the main highway. The area was unimaginably isolated and if the car had remained bogged, it was quite possible we could have succumbed to the heat. A very frightening experience which gave us food for thought about outback travel.

45

ALL IN THE GAME

s far back as 1962, applications had been made to the Australian Broadcast Control Board for a licence to open Melbourne's third commercial television station and in November of that year, hearings from six applicants were held. The hearings lasted only four weeks and by April 1963, Mr Reginald M. Ansett, the head of Ansett Transport Industries Ltd., had been granted a licence to own and operate Melbourne's fourth television channel, Austrama Television Pty. Ltd., to be located in Nunawading. Viewers were encouraged to have their old television sets modified to receive the new Channel's signal and in April 1964, ATV-0 started transmitting test programs ready for its grand opening later in the year. The months flew by and I was back in Keith's office signing a fourth contract with Channel 7, marking my eighth year in television.

Keeping up appearances was a daily routine and getting my hair professionally coiffured always seemed to be a waste of precious time, but was part and parcel of maintaining good grooming. While the girls fussed with my hair, usually I would either read a book or figure out the *Australasian Post's* mammoth crossword puzzle. One day there was much excitement in the third floor Salon and I soon found out that there was a flurry of activity taking place on the balcony of the Melbourne Town Hall, directly opposite the hairdressers. The girls beckoned me over to the window to witness the Lord Mayor welcoming *The Beatles* to Melbourne. We all waved to the 'Mop Top' foursome John Lennon, Paul McCartney, George Harrison and Ringo Starr and they waved back. Although I was not aware of it at the time, an historic event was taking place before my eyes. Beatlemania had arrived.

To celebrate another twenty-fifth birthday, photojournalist Frank Howe had taken a rather glamorous picture of me accompanied by a small eight year old admirer, for the cover of *Listener In-TV*. After it appeared in print the publication received a number of compliments about Frank's photographic excellence and the editor, Perc Dunstone, challenged him to take another equally glamorous shot for the next edition to accompany journalist Mary Maxwell's feature story: HOW TO STAY 25 FOR YEARS. My age was a running joke and the newspapers always good-humouredly poked fun at it. Twenty-five was a good number to stick with and Mary's subject matter was about the secrets of staying young. I never considered myself an expert in this field, however, some people thought otherwise and I was often a spokeswoman on the topic. Luckily my past modelling experience provided a great deal of knowledge in this area so I was able to pass on pertinent facts which were helpful to the uninitiated and that in itself brought great satisfaction. I always did the best with what God gave me and that's about all anyone can do. Aging is a progressive part of life and if one lives long enough, no matter what happens it will play catch-up.

Dozens of invitations continued to arrive weekly to open fetes, fairs and any number of charitable galas. As many as possible were accepted, but time was of the essence and many had to be declined. Almost all of the major hospitals and fund raising organisations called for appearances at one time or another and there was even an invitation from Sir Dallas and Lady Brookes to attend a Government House garden party to aid the Red Cross.

Then there were the regular file of International quest stars who appeared in concert, or clubs. My presence was constantly requested at the receptions held in honour of these celebrities and I got to meet many exceptionally talented people.

I never forgot the generous hospitality extended to me during my world tour and I vowed to return the compliment one way or another by inviting and entertaining dozens of visiting artists to my home. Amongst them was American actor-comedian Buddy Lester who was a regular guest. Buddy appeared on almost all of the television variety and talk shows in the United States and enjoyed featured character roles in Jerry Lewis movies. He was also cast with the famous 'Rat Pack,' Frank Sinatra, Dean Martin, Sammy Davis Jnr., Peter Lawford and Joey Bishop in the movie *Ocean's Eleven*. He went on to guesting in many Hollywood television series including playing the role of Nick in *The New Phil Silvers Show*. Buddy, Jimmy and I enjoyed many good times together and have remained friends for dozens of years. Buddy's brother Jerry Lester, was host of the 1950s smash hit television series *Broadway Open House*, which was the forerunner of the *Tonight Show* in New York.

Another house guest was English recording star, singer and impressionist Dickie Valentine. His show business career began as a pre-schooler in the British movie *Jack's the Boy*. Later he became a singer and in the fifties, made a succession of recordings in the top twenty, including some number one hits. Probably his biggest was *Finger Of Suspicion*. Amongst others, some of his amazing impressions were those of singing legends Nat 'King' Cole, Johnny Ray, Mario Lanza and Sammy Davis Jnr. He was considered one of England's biggest teen-idols. As a house guest he was thoroughly at ease and absolutely charming. He offered me a colourful children's song to perform. Instead, I invited him to sing it on the show himself. As a favour to me, he accepted without hesitation or a fee.

British stage, recording, radio and television singing star Alma Cogan was also a visitor to our home. Some of the stage shows she appeared in were, *Oliver*, *High Button Shoes* and *Sauce Tartare*. In the 1950s she was probably England's top female recording artist, with just under twenty songs in the hit parades. At one of her recording sessions Paul McCartney graciously played back-up tambourine. She not only had her own television show, but became a prolific song writer using the pen name of Al Western. Alma was appearing in Melbourne's Union Plaza showroom, and on a day off, along with her musical director Stan Foster, joined us for dinner. Clutching my bone china tea pot, she taught me the fine art of English tea making and light heartedly chided me for not having the pot well 'seasoned.' At the time, we in the children's show were promoting yo-yo manipulation. I happened to have some of those little fun devices at home for promotion practice. Alma demanded a demonstration and within no time became a master at 'walking the dog', 'rocking the cradle,' etc. Returning to England, she had one of the yo-yos tucked into her luggage as a memento. Later, both Dickie and Alma were sadly lost to us by their premature demise.

When Eddie Cole, brother of Nat King Cole, was in Australia promoting his latest record, he and his wife Betty were welcome guests at home. They were fond of Chinese food, so I went to my favourite Asian restaurant armed with an assortment of large saucepans and brought home an Oriental banquet. Together we feasted on deep fried prawns dipped in a variety of sweet and hot sauces, marinated sliced pork, chicken rolls, dim sums, stir fried chicken with vegetables and almonds, beef and mushrooms plus lashings of fried rice.

Eddie was a premier International cabaret act and like his brother, an accomplished pianist and singer. He and Nat got their first major exposure when they joined Broadway's touring show revival of *Shuffle Along*. At that time, Eddie played bass. In his cabaret act, he featured a calypso style straw hat adorned with paper currency collected from every country he had visited, including Australia. Eddie and Betty were a lot of fun to be around, very appreciative of my hospitality and before leaving for the united States, sent a beautiful bouquet of flowers.

At a reception for the legendary radio, television and motion picture star Jack Benny, the assembled guests were enthusiastically milling around him, so Jimmy and I retreated to a quiet corner of the room. Just prior to the reception, Jack had seen the children's show on television. He noticed us sitting apart from the throng and being the gentleman that he was, came over, introduced himself (hardly necessary) and complimented me on my work. The conversation flowed as though I was talking to an old friend and before leaving the reception arrangements had been made for Jimmy and me to be his personal guests at the Comedy Theatre where he was appearing. In front row seats, we witnessed a brilliant performance and after the show, were escorted to Jack's dressing room where we joined other guests Diana Trask and husband Tom Ewen. When Jimmy suggested telephoning the private Musicians' Club to request the dining room remain open for us, Jack was delighted. Diana and Tom also came along for the late-night-bite and as we were in the MGB, it was agreed that Jack would travel in their station wagon. It was a great night, the chef laid out a tasty supper and we all stayed later than any of us had intended.

Even though Jack was about seventy years old at the time, he was sprightly and insisted upon riding back to his hotel in the MGB. Under normal circumstances Jimmy did the driving, however, on this occasion I was wearing a tight fitting sheath dress and climbing into the limited space in the back was not possible, so I took the wheel while Jimmy squeezed into the rear seat. On the journey to his hotel and during the many happy hours we subsequently spent together, Jack kept us entertained with stories from his past, injecting humour at every opportune moment.

Starting out in vaudeville as a violinist, his unique sense of humour crept into the act and eventually he became the master of all masters of comedy timing. He owned and played one of the world's most coveted Stradivarius violins and incorporated much humour from his alleged bad musicianship. In actual fact he was a fine violinist who as guest artist played with many of the world's great symphony orchestras, often helping to raise large sums of money for the Musicians' Benevolent Fund and other charitable organisations. In his comedy routines, he portrayed the believable character of a stingy man. We kept this in mind as he related how he came to be in the possession of the Stradivarius violin, confessing that it had belonged to his great grandfather who, when he died, bequeathed it to his grandfather, who bequeathed it to his father, who in turn, SOLD it to Jack.

An adorable, articulate, interesting man, he talked about colleagues and sadly told of his ailing friend Eddie Cantor, who at age seventy-two was seriously ill. He spoke often of his close friendship with George Burns, the only person who could genuinely break him up on stage. They couldn't have been closer if they'd been brothers. His time in Melbourne was far too short. Each meeting with him was a great learning experience and I will never forget him.

Journalist Pat Weetman from *New Idea*, asked for an at home interview. Unlike today's colourful showy editions of the nineties, *New Idea* used to be a rather reserved homey magazine. Although it was not customary to grant the press access to our private retreat, there were certain exceptions and Pat's was one of them. I felt this magazine would reach a further circle of readers and be beneficial in promoting the children's show. While Pat sipped Jimmy's freshly brewed coffee, she jotted down pages of notes and titled the feature story, COFFEE WITH PRINCESS PANDA in which she described the residence as a palace, in keeping with my television title. She wrote about the interior decoration, furnishings, garden, home making and entertaining. The reaction to the story was pretty overwhelming. I received hundreds of letters from readers asking where and how they could obtain different decorating items described in the story. The curiosity of people and the power of the pen was once again astonishing.

The children's show continued to dominate the ratings. During one evening's performance I asked a small boy of kindergarten age to relate a riddle when suddenly he burst forth with a song. This diversion was not unique except that this time the Child Welfare Department claimed they had received a complaint and under the Children's Welfare Act, any child under age seven was prohibited from entertaining on stage, radio, or television. In addition, the Social Welfare Department must issue permits for children age seven and over. The chief inspector argued the point with HSV-7 executives and eventually conceded the child was not set-up, but was acting spontaneously and no action was taken.

After seven years of television, Channel's 7 and 9 were the only commercial stations competing for advertising revenue. The ABC was supported by tax payers and not required to vie for the lucrative pounds, shillings and pence. Now the time had come and Melbourne's third commercial television channel, Austrama's ATV-O, officially opened in August 1964. They were quick to grab a market share and the advertising 'pie' had to be split three ways. A lush opening night extravaganza paved the way, followed by a weekly variety talk show with the suave good looking Ray Taylor at the helm. Nancy Cato hosted their children's show and later regularly appeared in a scripted fantasy series *The Magic Circle Club* with Ted Dunn, Ernie Bourne and John Michael Howson. To counter GTV-9's news anchors Eric Pearce and Jack Little, and HSV-7's Geoff Raymond and Brian Naylor, ATV-0 engaged the team of Barry McQueen, John Royle and Philip Gibbs. A steady supply of American films and series provided a solid basis for regular programming and the station was up and running.

Popular TV Times journalist, Marsha Prysuska sought me out for another cover and feature story PRINCESS PANDA LIVES HAPPILY EVER AFTER. She wanted to know why, after four years of marriage, Jimmy and I were still so happy when so many couples were experiencing problems? This type of interview was always a little uncomfortable but Marsha managed to write a pleasant article which gave some insight as to how a good relationship could be effected. It was quite true that our private life had taken on a calm and joyous status. We were always together except when working in our individual shows and this brought a closeness none could match. It was almost idyllic. The main ingredients for our happiness were love, trust and honour, each of which we practiced. Marsha covered the story with sensitivity and good taste. She was a particularly likeable journalist and I always enjoyed her company during interviews.

Meanwhile, an offer from a Sydney Theatre production company, who wanted me to play the Fairy Godmother in a pantomime for the upcoming holiday season, was very tempting indeed. Unfortunately the season conflicted with my Channel 7 commitments and the very flattering proposal had to be turned down. A disappointment, but not the end of the world.

One day around election time, while sitting in my dressing room, Vic's voice could be heard from the make-up department next door. Needing to speak to him about a comedy sketch, I finished dressing and approached the make-up room calling out his show name, 'Funnyface!' Then I was stopped in my tracks. Looking back at me from the make-up chair was not Vic 'Funnyface' Gordon who had since vacated the chair, but Deputy Prime Minister and Country Party leader John McEwen being readied for an election telecast-taping. He laughed at the intrusion, so to break the ice I told him the only political joke 1 could recall at the time, which went something like:

> A leading businessman stated that he would not run for the office of County Treasurer explaining, 'I live in a mansion with four luxury cars, a yacht and a wonderful family and I don't want to have to leave it all and move to Argentina!'

Jimmy and 1 always kept in touch with Joff and Bernie Ellen who lived in a sleepy little riverside village in Tarwin Lower, where Bernie's sister and brother-in-law owned and operated the local hotel. We had reserved a room for the end of December to see the old year out and the new year in. The hotel was crowded with celebrants including us. The dining room was festively decked out and a large table covered with a freshly laundered tablecloth and assorted tableware was set aside for Joff and Bernie's friends. Including Jimmy and I were, Graham Kennedy, Val and John Wesley, Greta and Mike Williamson, Dale and Frank Rich, Rosie Sturgess and husband Peter McMahon. It was a great night abounding with laughter and we danced the night away. I wore a lovely cocktail dress made in France of delicately woven super lightweight white wool. Of course the dress was doomed when something from the dining table bounced on to my lap.

A couple of days later in Melbourne, Jimmy delivered the dress, amongst

New Years Eve at Tarwin Lower. Rosie Sturgess (back) with Joff Ellen. Front – Graham Kennedy and Panda

other items of clothing, to the dry cleaners. When he returned to pick them up, the dry cleaner told of an overnight robbery at his business and all of our dry cleaning was gone. Sad to say my expensive little Paris import would not be seen on television where I had planned to wear it on the annual Children's Hospital Telethon.

Now at the beginning of 1965, over at GTV-9 their children's show ratings had slumped and management's decision to replace it with film was a shock to everyone, in particular its cast. The show had been running in various forms for about seven years. Our good friends Geoff Corke and Joff Ellen were relocated to alternative live shows as were the rest of the cast, but the show's demise was bad news for children's entertainment. It affected not only the cast, but everyone connected on the production side and when this kind of situation arises, creativity flies out the window. All in the television industry were concerned about replacing home grown local productions with imported movies. It seemed incredulous that GTV-9, noted for nurturing live entertainment, would follow this path. It was quite a blow and caused an uneasiness in the industry regarding all live entertainment.

Also in January, wedding bells were in the air. Anne Watt and her handsome boyfriend Brendan McKenna married. Sweethearts for a long time, it was a fairytale romance. They met on the set of the children's show where Brendan was a cameraman. The wedding ceremony took place in Middle Park's Our Lady Of Mt. Carmel church and the couple were blissfully happy. We were all there at both the church and reception and they were given a splendid send off on their honeymoon.

While Anne was away, we were delighted to have as her substitute, young newcomer, singer olivia Newton-John. As Anne already had the title 'Lovely' Anne, we dubbed her 'Pretty' Olivia. (Some years later someone changed the history books and re-titled her role as 'Lovely Liv.') Although quite inexperienced, she oozed beauty and talent and carried out all of Anne's duties with confidence. She was warmly received by both the cast and viewers and went on to appear in many other Channel 7 productions. Later she partnered the equally talented and attractive singer Pat Carroll and ventured overseas. The rest is show business history. When Anne and Brendan returned from their honeymoon and resumed work, like most newly-weds, they were teased relentlessly about starting a family.

Soon it was time for the 1965 Moomba Festival. Channel 7's two top rating shows *Sunnyside Up* and our children's show were presented from the Myer Music Bowl on Friday March fifth. The outside broadcast van, cameras, sound equipment, lighting and stage settings were all in readiness for a couple of hours of rollicking entertainment. It was estimated that 100,000 people massed at the location to experience the thrill of a live telecast with their favourite television entertainers. It was one of Channel 7's most outstanding successes.

On signing yet another contract with Channel 7, I announced that this would be my final year working on camera. With thousands of hours of television experience behind me, producing shows was an obvious next step to pursue. For further experience and inspiration Jimmy's and my plans included an extended exploratory tour of the television and music industry in the United States. However, at this point in time, everything would have to be put on hold, until my obligations to Channel 7 were fulfiled.

The annual *Sporting Globe*-3DB-HSV-7 Royal Children's Hospital appeal was upon us once again. I was scheduled to visit the children in their wards and while there, participate in a photo shoot for the cover of *Listener In-TV* to promote the appeal. Visiting the hospital was always a bitter sweet affair. The pleasure displayed on the children's faces when I called on them was enough to compensate for my sadness at seeing those who were seriously ill and dying. The most compelling image I have of that day was a tiny infant in the Intensive Care Unit hooked up to life support with little hope of recovery. It all seemed so futile. How the doctors and nursing staff coped daily with their brave little patients is beyond comprehension. Their dedication is an inspiration to all. Each Good Friday's appeal surpassed the last and a special evening celebrity hour was traditional fare. I was programmed to sing and dance with the Channel 7 dancers and along with Vic was cast in a sketch with Syd Heylen, Maurie Fields and Val Jellay, which we enjoyed as much as the audience.

Back at the studios of Channel 7, all of our sponsor's products were carefully locked in the property bay's cage to protect them from theft. Following our daily production meetings, assistant producer Peter De Silva, a production staff treasure and his right hand man Bob Barnes would prepare the commercial products on their display tables in readiness for the rehearsal and show. While he and Bob were busy with cue cards and other pertinent duties, some of the products were disappearing. They searched high and low for them but to no avail. Everyone was put on alert to be on the lookout for the culprit. Eventually Peter and Bob, like Sherlock Holmes and Dr Watson, set a trap and laid low for the perpetrator. Their efforts were rewarded when they discovered it was a female entertainer from one of HSV7's other productions. She was reprimanded and let off with a warning and the problem was solved with a minimum of embarrassment to her.

Peter was always there when one needed anything at all. At one time, a publication wanted a quick photoshoot with a decorated cake to coincide with another of my twenty-fifth birthdays. At such short notice there was no time to call at a bakery and the canteen had only cup-cakes on hand. Peter volunteered to make a fake cake with bits and pieces from the property department. It turned out to be a masterpiece. The only part missing was 'Happy Birthday.' Having done such a good job of the decorating, he wasn't about to spoil it by slipping up on the written words. Not to worry though! He went to the Art Department and asked if they could handle it. Well, of course they could. Unfortunately, the chosen artist had just returned from a liquid lunch and with a masterful flourish swept across the cake writing 'Happy Birthday,' and as he ran out of space, trailed the last couple of letters over the edge. We were stupified. The artist, Peter, the photojournalist and I looked at each other and realising the silliness of it all simply burst out laughing. It mattered not. With just the right camera angle, no one could tell the difference.

By mid year, Channel 9 planned a special edition of *In Melbourne Tonight* to celebrate its 2,000th show. No one could have predicted the wrangle that went on between Channels nine and seven over me. Nine had requested that I make an appearance with Graham in my former segment of *IMT*. Seemed simple enough, except that Seven would only agree if Nine loaned Graham for an equal exchange in one of their variety shows. Nine argued that I was a veteran member of *IMT* and viewers would understandably expect to see me on the special and that Graham on the other hand had not made appearances on Seven and therefore would not be expected to do so. Seven argued that my contract was exclusive and any agreement would have to be reciprocal. The result of the bickering was a stalemate and there was no winner in this heated dispute.

The Channel 7 executive pool made a decision to have me, along with Happy and Vic, host a daily 90 minute movie at 5:00 p.m., following a half hour variation of our usual children's show which would start at the earlier time slot of 4:30 p.m. They were already showing cut up, full length movies in serial form but abandoned that idea to introduce the 90 minute uncut version. Hosting the movies they said, would add our personal touch and invite a broader spectrum of viewers to the program, upping the ratings and revenue. With a new contract and my decision to move into the production side of television, I thought it would be an ideal transition and began to devote more and more time into research and development of ideas for the future.

Following Robin's sixteenth birthday Jimmy and I promised to secure a used car to enable him to strip and rebuild it in readiness for his driver's licence and entry into University in 1967. He had planned an electrical engineering career and the experience of rebuilding a car was an exciting prospect for him. As it happened, one of Jimmy's musicians offered for sale a small black Morris 8 in reasonably good condition. Jimmy thought it would be an ideal car for the make over project. Robin was delighted when he saw his prize and promised we would not recognise it after its rejuvenation. We would wait and see.

ATV-O'S Ted Dunn called into the children's show to invite Jimmy and me to visit The Magic Circle Club's weekend taping. We were happy to accept the invitation and found Ted and the cast including Nancy Cato, John Michael Howson and producer Godfrey Philipp to be very friendly and welcoming. As our show did not follow a story line per se, it was interesting to observe their strictly scripted production. We were particularly impressed with Ted's outstanding colourful costume creations. As well as playing 'Fredd Bear' in the series, he was an exceptional dress designer and outfitted the entire cast in appropriate style. His television destiny was cemented by his talent.

Ted was also a gracious host and when he heard Vikki Hammond and her husband Bill Forbes were about to sail for England to visit Vikki's homeland, he threw a big shindig to send them happily on their way. Jimmy and I were there and among the other party goers were Toni Lamond and husband Frank Sheldon, Mary Hardy and Julie McKenna. With an abundance of professional singers present, *Auld Lang Syne* never sounded so sweet.

Another generous host was our dear friend Joe Latona. He had travelled the world along side his show business partners with their act 'Latona, Warren and Sparkes.' They were a star attraction at the Stardust Hotel and Casino in Las Vegas, appeared on television's *Ed Sullivan Show* in New York and Royal Command performances in London and Europe. Joe was show business savvy, an inventive choreographer and producer and there was little he didn't know about stage blocking. He was the complete showman, producing the *Graham Kennedy Show, Delo and Daly* and other memorable television and stage extravaganzas.

His parties were always fun. He had the knack of mixing guests to create an atmosphere of intellectual diversity. We were regulars at his Alexandra Avenue apartment and each time we were there past friendships were rekindled. One memorable evening, old friends from J.C. Williamson Theatres, Betty Pounder and Prima Ballerina Kathleen Gorham held our hands and guided us as we pranced around the room, Greek dancing to the theme music of *Zorba the Greek*. There we were, tripping the light fantastic with one of the world's greatest ballerinas and no one thought twice about it, we just enjoyed the moment. To us, Joe was one of the family, who often stayed over night when he came to visit.

In the female league of hosts was June Bronhill, Australia's darling of popular classical music, who had audiences falling at her feet wherever she performed. At one of her fashionable parties, Jimmy had again rewritten some musical excerpts from various operas with special comedy lyrics and handed the parts out to June and her guests, practically all of whom were professional opera singers. It was an immediate success. They sight read the music and lyrics and had the walls resounding with song.

We were having a great time, but it was not one of my better health days and during the levity, dread set in at what I could feel coming on. My heart started rolling over with its irregular beats and the familiar side effects caused further distress. Jimmy carefully guided me to a quiet place in the townhouse where I quickly got into fainting mode, while Jimmy pressed cold wet towels on my brow and nape of the neck. This technique sometimes fended off a complete blackout and luckily it worked this time around. On the way home, feeling weak, fatigued and not at all well, I figured the fun definitely outweighed the health problem. June thoughtfully telephoned to make sure everything was alright and that we arrived home safely.

Over the previous year, Jimmy had a couple of mishaps on the studio set. The first time, he tripped on a camera cable and broke a bone in his foot. The doctor didn't put the foot in a plaster cast, instead sent him to a special cobbler who fitted one of a pair of shoes with a metal plate to immobilize the foot and stop it from bending when walking. To our surprise, the bone set correctly in just a short period of time and it was back to wearing his fashionable shoes again.

The second incident occurred while he was conducting the orchestra. A large audio speaker fell on him and as he tried to save himself from the weighty piece of equipment, a bone in his hand fractured. True to his medical beliefs, the doctor once again opted for no plaster and strapped the hand with a special bandage. The method worked fine until about midnight. The pain had worsened and Jimmy could endure the agony no longer. When I telephoned the doctor, he told me to cut a specific part of the bandage and all would be fine. Another hour later, the pain had not subsided so I called the doctor again and he was there in a flash. On examining the hand which by this time was quite swollen, he realised the bandage was bound too tightly, dangerously slowing down the circulation. Carefully re-binding the damaged hand, the pain subsided and the doctor was on his way to another patient in need.

Then there was the time Jimmy was carving a leg of lamb and accidentally sliced a deep cut in his hand.

We couldn't stop the bleeding, so again called the doctor to ask his advice. He volunteered to call around immediately and tend to the problem. He decided the wound would have to be sutured. Rummaging in the pantry, I provided him with a small saucepan into which he poured water and then placing it on the stove, proceeded to sterilise a needle. During the suturing, which took place without a local anaesthetic, he jabbed at the wound and apologised for the needle's bluntness. As Jimmy winced, he believed the doctor when he confided that he had not used this particular needle since he was in the Punjab in northwestern India during world war two. Our doctor was quite a character. Once while playing polo, he fell off his horse breaking a limb. Refusing a plaster cast, the limb was strapped in bandages in the same unconventional method used on Jimmy's broken bones. He continued working at his medical practice while the fracture healed and was back on his polo pony, bandage and all.

46

BIDING TIME

hanges to the children's show in the coming year did not alter my plans to enter the realm of production. My confidence was high at the prospect of producing shows and nothing could dissuade me. When we returned to work in the new year, Jimmy resumed his position as Channel 7's musical director while I was scheduled, along with my colleagues to make a pilot for a new half hour children's show. There were meetings and more meetings. Suggestions from the executive pool were laid end to end on the table until finally, after a couple of weeks of discussions, they submitted a half hour adventure series as the most likely pilot. It was eventually videotaped and not unexpectedly, rejected.

The script and story line were considered weak and unconvincing. While I was biding my time waiting for Channel 7 to make a decision about a future children's show, Jimmy was busy with music for the high rating *Sunnyside Up* as well as the national *Bob Crosby Show* which was produced alternately from the Sydney studios of ATN-7 and HSV-7's Teletheatre in Melbourne and to which I was asked to make guest appearances. Bob flew in from Sydney every second week and presented a bright late night variety show which garnered comfortable ratings.

Still playing the waiting game, I was being paid my substantial salary for doing little more than guest appearances. A new children's show was sidelined and at the conclusion of my contract, I received a charming letter from Brian Ferguson, supervisor of live programming at Austrama Television Pty. Ltd. (ATV-0) in Nunawading. Regarding an offer, he said:

> ...We have some interesting plans for the near future, both within our current operation and beyond it as well ... so I wish to paint a rainbow, although the pot of gold is a little further away ... I do not wish to leave the matter up in the air and so we will get in touch with you as soon as possible ... Meantime we send our love and best wishes...
>
> Brian.

From the Australian Broadcasting Commission, Program Director A.W. Wyndham asked me to telephone his secretary to arrange a convenient time for a meeting. I was put in touch with the ABC Drama department where I was offered a role in George Bernard Shaw's play *The Apple Cart*, which they proposed producing.

The biggest surprise came from Channel 9's Program Manager Rod Kinnear, who telephoned and invited me to meet with him in his office. He welcomed me with open arms and after some congenial chit chat, offered me a role in Channel 9's news department presenting the weather, alongside Eric Pearce. I was not sure that it fitted my character and asked for an extension of time to make up my mind. When Rod called me back to his office for another meeting, before I had time to discuss the weather role, he dropped the biggest surprise of all by disclosing that Graham, who hosted three *IMT*'s weekly, was about to take a vacation for a period of two weeks and that Channel 9 would be engaging six individual hosts during his absence. Rod generously offered me the opportunity to be one of the hosts. Flattered indeed, I was to be the only woman amongst five males. I accepted without hesitation. It was like going home.

The fact that over at Channel 7 they'd left my production plans on hold and I'd had little to do over the past few weeks now seemed unimportant. Everything was jumping. It was back into the swing of live television at my old stamping ground.

When Channel 9's publicity department announced the news to the press, the headlines crowed:

PANDA ON IMT SHOW.

PANDA RETURNS TO HOST IMT.

PANDA'S TV COMEBACK ON IMT.

PANDA REIGNS AGAIN ON IMT.

PANDA RETURNS TO COMPERE IMT SHOW.

PANDA RETURNS TO IMT.

The other hosts were TCN-9's Don Lane, a jewel in the area of variety-talk shows; Eric Pearce, respected and dearly loved head anchorman of GTV-9's news department; Pete Smith, experienced disc jockey and witty television presenter; Tony Charlton, champion sportscaster; and Frank Wilson, fine actor and television presenter.

Rod appointed Frank Sheldon my producer and I couldn't have been happier. Frank was married to Toni Lamond and understood perfectly the female aspect of television entertainment, recognising my every need. He put at my disposal, musical director Ron Rosenberg, choreographers Gladys Raynor and Russell Stubbings, comedy producer Johnny Ladd, script writers Mike McColl-Jones and Freddie Parsons and the comedy team of Joff Ellen, Rosie Sturgess, Johnny Ladd and Patti McGrath. My other guests were Bert Newton, Vikki Hammond, Ted Hamilton and teen idol Merv Benton. I even had Eric Pearce to introduce the contestants on the prize wheel. Frank directed me to a Collins Street boutique where I was outfitted with several beautiful gowns into which I would change throughout the evening.

The show was to be a departure from the usual fare and Frank made certain I was showcased in every possible facet of the entertainment. There was a lot to learn and every aid was placed at my finger tips including the offer of detailed cue cards. At times cue cards can be critical, but I have always felt that committing everything to memory, as we did in the theatre, made for a more confident performance so I set out on the learning trail immediately.

Remembering lyrics posed no great challenge, nor did the choreography which was designed to suit my capabilities. The script writers dazzled me with their wit, coming up with smart, funny sketches and I settled down to rehearse and get the best out of them. Fittings for the changes of gowns required considerable time and although they were glamorous, great care was taken to see that lightning fast changes were feasible.

All of the introductions and back announcements were flexible to suit me. Still to come were scripts from the advertising agencies for live commercials.

Each of these I also committed to memory and when the big night arrived, I was as prepared as anyone could possibly be.

The opening brought the audience to their feet when the ballet chorused *Hello Panda* to the music of *Hello Dolly*. The applause was deafening and one could feel the electricity in the air. It was a memorable homecoming.

Vikki had given birth to her infant son just weeks before I asked her to appear as one of my guests. After she had sung her solo *An Occasional Man* to the male dancers, I joined her in a duet of *The Doodlin' Song*. Bert had been off television for many months, and I was delighted to welcome him back on my *IMT*. As always, he was magnetic, sparkling and loads of fun. Along with Joff, Rosie and Patti, Bert appeared in a sketch playing the role of my boyfriend. Later I invited him onto the set where he produced a bunch of comedy telegrams which took a rise out of me and reaped some big laughs. The genteel Johnny Ladd and I played out a comedy sketch, with Johnny as a psychiatrist and me the patient. Another segment had me singing and dancing with the ballet in an innovative routine choreographed by Russ Stubbings. Baladeer Ted Hamilton, who had been a member of the Sydney produced Digby Wolf shows and pop star Merv Benton both added their distinctive talents and individually wowed the audience.

The reviews following the show were all favourable. In essence they all agreed with *The Age* which stated:

> *Panda ... much-in-the-news personality popped up again from GTV-9 last week to compere an edition of IMT, and thoroughly delighted her fans.*
>
> *She looked well, very capable, quite smart, and her handling of the program was more expert than some others who have stood in for Graham.*
>
> *She thoroughly intrigued female viewers by making no fewer than eight changes of clothes providing a solo running fashion parade through the program...*
>
> *GTV-9 could do worse than call Panda back into IMT occasionally ... her stocks have gone up.*

Hundreds of cards, letters and telegrams of congratulations were delivered to the studio, including one from GTV-9's then General Manager, who wrote:

> *I just wanted to write and congratulate you on your program last night.*
> *We got many calls from viewers to say how much they enjoyed it.*
> *It was great to have you back with us again.*
> *Sincerely*
>
> *Nigel Dick.*

The complimentary headlines following the high of such a successful show left an afterglow which lingered on. However, the die had already been cast and I was content to follow through with plans for entering the off camera phase of production. The timing to ring down the curtain on this chapter of my life felt right and although the studio lights still shone brightly, this had been the perfect night to take my final bow and exit gracefully. Overtures to continue on camera tempted me still, but the idea of retiring while on top decided my future and I retreated from the public eye.

To embrace a normal urban life proved difficult. Dining in restaurants, attending theatres, or a simple shopping spree continued to attract just as many well wishers, admirers and autograph seekers as always. It seemed I was to be permanently deprived of anonymity. Unfortunately, one can not close the door on fame.

The insatiable appetite of the press continued with their feature articles, but now they were writing about where I might be or what 1 might be doing, my health and other pieces of gossip, none of which was 'from the horses' mouth' as they say. They accused me of 'doing a Garbo' (in her quest for anonymity, legendary movie actress Greta Garbo was alleged to have once said, 'I want to be alone'). Our unlisted telephone number and Jimmy's capacity to parry all attempts for interviews made the situation tolerable and I wistfully dreamed that complete withdrawal from being a public figure would soon become a peaceful reality. It never happened.

At this point in time, Robin's car restoration was governed by his school work and as he was deeply immersed in study for a University scholarship, there was much concentration and reams of reading matter and note-taking to do. Nothing could stop him and we were there for him every inch of the way. He needed no prompting and it was clear to us that he would succeed in his endeavour. However, we would wait in anticipation for the official outcome.

Even though it was generally known I had retired from on camera appearances, offers continued to come in. Another telegram asked:

> WOULD APPRECIATE IMMEDIATE ANSWER REGARDING PANDA'S AVAILABILITY FOR MCC (Channel O's 'Magic Circle Club')
>
> KIND REGARDS GODFREY (Philipp).

What a pleasant surprise it was. Godfrey was formerly at GTV-9 and now creator and producer of Channel O's 'Magic Circle Club.' I was disappointed to have to decline his offer, especially after ATV-O's Brian Ferguson's earlier encouraging letter, but show business has a way of turning up opportunities at the most inopportune times.

The Sydney based Sadler Theatrical Agency offered me the starring role in a live childrens' theatre production at David McIllwraith's Lido Theatre in Russell Street, Melbourne. Stage promoter Ivan Vander, director of Melbourne's Permanent Children's Theatre, wanted me to appear regularly in his shows to give them a popular TV touch. The first show *Trumbo The Clown*, an original story was to be produced and directed by the very talented actress-writer Bunney Brooke. I was somewhat tempted to accept the offer but plans for a long term commitment conflicted with my future aspirations and I decided against it.

This holiday season, Jimmy and I briefly vacationed in Sydney where we met up with friends Annette Klooger and Ray Taylor. Singer Annette, a one time regular on *IMT* presented her own television variety series on ABV-2. Talk show host and actor Ray, formerly with ATN-7 and ATV-0 had just completed a starring role in an ABC television play. We had much to talk about and spent New Years Eve together at a Double Bay restaurant in close proximity to the Yugoslav Consulate. While we enjoyed a splendid dinner and the company of our good friends, not long after the New Year had rung in, there was a huge explosion which shook the entire restaurant and all of those within. We learned that the explosion came from the Consulate premises nearby. It had been bombed and sustained severe damage, but luckily no one was hurt. There was a mass exodus from the restaurant and car park. We may not have been at the head of the exiting crowd, but we were not far behind.

On our return to Melbourne, we were over the moon with Robin's news from the Commonwealth Scholarship Scheme of the Education Department-Victoria, which stated:

> *Your results in the Matriculation Examination have gained for you an award of a Commonwealth University Scholarship for 1967. We congratulate you on your success and hope that this achievement will be followed by many more in your chosen field of study ...*

His dedication to studying had paid off. Now he could relax and for a little while enjoy the pleasure of restoring his car.

Shuffling through my mail often brought pleasant surprises, one of which read:

> *Dear Panda,*
>
> *For the first time, Tikki and myself are going to appear in our late supper review on Wednesday, Friday and Saturday nights ... Also in the cast will be Betty Bobbitt and Terry Norris, so naturally the theme of the show had to be TV... I am writing to ask permission to name the show 'WHATEVER HAPPENED TO PRINCESS PANDA' ... Please let me know what you think.*
>
> *Best regards,*
>
> *John (Newman).*

Tikki and John's theatre restaurant 'The Gods' was without a doubt one of the most popular theatre night spots in Melbourne and was frequented by theatre goers and show business people alike. I happily agreed to Tikki and John's request and the show opened to packed houses and favourable reviews.

And yet another offer turned up. This time from independent producer John Collins, who proposed a television show designed for an adult audience, loosely based on Art Linkletter's, *Kids Say The Darndest Things*. In fact though, the concept was more or less the same interview segment I used to present in the children's show. It was to be expanded into a full length program. I was told that my reputation for handling children on television was legendary and the powers that be knew that if anyone could tackle a show of this nature, I would be their choice. Although it was to be a Channel 7 presentation, there was even talk of joining ranks with Channel O's 'Pied Piper' show. No matter which way it was proposed, like all of the other offers, this too I declined.

With the distinction of a scholarship, Robin had enrolled at University. Every afternoon I motored to the campus to pick him up, whereupon he would take out his learner plates, attach them to my MGB sports car and proceed to practice his driving all the way home. The experience was invaluable to him and gave me great pleasure observing the gradual improvement in his driving skills. Shortly thereafter he was tested and received his driver's license. As part of his vehicle's restoration, Robin asked if I would re-design his car seat covers. It was a huge challenge for me to take on. Following directions, I had previously made drapes, but never upholstered anything before. Agreeing to give it a try, he removed the seats from his car, supplied me with yards of light coloured, almost white deerskin naugahyde and left me to my own devices. First, I stripped the old cover from the rear seat and then those from two Volkswagon seats he was substituting for the passenger and driver's area. Carefully unpicking all of the stitching from the old covers, I laid them out on rolls of brown paper and made patterns. With these I cut the naugahyde to match and set about sewing the pieces together with all of the ribbing in the right places. My electric sewing machine stood the test remarkably well and the end result was three very attractive seats ready to be re-installed in the car. Robin's pleasure was obvious and I was prouder than a peacock. We worked out patterns for the interior of the doors and roof lining which he later carefully set in place. Robin had ingeniously adapted and installed Volkswagon headlights, tail lights, traffic indicators, windscreen wipers and various other improvements to bring the vehicle up to date, including re-wiring the entire electrical system. All of this he did by himself, solely with the aid of a workshop manual.

Technically, the car was ready to be registered. On this auspicious day, he and Jimmy ventured into the Motor Registration Department. All of the modifications passed the inspection and with a grin from ear to ear, he received his registration plates.

While enjoying the pleasures of one of Joe Latona's soirees, 1 got caught up in a conversation with Vikki Hammond and husband Bill Forbes regarding the rejuvenation of Robin's car and his final step to have it re-ducoed. Bill volunteered to spray paint the vehicle. All Robin had to do was supply the paint in the colour of his choice.

Jimmy and Bill set a date and to make it a special day, Vikki invited us all over to the house for lunch. A heavy fog had started to lift early on the appointed day. Robin and Jimmy gave the car a final rub down and were on their way. By the time I arrived, the spraying was well in progress and with our movie camera, Jimmy was recording the event for posterity. When the last squirt of paint found its mark we all stood back to admire this stunning, as new vehicle, gleaming in its new 'Monza red' duco. After Vikki served us a luscious lunch, Robin, who was champing at the bit to take to the road, thanked Vikki and Bill profusely and at long last took his leave, disappearing into the afternoon mist to enjoy his labour of love.

Jimmy and I were planning our journey to the United States of America and there was a swag of overseas correspondence coming and going. To enable us to enjoy an obligation and publicity free tour, we decided not to let anyone locally know of our plans. Friend Buddy Lester, had cleared a path for us by opening the doors of the television and music studios in Los

Angeles to observe behind the scenes of one of the world's most high powered industries. Former publicity chief at Channel 7, Dick Voumard, was now an executive with Qantas airlines. We confided our plans to him and he reassured us that our privacy would remain intact. He further suggested, as we would already be in the Americas, we should shoot down to Mexico City and enjoy the pleasures of Old Mexico, adding this fascinating side trip to our itinerary.

47

U.S.A. Here we Come

Our carefully laid plans were now under way. After a brief stay in Honolulu to soak up the sun, our sights were focused on Las Vegas, the entertainment capital of the world. We were scheduled to arrive there about midnight, fly over the brilliantly lit city, then catch a 2:00 a.m. show. The connecting incoming flight from Seattle, Washington was snowbound, leaving us stuck in the San Francisco airport for three long hours.

When we touched down at McCarran Field airport in Las Vegas, we were fortunate to share a limousine with a local casino maitre d' returning home from vacation, who gave some pertinent advice and pointed out places of interest like the famous Flamingo Hotel-Casino on 'The Strip' (Las Vegas Boulevard) , where in 1946 the flamboyant and notorious Benjamin 'Bugsy' Siegel created and opened this gambling and entertainment mecca. Following years of building and re-building, the only original section of the Flamingo remaining is 'Bugsy's' rose garden which was left intact for historical reasons.

Stepping out of the limousine under the canopy of Howard Hughes' Desert Inn Hotel-Casino and Country Club at about four in the morning in a sleep deprived state, we registered at the desk. While a bellboy continued up to the suite with our luggage, we wandered across 'The Strip' to the quaint, original Silver Slipper Casino for a bacon and egg breakfast. From the restaurant one could hear slot machines spinning, the rolling of dice and yowls of encouragement as someone won at the Craps table. The distant strains of a country and western singing group could be heard drifting in from the lounge-bar. Too tired to take it all in, as daylight emerged and crept over the distant Sunrise Mountain, we sauntered back to the Desert Inn where sleep swept us into dreamland for hours, in readiness for a week of crackerjack entertainment.

There were big shows at every major casino including the Dunes, Sands, Tropicana, Desert Inn, Stardust, Sahara, Hacienda, Frontier, Thunderbird, Riviera, Las Vegas Hilton, Caesar's Palace, MGM Grand and Landmark. With the passing years, as fast as the the old casinos are demolished, bigger and more elaborate establishments replace them. The original old Downtown Las Vegas, affectionately known as 'Glitter Gulch,' attracted tourists in the thousands to gaze in wonderment at the millions of dazzling multi coloured lights adorning the Four Queens, Lucky Strike Club, Golden Nugget, Binions Horseshoe, the Mint and Pioneer Club.

Until we experienced it, an open twenty-four hour a day community seemed unimaginable. At any time, one could shop at supermarkets, drugstores, deliver or pick up dry cleaning, get a car serviced, stroll from one casino to the next, or shop 'til one dropped. For prospective brides and grooms, day or night, any number of Wedding Chapels could be located interspersed between the casinos. However, the piece de resistance was the twenty-four hour entertainment scene. There were small open lounges with young up and coming performers spreading their wings and becoming established. The plush, intimate lounges were home to famous show business idols in their prime like Tony Martin, Vic Damone, Shecky Green, The Mills Brothers and others of their ilk. The major showrooms featured the upper echelon of super-stars. Some of whom could be seen throughout the year were Jack Benny, Johnny Carson, Debbie Reynolds, Sammy Davis Jnr., Frank Sinatra, Peggy Lee, Wayne Newton, Count Basie, Ann Margret, Jimmy Durante, Dean Martin, Joey Bishop, Petula Clarke, Liberace, Elvis Presley, Shirley MacLaine, Duke Ellington, Dianne Carroll, Harry James, Steve Lawrence, Eydie Gorme and numerous others, all accompanied by full size orchestras performing to SRO audiences. Other casinos presented sensational star spangled production shows like, the *Lido de Paris*, *Folies Bergère*, *Casino de Paris* and one or two shows direct from Broadway, all in the same city at the same time.

U.S.A. Here We Come

A smorgasbord on offer and we took in every show that could be crammed into our week-long stay. We'd seen the best live entertainment Las Vegas had to offer, stayed at a beautiful Hotel-Casino Country Club and had the time of our lives. To take up residence there, would be like living in show business heaven. We didn't realise it at the time, but Las Vegas was to play an important role in our future.

In Los Angeles I renewed old acquaintances from my previous trip. Jonathan Daly came down from Santa Barbara and invited us to visit he and Marlene at their home. Our good friend Buddy Lester who was on tour with Woody Herman and his famous 'Thundering Herd' Orchestra had arranged to access us behind the scenes of television productions and sound recording studios via one of America's top studio trumpet players Pete Candoli, who was married to motion picture actress Betty Hutton. Pete went far beyond anything we could have asked of him, taking us to rehearsals and television shows in which he was involved like the *'Carol Burnett, Jonathan Winters*, and *Red Skelton* shows. In addition to a sound recording date for *The Mod Squad* there was also a recording session at Capital Records with Paul Anka.

Talking one on one with television producers and directors brought me up to date with the latest developments, while Jimmy was in musical heaven discussing arranging with the *créme de la créme* of music, Earl Hagen, Paul Weston, David Rose, Peter Matz and Don Costa, all of whom were generous with their valuable time. We witnessed the filming of *Get Smart* starring Don Adams and Barbara Feldon and another critically acclaimed show of the time *He and She* featuring husband and wife team Paula Prentiss and Richard Benjamin.

At Jonathan Winters rehearsal we caught up with CBS cameraman Brian Phyllis, formerly of GTV-9. He had married a member of an American singing group the Starr Sisters and was now living in California. During a rehearsal break we all adjourned next door to the Farmer's Market for a bite to eat, talk television and reminisce about Australia.

The laughs came hard and fast at each of Carol, Jonathan and Red's rehearsals. During one of Red's famous Clem Kadiddlehopper sketches, he was standing next to a tethered cow. As the rehearsal progressed, the bovine deposited a large cow-pat right in the middle of the set. Walking away from the animal and pointing to the floor, Red announced:

'I'm not coming back 'til that heals up!' As a boy he worked in a medicine show and like his father, went on to become a circus clown. His success on radio was phenomenal and motion pictures elevated him to international stardom. He was loved most of all though for his television shows. In the 50's and 60's the *Red Skelton Show* was viewed more than any other show on television with the exception of *Gunsmoke*. Red received many awards during his lifetime including Emmys and an Academy Governor's award.

Jonathan Winters also worked in radio and it is alleged that when he couldn't get guests for his shows, he invented them, masking his voice, creating various characters. After guesting on most of the top American TV shows he presented his own successful television series in the 50's, 60's and 70's and was very much revered by his peers.

Carol Burnett is one of those extraordinary talents and like myself was a creation of television. Her show ran successfully for twelve years and she too won several Emmy awards. As were Red and Jonathan, Carol was especially friendly, likeable and very funny.

Some months before the trip, we'd taken a crash course in the Spanish language in preparation for our Mexican tour. Mexico City was enormous. A taxi transferred us from the airport to a charming old Mexican hotel, 'The Montejo,' situated on the Paseo De La Reforma, a beautiful tree lined Avenue dotted with handsome sculptures. Making the effort to speak Spanish made a big difference. Everyone went out of their way to be helpful. We spent the first evening listening to a legendary Mariachi Band at the Maria Isabella Hotel, a romantic introduction to this enchanting city.

As our Spanish was not altogether fluent, for extended tours, we engaged an English speaking guide. The first major excursion was to the Toluca market place in a small community about sixty miles from Mexico City. Here, in the hustle and bustle of busy trading, we purchased some heavy, hand knitted natural lanolin woollen jackets for Robin and Jimmy and a hand woven serape for me. Added to these items were a copper urn and chess set which helped bulge our luggage.

On the way back, our guide drove us to an ancient monastery high in the mountains and as we stepped from the vehicle a small child asked in broken English, if the guide would let him watch the car for a peso, to which the tour guide replied,

'And who's going to watch you?'

On another full day tour, we attended a performance of the *Ballet Folklorico*. This show was staged in a very old theatre which over the years had sunk several feet into the unstable earth. Instead of steps leading up, we found ourselves stepping down into the foyer. With our guide in tow, we sauntered down the aisle to our reserved seats. When the curtain went up, we were rivetted by a brilliant, colourful, toe tapping, finger snapping, Mexican theatrical experience.

From there it was on to Xochimilco with it's network of irrigation canals and floating flower bedecked gondola like boats with gondoleros propelling them along by wooden poles. Along the banks of the canals one could see silhouetted against the skyline, the sombrero clad vaqueros sitting astride their horses, looking down on the picturesque scenes below. For a few pesos, a Mariachi band in the colourful flat bottomed pleasure craft, tied up to our boat and serenaded us with traditional Mexican music as we munched on freshly made Enchiladas.

Next we were escorted to a bull fight. The stadium was a massive concrete structure with dangerously precipitous steps. One had to rent cushions to pad the solid rock-like seats. Bullfighting was a part of the culture we found difficult to accept. It was too gory for our stomachs. One finds oneself rooting for the bull and on this occasion in one of the fights, the bull won. The matador was quickly protected by his minders and was not seriously injured, at least by matador standards. He was rushed to hospital and the bull was set free to live another day. As dusk set in, our guide drove us to Garibaldi square, a large open spaced plaza where Mariachi bands gather and play their rousing traditional music. This rounded off a very exciting week of sight seeing and adventures. For the first time in many years, I was able to enjoy the luxury of anonymity, which gave me much food for thought.

Following an exhausting thirty-two hour flight home and twelve hours sleep, we were ready to face the world. This four week exhilarating experience was to change the course of our lives forever. Jimmy and I talked constantly of living in Las Vegas and at the first opportunity we made application for residency in the United States of America. Unless we were absolutely sure of an embarkation date, which would be many months away, we vowed to keep our plans confidential.

Inspired by our experiences in America, I immediately resumed writing the show I'd been working on prior to our tour. There was much research to be accomplished still and costing to be determined. Keith Cairns had furnished me with a rundown of costs and how budgeting could be achieved. The show would be aimed squarely at women and homemakers. I was confident that Channel 7 would approve it and put it to air. After finally submitting a comprehensive format, the waiting game began.

At the same time, Norm was putting together a new variety series, *A Guy Called Athol* starring Athol Guy formerly of The Seekers. The line-up of talent included Pat Carrol (Olivia Newton-John's one time singing partner and friend) , duo Bill 'n' Boyd, Bruce Woodley (also from The Seekers), politician Andrew Peacock, the Joe Latona dancers and Jimmy conducting the HSV-7 orchestra. Norm asked Jimmy to write a theme for the show and have me write the lyrics. It was a snap. The words and music simply fell into place.

Although my new production was yet to be confirmed, *TV Times* reported that Channel 7 and I were in discussions with a show in view. A short time later Channel 7 started promoting another new program. Tuning in to monitor it, I was stunned. As it unfolded, a most remarkable coincidence was taking place. There was an astonishing resemblance to the format I had submitted. I was dumbfounded, flabbergasted and beside myself with disbelief. Spinning around in my head were the familiar words,

'Trust in God, but tie up your camel!' Deeply hurt and feeling utterly betrayed, I considered my options. Another of my completed projects was a game show, which up to this time had not been submitted, so in an act of contempt and telling no one, I withheld the format then deliberately and abruptly withdrew from the television industry, declining all offers and interviews and vanished into seclusion.

Meanwhile the press continued pursuing me. resisted their overtures. Undeterred, their headlines persisted:

WHATEVER HAPPENED TO PANDA? ... OUR ONLY FEMALE TV SUPERSTAR HAS GONE INTO HIDING.

THE PANDA MYSTERY.

PANDA... WHERE IS SHE NOW?

WHERE'S PANDA GONE?

WHATEVER HAPPENED TO PRINCESS PANDA.

While I licked my wounds, Jimmy was busy with *A Guy Called Athol* and the revival of *Sunnyside Up* which had been on hiatus. Over the years, Channel 7 tried and tested many shows. One in particular which held great potential was a pilot of *The Young Entertainers* starring Ian Turpie, Olivia Newton-John and Pat Carroll. It was a delightful presentation, but was scrapped before it even got to air. A pity. There seemed to be no accounting for some executive decisions.

All of my concentration was now directed at our move to Las Vegas. The process was not especially complicated, simply time consuming. We eventually completed the paper work required for entry into the United States and received our green cards. The time had come to sell our house and painstakingly sort out what we would or would not take with us. The real estate agent was particularly understanding about our privacy. We had requested no FOR SALE signs on the property and no address published in the newspaper advertisements. They carefully screened a handful of prospective buyers before showing them through the home and it was sold within days.

Time was running out. After nearly ten years as Channel 7's musical director, Jimmy parted company with the network which enabled us to finalize our plans. He called an international removal company for a quote. They came, wandered through the house measuring and taking notes, before leaving to work out the final estimate. That same evening we received a phone call from Norm telling us he'd heard that we were moving to the United States. At this point in time, the only people who knew about our plans were Robin and our immediate families, who were all sworn to secrecy. Someone from the moving company had broken their code of ethics and leaked the information. To avoid press coverage, we abided by our original decision of not telling anyone about our plans and side stepped the question of our impending departure.

By this time Norm had left Channel 7 and returned to Channel 9 as executive producer of *IMT*. He asked if I would do him a favour and consider rejoining the show. As this was a good opportunity to put an end to the rumour about our leaving, I agreed. Channel 9 also persuaded Jimmy to become a judge on *New Faces*, so our well kept secret would now be shielded by these television appearances. Nobody had the slightest inkling that we were off to the United States within a matter of weeks.

A ratings war was going on between Channel 7's *Mike Walsh Show* and Channel 9's *IMT*. Graham, no longer associated with Channel 9, was scheduled to appear as one of Mike's guests. Channel 9 countered this by programming me to appear opposite Graham on Jimmy Hannan's *IMT*. The headlines spelled out:

PANDA ON IMT AGAIN?

PANDA COMES OUT OF HIDING.

PANDA, SHE'S COMING BACK TO TV.

PANDA'S TV COMEBACK.

TV RETURN FOR PANDA.

PANDA RETURNS.

PANDA MAKES TV COMEBACK.

The evening before my appearance, George Wilson telephoned from Channel 9's publicity department and asked me to do a special interview with the *Herald*'s highly regarded journalist, John Sorell. I had planned to spend the evening resting to ensure my work on *IMT* would be smooth and relaxed. However, George was very persuasive and instead of resting, I showered, applied make-up, dressed and was on my way into Channel 9 where a hairdresser was standing by to coiffure my hair in readiness for the interview. Eventually I made my way to the board room where Norm and a gathering of nine's VIPs were chatting with John Sorell. Introductions followed and in a very relaxed atmosphere, John and I participated in a pleasant exchange of questions and answers. While this was going on, *Herald* artist 'Peter' proceeded to sketch me and a photographer snapped pictures of the meeting. John was quite a charmer and the next day I was amazed to find that his amusing, tongue in cheek article had covered over half of the *Herald*'s page two. As a promotion for *IMT* that night, it couldn't have worked out better.

On the night of the show, there were dozens of telegrams and floral bouquets from friends and colleagues amongst whom were Bert Newton, Mike McColl-Jones, John Michael Howson, Mary Hardy, Ian Rainsford (Darrods), Vikki Hammond and husband Bill Forbes, Ron Tudor (record producer), Val Jellay and Maurie Fields, Evie Hayes, Eric Pearce, Joe Latona, Peter DeSilva (HSV-7 producer), Rod Fowler (FowlersVacola) and so many others. There was also a note from GTV-9 management.

> *Dear Panda,*
>
> *It's wonderful to have you back with us again after such a long time.*
>
>> *All the very best of luck tonight, and you know that everyone in the station is with you.*
>
> *All the best,*
>
> *Ian Holmes.*

My role was to participate in *IMT*'s new game, where a bow and arrow apparatus was attached to a television camera, which in turn was aimed at a target. As the operator, I directed the cameraman via a television monitor to move the camera this way and that, then finding my mark on the bull's-eye, called out 'Fire!' The cameraman triggered the apparatus and when the arrow hit the center of the target, cheers echoed from the audience and a lucky viewer landed one of the show's big prizes.

In another segment I was to present a commercial for Fowler's Vacola, 'Flame' fire lighters. The set designer had prepared a sophisticated setting with the ignited fire lighters elegantly displayed in a candelabra positioned on a decorative table. Halfway through my commercial spiel, the fire lighters began to teeter and suddenly crashed down onto the floor. it was like all hell had broken loose. As I dodged the flames and the staff reached for extinguishers, Jimmy Hannan ran onto the set, grabbed me and we did an impromptu interpretation of The Ritual Fire Dance, stomping out the lighters with our feet. It was quite hilarious and one of those rare moments where live television sometimes finds itself. A couple of days later, Mike McColl-Jones gave me a letter from the advertising agency.

> *Anderson White Advertising*
>
> *To Mike McColl-Jones. Dear Mike,*
>
>> *Shortly after you called me this morning I had a call from the managing director of Fowlers who asked me to pass on to you and Channel 9 his congratulations for the wonderful re-introduction of Panda to Melbourne television.*
>>
>> *I personally thank you for giving us the opportunity of allowing one of our clients to be associated with such a successful venture.*
>
> *Kindest personal regards,*
>
> *Anthony A. White.*

Norm wanted me to appear weekly on *IMT*. I was very apprehensive about accepting, as the departure date was closing in.

Our calendar had reached bursting point. We were invited to participate in a gala celebration of *IMT*'s birthday held at the Southern Cross Hotel and televised live to air. A splendid time was had renewing old acquaintances with GTV-9 pals Norm, Graham, Bert, Joff, Rod Kinnear, Colin Bednall, Rosie Sturgess, Patti McGrath, Jimmy Hannan, Stuart Wagstaff, Barry Crocker, Kamahl, Frank Wilson and Elaine McKenna. We talked long into the night about the good old days.

Another celebration was with Robin, now a young man and deeply immersed in the University education system. For his twenty-first birthday, we treated him and his young friends to dinner and a show at the Chevron Hotel. It was a very happy occasion. We arranged a financial backup, allowing him to move into the all male Mannix College to concentrate without distraction on his final examinations. Mannix College was affiliated with the University and he fitted in like a glove.

An alternative international removal company was engaged to pack and ship our furniture and other belongings to the United States, which they did under the strictest of confidence. Once our chattels had gone though, we were virtually living out of suitcases in an all but empty house. Fortunately, the dealer to whom we'd sold our cars, agreed to let us keep one until our last hours in Melbourne, so we remained mobile.

The day of departure was upon us. Robin collected the last vestiges of the house contents and we were on our way. After telephoning Norm and Joe Latona from the airport informing them of our move and to say goodbye, we embarked on our large scale adventure, to live an American dream. Meanwhile back in Australia the media had the last word:

PANDA OFF TO U.S.

PANDA TO U.S. SHOCK FLIGHT.

PANDA QUITS AUSTRALIA IN SURPRISE MOVE.

PANDA, JIMMY IN LAS VEGAS.

48

EPILOGUE

Hand in hand we ventured into the unknown. Having the courage to uproot ourselves from a secure, comfortable and lucrative lifestyle to start all over again was a big challenge. We were not simply moving to another house, suburb, city or even a state, but to another country. A bold move indeed. Not revealing our plans to anyone was a wise decision as it eliminated any negativity on the part of would be dogooders and left us with no doubt that even without the certainty of success our future held more than could be imagined.

With complete anonymity we leased an attractive air conditioned, security controlled Las Vegas apartment located in the vast, scorching Mojave desert. When our furniture arrived we moved to Paradise Valley into a sparkling new house which we later sold and eventually relocated into the private Las Vegas Country Club, resplendent with golf course and everything anyone could wish for. Jimmy became resident musical conductor for the showroom of the famous Las Vegas Flamingo Hilton Hotel and Casino, and in tandem with this, together we operated a music preparation service providing original compositions, arrangements, copying, commercial jingles and television scores and layouts. I enrolled in a communications course at the University Of Nevada, Las Vegas, trading show business for writing. Robin graduated from University with a degree in electrical engineering and in due course achieved a Doctorate of Philosophy.

The sequence of events in my life produced a few bruises, however, these were outweighed by the spectacular rewards. From my humble beginnings in rural Western Australia I soared through the glittering corridors of Vaudeville, musical Comedy, Opera, Fashion and Photographic Modelling, took on the title of Magazine Columnist, distinguished myself as a television star, was presented with several Logie Awards and lived a wonderful life in the United States of America. Counting all of my successes the most gratifying was climbing the mountain.

Puppet, Puppy and Panda

INDEX

Abbot, Bud, 109
Acfield, Bill, 180
Adams, Don, 249
Allen, Marty, 109
Allen, Steve, 95
Amadio, John, 109
Ames, Neil, 141, 142, 145
Amsterdam, Morey, 109
Anderson, Susan-Gaye, 94, 203
Andrewatha, Arlene, 80
Ann Margret, 248
Ansett, Reginald, 225
Armstrong, Louis, 110
Astaire, Fred, 114
Auckett, Marie, 73
Ayling, Jack, 98, 128
Baker, Dorothy, 89, 120
Ball, Lucille, 153
Banks, Norm, 192
Barassi, Ron, 202
Barling, Morrie (Slim), 43

Barnes, Bob, 233
Barry, (neighbour), 94
Barry, Alan, 48
Bartlett, Nancy, 194
Basie, Bill (Count), 248
Beames, Billy, 89
Bednall, Colin, 86, 91, 92, 99, 127, 131, 132, 163, 165, 167, 175, 183, 185, 256
Bednall, Marion, 106
Benini, Bruno, 68, 70
Benini, Hilda, 68
Benini, Mario, 68
Benjamin, Richard, 249
Bennetts, Don, 94, 98, 114, 165, 167, 168, 172, 173, 174, 178
Bennetts, Rev, 165, 167, 174
Benny, Jack, 228, 248
Benton, Merv, 240
Bergen, Edgar, 214
Berry, Jeanette, 172
Biddle, Rod, 111, 120, 168, 174

Bilceaux, Joan, 77
Bill 'n Boyd, 251
Bishop, Joey, 227
Blaskett, Harry, 109
Blaskett, Ron, 94, 101, 109, 120, 146, 203
Blau, Hans, 81
Blau, Robert, 82
Bleach, Max, 89
Blencoe, Lorys, 35, 36, 41, 45
Blue, Ben, 142
Bogart, Humphry, 145
Bond, Ward, 142
Boone, Pat, 152
Bourne, Ernie, 230
Bourne, Shane, 109
Bourne, Stan, 109
Bowkett, Jack, 101, 153
Bradley, Sheila, 214
Brady, Philip, 153
Broadway, Shirley, 117
Bronhill, June, 236
Brooke, Bunny, 243
Brookes, Sir Dallas, 219
Brown, James, 215
Brox, Guus, 117
Bryant, Bert, 83
Buckley, Maggie, 40, 41, 42, 43, 48
Bunning, Gaynor, 94
Burnett, Carol, 249
Burns, George, 229
Burns, Phil, 171, 178
Burns, Robert, 60
Burr, Raymond, 190
Burrowes, John, 124, 165, 180, 197
Byington, Ann, 137
Cadee, Ron, 192
Cagney, James, 144
Cairnes, Keith, 182, 183, 188, 199, 207, 218, 225, 244
Campbell, Jean, 58

Candoli, Pete, 249
Cantor, Eddie, 229
Cantrell, Lana, 144
Carroll, Bruce, 35, 39, 46, 48, 49
Carroll, Dianne, 248
Carroll, Ernie, 94, 203
Carroll, Pat, 232, 252
Carroll, Roger, 49
Carroll, Tom, 48
Carter, Benny, 152
Carter, Don, 94
Cassavetes, John, 141
Cato, Nancy, 230, 235
Chappel, William, 60
Chappelle, Albert, 60
Charlton, Tony, 83
Clancy, Jackie, 117
Clark, Bruce, 109, 118
Clark, Dick, 195
Clark, Joan, 101
Clark, Martin, 89
Clarke, Petula, 248
Clemenger, John, 86, 87, 88
Clemens, Bob, 109
Clooney, Rosemary, 95
Cole, Eddie, 103, 227
Cole, Nat ìKingî, 110
Collins, Bill, 112
Collins, John, 244
Colville, Peter, 186
Como, Perry, 95, 135, 136, 142, 195
Cooke, Elisha, 142
Cooper, Gary, 104
Cooper, Peter, 219
Corke, Geoff, 82, 83, 86, 88, 91, 93, 94, 98, 106, 108, 120, 127, 153, 164, 192, 203, 204, 232
Costello, Lou, 109
Coulson, Kevin, 204
Cowan, Joan, 58

Index

Crane, Steve, 140
Crawford, Curtis, 188
Crawford, Ian, 89
Crocker, Barry, 256
Croft, Colin, 60, 61, 62
Crosby, Bob, 187, 190, 238
Cummings, Sandford, 145
Curtis, Leo, 64, 65
Curtis, Tony, 141
D'albora, Gwen, 150
D'albora, Ron, 150
D'Arcy, John, 94, 117, 202, 203, 220
Dali, Salvador, 137
Dalton, Paul, 115
Daly, Jonathan, 153, 173, 199, 204, 216, 220, 221, 228, 249
Danaher, Kath, 153
Daniels, Billy, 110
Dargie, Horrie, 89, 120, 149, 153, 154, 164, 191, 199, 204, 207
Davey, Jack, 95
Davey, Lorraine, 187, 193
Davis, Ron, 89, 163, 164
Davis, Sammy Jnr, 227
De Lisle, Gordon, 70
De Lyon, Leo, 109
De Silva, Peter, 233
De Valois, Dame Ninette, 79
Dearth, Harry, 94
Delacruz, Katy, 101
Delavale, Ike, 40, 41, 42, 43, 48
Delo, Ken, 153, 173, 220, 221, 228
Devine, Florence, 36
Dick, Nigel, 127, 160, 169, 241
Douglas, Mike, 147
Douglas, Molly, 133
Dow, Tony, 141
Doyle, Peter, 202
DuCane, Diane, 172
DuCane, Marie, 172
DuCane, Terry, 172
Duff, Marlene, 180
Duncan, Arthur, 153
Dunham, Katherine, 109
Dunn, Ted, 230, 235
Dunstone, Perc, 116, 189, 226
Durante, Jimmy, 248
Durham, Judith, 203
Dyer, Bob, 95
Eden, John, 187
Edgar, Richard, 60
Edwards, Eddie, 217
Edwards, Jimmy, 187
Edwards, Margaret, 72
Ellen, Bernie, 109, 170, 172, 231
Ellen, Cheryl, 165, 172, 174, 180
Ellen, Joff, 101, 103, 109, 111, 115, 117, 119, 120, 128, 149, 153, 155, 156, 164, 165, 172, 180, 203, 204, 231, 232, 240, 241, 256
Ellen, Russell, 172
Ellinger, Ed, 139
Ellinger, Maria, 139
Ellington, Duke, 248
Elphic, Jeanette, 73, 76
Ennor, Vlamai, 165
Epstein, Mr, 81, 82
Ewen, Tom, 228
Farrow, Moira, 83
Faulkner, Chuck, 217
Feldon, Barbara, 249
Fennell, Willie, 57
Fent, Robert, 98
Ferguson, Brian, 239, 242
Ferrier, Noel, 94, 95, 97, 180
Fiddess, Buster, 185, 186, 187, 188, 189, 191, 192, 204
Fields, Marty, 220
Fields, Maurie, 209, 220, 233, 254
Fitzgerald, Bob, 127, 140, 141, 142

Fitzgerald, Ella, 110
Flemming, Claude, 56
Forbes, Bill, 235, 245
Ford, Judy Anne, 94
Forwood, Edgar, 62, 63
Foster, Stan, 227
Fountain, Jim, 180
Fountain, Joy, 78, 87, 88, 91, 97, 120, 121, 149, 155, 165, 170, 171, 180, 222
Fowler, Rod, 254
Fox, Ernest, 83
Fox, Peter, 70, 72, 81, 83, 86, 189, 190
Francois, 58, 59, 60, 61, 62, 63, 64, 65, 66, 67, 68, 69, 73, 74, 77, 78, 79, 80, 82, 107, 124, 125, 165, 191
Freberg, Stan, 109
Fulton, Margaret, 182
Gallagher, Lee, 80
Gardner, Ava, 114
Garland, Deborah, 181
Garner, James, 144
Gay, Louise, 49
Gertler, Alf, 162
Gibbs, Philip, 230
Gilbert, Honest John, 204
Gilbert, Melissa, 152
Gilbert, Paul, 152
Gitsham, Dorothy, 77
Goldberg, Mr, 132
Goldsmith, Brian, 79, 80
Goldstone, Phillip, 86, 87, 88, 91, 92, 99, 100
Goodlet, Ronnie, 73
Goodman, Isador, 204
Gordon, Vic, 186, 195, 198, 200, 202, 204, 207, 208, 211, 216, 217, 219, 230, 231, 233, 234
Gorham, Kathleen, 64, 235
Gorme, Eydie, 248
Gorton, J,G, 213

Grade, Lew, 127, 131
Grant, Cary, 142
Grant, Earl, 152
Green, Mishel, 140
Greenstreet, Sydney, 145
Grey, Pamela
Grizzard, George, 137
Guest, Clifford, 142, 144, 145, 146
Guest, Dana, 142
Guy, Athol, 165, 251, 252
Gyngell, Bruce, 186
Hagen, Earl, 249
Haines, Jimmy, 47, 48, 50
Haley, Bill, 110
Hamilton McIllwraith, David, 79
Hamilton, Ted, 240
Hammond, Happy, 94, 98, 156, 180, 181, 199, 202, 203, 211, 217, 220, 234
Hammond, Vikki, 193, 204, 221, 235, 240, 241, 245, 254
Hampton, Lionel, 137
Hancock, Tony, 216, 217
Handfield, Esta, 76
Handfield, John, 76
Hanlon Jnr,, Tommy, 153
Hannan, Jimmy, 253
Hansen, Wendy, 101, 131, 132, 133
Hardy, Mary, 180
Harris, Rolph, 114
Harris, Stan, 109, 202
Harris, Ted, 83
Harrison, George, 226
Harrison, Wilma, 60
Hartley, Ray, 139
Hartnell, Norman, 60
Hathaway, Ann, 221
Hawker, Johnny, 221
Hayama, Peggy, 152
Hayes, Evie, 51, 55, 69, 94, 96, 112, 117, 153, 170, 171, 178, 179, 192, 254

Henderson, Brian, 186
Hennessy, Richard, 61, 85
Herrick, Bob, 145, 146
Heylen, Syd, 204
Hill, Karen, 73
Hitchcock, Alfred, 141
Ho, Don, 146
Holmes, Ian, 89, 156, 255
Homewood, Helen, 73
Hope and Keen, 187
Hope, Bob, 76, 77, 109, 115, 137
Hope, Tony, 129
Horn, Rudy, 117
Horsfall, Bob, 101, 120, 202, 203, 220
Horton, Robert, 145
Hosking, Roy, 117
Howard, Maureen, 217
Howe, Ci, 219
Howson, Denzil, 94
Howson, John Michael, 230, 235, 254
Hudson, Joe, 117
Hudson, Kenric, 204
Hutton, Betty, 110, 249
Jack, Judy, 95
Jackson, Betty, 72
James, Ginger, 52, 56, 60
James, Harry, 248
James, Heather, 44
Jay, Harry, 70
Jay, Phil, 60
Jellay, Val, 209, 220, 233, 254
Jepperson, Ritter, 70
Johnson, Ian, 83
Johnston, Kevan, 214
Jones, Ian, 112, 219
Jones, Tom, 169
Joy, Col, 151
Joyce, Eileen, 57
Kamahl, 256
Katz, Mickey, 109

Kaye, Danny, 144
Keating, Pat, 60
Kelly, Grace, 104
Kelly, Jack, 144, 145
Kelly, Nancy, 145
Kennedy, Graham, 87, 88, 89, 90, 91, 94, 95, 96, 97, 98, 100, 101, 102, 103, 104, 106, 107, 108, 111, 112, 113, 115, 116, 117, 118, 119, 120, 121, 122, 127, 128, 136, 137, 149, 150, 151, 152, 153, 155, 156, 157, 158, 161, 162, 163, 164, 165, 167, 168, 172, 173, 174, 179, 180, 182, 183, 184, 186, 192, 194, 216, 217, 231, 234, 235, 239, 241, 253, 256
Kennedy, Isobel, 70
Kent, Roma, 58
Kiernan, Pauline, 73, 76
Kinnear, Rod, 89, 163, 192, 239, 240, 256
Kirby, Corrine, 95, 196
Klooger, Annette, 89, 153, 158, 176, 204, 243
Knights, Harold, 186
Kogan, Alma, 114, 227
Kollis, Christine, 73
Kramer, Jack, 83
Kramer, Stanley, 114
Krauss, Bob, 147
Krupa, Gene, 110
Ladd, Johnny, 153
Laine, Judd, 61
Lake, Dawn, 217
Lambert, Tony, 141
Lamond, Toni, 94, 103, 114, 120, 195, 201, 204, 235, 240
Lancet, Judy, 72, 73, 83
Land, Edwin, 217
Lane, Don, 240
Langdon, Peter, 193
Langlands, Paula, 81
Larson, John, 204
Latona, Joe, 220, 221, 235, 236, 245, 251

Lawford, Peter, 227
Lawrence, Steve, 248
Lemmon, Jack, 131
Lenner, Geofrey, 188
Lennon, Hal, 35, 48
Lennon, John, 226
Lester, Buddy, 153, 226, 227, 245, 249
Lester, Jerry, 227
Lester, Miriam, 60, 61, 62
Lester, Shirley, 77, 87
Levant, Oscar, 143, 144, 152
Lever, Rod, 98, 110, 116, 216
Liberace, 110
Limb, Bobby, 185
Little, Jack, 91
Lockwood, Johnny, 117
Lorre, Peter, 145
Lowe, Len, 185
Lucas, Elly, 73
Lum, Bernice, 94
Lund, Don, 180
Lyons, Roy, 117, 202, 219
Lys, Betty, 153
Lys, Pauline, 153
Mack, Bobby, 60
MacKay, Barry, 127
MacLaine, Shirley, 131
Mahoney, Will, 44, 51, 52, 56, 117
Manion, Geoff, 192
Manuel, Jack, 193, 195
Marco, Johnny, 89, 153
Marshall, Wendy, 80
Martin, Dean, 227
Martin, Percy, 61
Martino, Al, 114
Marx, Chico, 57
Matey, Michele, 115
Mathers, Jerry, 141
Matz, Peter, 249
Maxwell, Mary, 226

McCadden, George, 134, 135, 139
McCadden, Hazel, 134, 135, 139
McCartney, Leah, 73, 74
McCartney, Paul, 226
McCloud, Peggy, 95
McColl-Jones, Mike, 153
McComas, John, 94
McCormack, Bill, 89, 94, 120
McEwan, John, 231
McFarling, Ian, 189
McGaven, Darren, 141
McGrath, Patti, 196, 240, 241, 258
McHarg, Alistair, 197
McKenna, Brendan, 232
McKenna, Elaine, 89, 101, 120, 149, 153, 170, 171, 203, 256
McKenna, Julie, 235
McKenzie, Doug, 202, 206, 207, 219
McMahon, Peter, 149
McManus, Mary Jane, 136, 137, 139
McManus, Tom, 127, 135, 136, 137, 139
McMillan, Bob, 146
McQueen, Barry, 120
Meddings, Betty, 60, 61, 62, 193, 219
Medina, Patricia, 141
Meehan, Valerie, 58, 62
Meldrum, Hazel, 60
Menzies, Sir Robert, 84, 110
Michael, George, 168
Middleborough, Gordon, 109
Miers, Gretta, 72, 73, 86
Miller, Tom, 86, 89, 96, 103, 152, 164, 172, 180
Millesi, Robert, 72
Mitchell, Guy, 190
Mitchell, Keith
Mockridge, Irene, 180
Mockridge, Russell, 180
Moncrieff, Gladys, 57

Index

Monroe, Vaughn, 114
Moody, Len, 215
Moore, Don, 117
Moore, Dorothy, 80, 192
Moore, Lily, 60
Moore, Patricia, 214
Moore, Red, 118
Moore, Roger, 145, 146
Moran, Phil, 48, 60
Morgan, Al, 152
Mortimer, Peggy, 45
Morton, Gary, 153
Muir, Christopher, 95
Murphy, Rose, 97
Murray, Fred, 60, 62
Musgrove, Nan, 103
Myers, Peter, 114
Naylor, Brian, 188
Newman, Bill, 94
Newman, John, 61, 114, 212
Newton, Bert, 95, 97, 98, 106, 117, 118, 120, 151, 153, 155, 162, 164, 165, 179, 186, 192, 201, 204, 240, 241, 254, 256
Newton, Helmut, 70, 77, 80, 83
Newton-John, Olivia, 232, 252
Nicholls, Rosa, 170
Nixon, Larry, K, 153
Norman, Pat, 193
O'Brien, Edmund, 142
O'Brien, Hugh, 111, 138, 139, 149, 150
O'Dea, Jimmy, 197
O'Hara, Maureen, 135
O'Keefe, Johnny, 217
Paar, Jack, 199
Packer, Sir Frank, 163
Pan, Hannah, 118
Parkinson, Jimmy, 103
Parsons, Freddie, 153

Peacock, Andrew, 251
Pearce, Eric, 94, 95, 169, 192, 230, 239, 240, 254
Peck, Gregory, 114
Perryman, Jill, 94, 214
Petersen, Keith, 94
Peterson, Oscar, 152
Pethard, Ken, 101
Philipp, Godfrey, 235, 242
Phillips, Donald, 55
Phillips, Gerry, 55
Phillips, June, 51, 55
Phillips, Norm, 55, 57
Phillips, Vera, 51, 55, 57
Phillips, Maisie, 55
Phillis, Brian, 89, 249
Pilita, 152
Pomeroy, Judy, 153
Porges, Albert, 129
Porter, Joey, 116, 117
Potter, Alf, 219
Pounder, Betty, 235
Powell, Jane, 114
Power, Tyrone, 144
Prentiss, Paula, 249
Presley, Elvis, 248
Previn, Andre, 143
Price, Vincent, 143
Prysuska, Marsha, 230
Purser, Warwick, 104
Quinn, Louis, 144
Radford, Shirley, 202, 214, 217
Rafferty, Chips, 214
Rainsford, Ian, 86, 88, 101, 247
Randall, Carl, 52
Rangott, Brian, 101
Rawady, Dennis, 89
Ray, Johnny, 110
Raymond, Geoff, 95, 117, 230
Raymond, Glenda, 196

Raynor, Gladys, 240
Reddy, Helen, 144, 165
Reynolds, Burt, 141
Reynolds, Debbie, 248
Rich, Buddy, 152
Rich, Frank, 117
Rickards, Harry, 37
Roberts, Helen, 117
Robertson, Geoff, 35
Rockefeller, Bobo, 137
Rofe, Carden, 71
Rofe, Stan, 192
Rose, David, 249
Rosenberg, Ron, 109, 118, 240
Ross, Kenneth, 71, 83
Rowlands, Gena, 141
Royle, John, 230
Rubinstein, Martin, 65, 79
Ruff, Val, 89, 91, 93, 108, 192
Russell, Bernadette, 94
Russell, Jack, 83
Sabrina, 113
Sampson, Henry, 136, 137, 138, 139
Scammel, Karen, 72
Schaefer, Carl, 144
Schildberger, Michael, 104
Seal, Elizabeth
Sheldon, Frank, 114, 120, 235, 240
Shmith, Athol, 71, 75, 83, 85, 175, 189, 219
Shmith, Bambi, 72
Shmith, Verna, 189
Shore, Dinah, 195
Sigley, Ernie, 94
Simmonds, Shirley, 81
Sinatra, Frank, 110
Skase, Charles, 188
Skelton, Red, 249
Skouris, Mrs,George, 137
Skouris, Spiros, 137
Skouris, Thana, 137, 138, 139
Smith, Pete, 153
Smith, Roger, 144
Sneddon, Billy, 104
Sorell, John, 254
Southern, Jerri, 152
Spargo, Alf, 209
Sparks, Betty, 60
Spencer, Amy, 91, 170, 172
Spencer, Dennis, 91, 172
Spencer, Diane, 91, 165, 174
Spencer, Norm, 86, 88, 89, 90, 91, 93, 95, 97, 98, 99, 100, 103, 105, 106, 108, 111, 114, 118, 120, 124, 126, 127, 128, 137, 149, 151, 152, 153, 154, 163, 165, 168, 172, 173, 174, 182, 183, 185, 187, 188, 189, 190, 193, 914, 199, 200, 201, 202, 216, 217, 220, 251, 252, 253, 254, 255, 256
Stainten, Philip, 103
Starr, Ringo, 226
Stevenson, Shirley, 77
Stewart, Andy, 195, 197
Stewart, Betty, 113
Stewart, Darryl, 187
Stuart, John, 84
Stubbings, Russell, 240
Stuckey, Hugh, 153
Sturgess, Rosie, 149, 153, 204, 231, 240, 241, 256
Sutcliffe, Berkeley, 60
Talbot, Henry, 80
Taylor, Ray, 243
Taylor, Tikki, 61, 87, 114, 212
Terry, Ron, 109
Thring, Frank, 115
Thurlowe, Deidre, 204
Tilbrook, John, 199
Tilton, Webb, 56
Todd, Hal, 104, 105, 120, 153, 164

Toppano, Enzo, 45
Toppano, Lou, 117
Toppano, Peta, 45
Trainor, Barry, 96
Trask, Diana, 89, 144, 192, 228
Traubel, Helen, 114
Trinder, Tommy, 109
Tudor, Ron, 254
Turner, Lana, 140
Turpie, Ian, 252
Valentine, Dickie, 114, 227
Vander, Ivan, 243
Vaughan, Sarah, 114
Vaughen, Terry, 79
Vee, Bobby, 195, 197
Versluys, Pierre, 91
Violaris, Helen, 72, 78, 79, 80, 94
Voumard, Dick, 219, 246
Wagstaff, Stuart, 256
Wakely, Janice, 73
Walker, Richard, 117
Wallace, George, 109
Wallace, George Jnr, 214, 217
Wallace, Olive, 202
Wallis, Shani, 97
Warner, Sir Arthur, 132, 163
Warren, Jeff, 214
Watkins, June Dally, 76
Watt, Anne, 202, 232
Weate, Kenny, 165
Webb, Wally, 211
Webber, Gweneth, 72
Webster, Leslie, 170
Weetman, Pat, 229
Welsh, Eric, 83
Wesley, John, 156, 182
Wesley, Val, 156, 182
Westmore, Jack, 117
Weston, Paul, 249
Whalen, Jackie, 109

Whalley, Pauline, 165
Wheeler, Jimmy, 117
Wheeler, Sydney, 56
Whimp, Doris, 41
Whitbread, Oscar, 95
White, Anthony, 255
White, Beryl, 82, 124
White, Charles, 82, 124
Whitehorn, Chris, 129
Whitten, Ted, 191
Widmark, Richard, 142
Williamson, Greta, 197, 231
Williamson, Mike, 193, 194, 195, 196, 197, 198, 231
Willson, Meredith, 139
Wilson, Frank, 193, 204, 240, 256
Wilson, George, 254
Wilson, Joan, 91, 92
Wilson, Madge, 35, 39
Wilson, Nancy, 152
Wilson, Sam, 91, 92
Winters, Jonathan, 249
Withers, Googie, 112
Wolf, Digby, 241
Wood, Wee Georgie, 44
Woodley, Bruce, 251
Wyndham, A,W, 239
Wynter, Mark, 197
Yates, Mr, 76
Young, Arthur, 81, 82, 89, 97, 101, 103, 114, 118, 153, 199
Young, Laurel, 170
Yule, Carol, 217
Zanuck, Darryl F, 137
Zimbalest Jnr., Efram, 144